Draw Me Near

Workbook

NANCY DOUGLAS

Copyright © 2007

ISBN 978-0-6151-3983-8

Nancy Douglas

Cover and layout design by Jimmy Douglas

Scripture verses taken from the Holy Bible, New International Version

All rights reserved.

No part of this publication may be reproduced, stored in a retrieval system, or transmitted in any form or by any means —electronic, mechanical, photocopying, recording, or otherwise – without the prior written permission of the publisher and copyright owner.

Dedication

This study is dedicated to my Lord and Savior, Jesus Christ, whose immense love and patience drew me closer to His side. I give Him all the glory for anything that is good. He gently called me to do this work and then faithfully sustained me throughout the entire nine months. I have been blessed beyond measure by simply getting out of His way and letting Him write. If I had known it was this simple, I would have moved aside long ago! I pray the Holy Spirit will move freely through this study to do the specific work He has designed for it. May it bring all glory, honor and praise to our God, the great "I AM."

Acknowledgements

I would like to thank six key people whom God has strategically placed in my life who have proven to be not only pillars in my life, but also in the writing of this Bible study.

Beyond measure, I thank my husband, Jimmy, my only true love, best friend, and confidant. He has supported me in every way for the past 23 years, never ceasing to speak the truth of God to me, even when I didn't want to hear it. His gifts of wisdom and truth have kept me on the straight and narrow. Thank you, dear!

I also want to thank my "Final Four:" Annette, Caren, Debbie and Monty. Of all the great prayer warriors who could have been chosen to pray over this study, God handpicked these four. Their faith in this project has astounded me and proven their great love for our Lord. During the nine months it took for me to write this study, they each ministered to me in distinctly different ways, each providing a perfect blend of love, support, and protection.

Annette, your gift of editing polished this study into a fine jewel. Your gifts and talents go far beyond a keyboard and I am so grateful you heard and responded to God's call to assist me in this wonderful journey. Caren, your gracious and faithful prayers have served to be a powerful rudder in this enormous project, which could have so easily gotten off course. Your strength and peace in the Lord are a great example to me. Thank you! Debbie, through you, God has provided me with my greatest friend. You always seem to know what I need before I need it and in so many ways, you are to me like Jonathan was to David. I am so glad the Lord put you in my life. And Monty, you have been my mentor through it all, guiding me in the wisdom of the Lord. You literally paved the way for this study by requesting it before it was ever written! Your faith spurred me on to do what I didn't believe was possible.

Last but not least, I want to thank my son, Drew, for editing this work after its final revision. You have been a gift from God to your father, sister, and me, since the day you were born. Much of what I write about in this book, you know all too well, for you have had to live with the pain of having a disabled sister, and all that goes with it. Working with you has not only been a joy and privilege, but has further revealed the great talent I suspected in you all along. May the Lord bless you and use you mightily all your days!

Introduction

Welcome, dear sister! I am tickled pink you have joined me for this study. The Lord has finally allowed me to fulfill the desire He planted deep within my heart years ago – to write my own Bible study. This desire wasn't always a tangible one I could have put into words but as I look back, I now see that this desire has always been there. This study has been long in coming but the time is finally here. I feel absolutely privileged to have you join me.

I not only love women but I also love to teach them. Perhaps I feel most comfortable with women because I am one. I know the struggles of being a teenage girl, a single young woman, a wife, a mother, a full-time employee, a full-time stay at home mom, a woman in mid-life crisis and the parent of a disabled child. I know what it's like to feel I must do everything perfectly. I also know the empty, sinking feeling that comes from knowing I can't possibly do it all perfectly.

Through all these phases of life, I learned that the key to a happy, abundant life is to draw near to God. However, it's very common to struggle to have a close, intimate relationship with God. In fact, it's actually normal. Don't ever feel as if you are the only one fighting this battle. I encourage you to join the crowd. And I have comforting news for you: although we may all be in the same boat, we don't have to be lost. A strong, healthy, vibrant relationship with God is not only possible, but precisely what He intends for each and every one of us.

We are in for a great adventure as we study together, pursue a more intimate relationship with God, and learn exactly how to find Him. Abundant healing awaits you as you begin to dig into His Word. It is my prayer that in these next ten weeks you will be transformed, never to be the same again.

We are going to fly high into the sky and dive deep into the ocean as we meet some of the godliest men of the Bible. It will be an exciting adventure and a wonderful journey. In the end, you will step onto the shore of the new Promised Land God has waiting just for you.

Maximizing Your Study Time

Over the next ten weeks, we will meet together in class for a time of lecture and discussion. You will have five lessons per week to complete on your own, each taking about 20-30 minutes. As you study, God will serve as your personal tutor, teaching you new truths as He transforms you. Each week there are two days off to rest, meditate, or catch up on any material not yet completed.

Before we begin, it's important to lay a firm foundation. Rather than plunging into the first lesson, let's first prepare our hearts and minds with some guidelines. They will help us develop a strong commitment to study God's Word each day so we receive all He has to teach us.

Guidelines:

- Determine to complete this entire 10-week study. Resolve to make this study a top priority in your life. If God has called you to do this study, do it completely.

- Pre-select a time each day to do your lesson. What time is best for you - early morning, late at night, or mid-afternoon? Choose a time when your home is most quiet and your mind most focused.

- Make sure your time alone with God is a quiet, uninterrupted time. This means that during this designated time, you will not answer the phone, respond to an email, or even answer the door. At first this may seem difficult, but determine to honor this time as the Lord's.

- Begin your daily study time in prayer by asking God to:
    o Protect your heart and mind from anything that might distract you from hearing Him.
    o Help you hear Him clearly.
    o Help you to implement all that He has to teach you.

- Make it your goal to do one lesson per day. Completing more than one lesson a day will dilute what you learn. Being in a hurry is a sure way to quench the Spirit and miss what God has to say to you. If at all possible, begin doing your daily lessons the day immediately after we meet for class. Don't wait a day or two to begin. Save your two days off for later in the week in case they are needed then.

- If you get behind in your lessons, continue to attend class. The enemy will tell you there is no point in coming if you haven't done all your work but don't listen to that lie. He will tell you that you are a failure and will be judged for falling behind. Don't listen to that lie either. Come anyway and resume your weekly lessons with the class. You can always go back and complete what you have not finished at a later date. In fact, God may use that material to make a greater impact on you at that future time. So even if your workbook is not complete, join us each week.

If you determine to go by these few simple rules each day for the next ten weeks, you will provide yourself with a firm foundation for this study. Drawing near to God involves willpower and grit but I assure you it will get easier over time. If you are new at studying the Bible, take comfort in knowing God is with you and will help you.

TABLE OF CONTENTS

TABLE OF CONTENTS 12

Week One 17
Day 1 - The Power of Communication 17
Day 2 - Communication Breakdown 23
Day 3 - The Danger of Self-Diagnosis 29
Day 4 - The Spiritual Infant 35
Day 5 - Seeking Spiritual Maturity 41

Week Two 47
Day 1 - Sin and Sincerity 47
Day 2 - The Fork in the Road 53
Day 3 - Knowing God 57
Day 4 - The Age Old Tool 63
Day 5 - The Danger of Role Reversal 67

Week Three 73
Day 1 - The Throne of Your Heart 73
Day 2 - The Image of God 77
Day 3 – Christ - The Pure Reflection (Part One) 83
Day 4 – Christ - The Pure Reflection (Part Two) 87
Day 5 – Christ - The Pure Reflection (Part Three) 91

Week Four 95
Day 1 - The Committed Life 95
Day 2 - Setting Your Heart On God 99
Day 3 - Expectations of a Heart 105
Day 4 - Hidden Agendas of the Heart 111
Day 5 - Finding Our Heart's Hidden Agenda 115

Week Five 121
Day 1 - Fearfully and Wonderfully Made 121
Day 2 - Matthew 127
Day 3 - Mark 131
Day 4 - Luke 137
Day 5 - John 143

Week Six 149
Day 1 - Pride, the Roadblock to Intimacy.. 149
Day 2 - The Battle of True Submission 155
Day 3 - Clinging to Our Clocks 161
Day 4 - Humble Yourself and Be Exalted 167
Day 5 - Waiting on God 173

Week Seven 177
Day 1 – Worship: Our Vital Perspective.. 177
Day 2 – Worship: Our Eternal Act 181
Day 3 – Worship: It's In Our Spirit, Not Our Location 185
Day 4 – Worship: It Isn't About Us 189
Day 5 – Worship: It's About God! 195

Week Eight 199
Day 1 - Our Daily Bread (Part 1) 199
Day 2 - Our Daily Bread (Part 2) 205
Day 3 - A Spotlight on Prosperity 211
Day 4 - Daily Bread for the Mind 217
Day 5 - Daily Bread for Our Spirit 221

Week Nine 227
Day 1 - Standing Firm 227
Day 2 - The Armor of God 233
Day 3 - Bondage of the Enemy 239
Day 4 - Attacks of the Enemy 245
Day 5 - Detecting Subtle Lies 251

Week Ten 257
Day 1 - The Narrow Road 257
Day 2 - Daily Discipline 261
Day 3 - Our Teacher and Our Reminder 267
Day 4 - The Lonely Road 271
Day 5 - Your New Journey with God 275

Week One

Day 1 - The Power of Communication

"Then they said, "Come, let us build ourselves a city, with a tower that reaches to the heavens, so that we may make a name for ourselves and not be scattered over the face of the whole Earth."
Genesis 11:4

Have you ever heard someone pray and thought to yourself, "Wow, I wish I could pray like that!" Although many Christians today claim to pray (and most will admit prayer is important), you find few who faithfully pray on a daily basis, year after year. It's these who have passion and intimacy with God who have a track record to prove it. When you ask them to pray, you know they will. Their passion for, and belief in prayer, stands in stark contrast to the blank, awkward stare some give at the mention of prayer.

In general, there are two types of people:
1. Those who believe and actively pray on a regular basis.
2. Those who advocate prayer, yet pray sporadically.

There are many varying degrees of dedication to prayer. Some people believe in God but fail to pray on a regular basis until they are in great need. Others pray on a very regular basis however their prayers are shallow and repetitive. They faithfully go through the motions but their hearts lack the passion to intimately communicate with God.

Our goal in this study is to learn to pray in a way that pleases God and brings us closer to His heart. When we lack communication with God, it is never His fault. God wants to communicate with us. Communication breakdown always occurs on our end. Once we humbly accept this never changing fact, we will be able to draw near to God in a new way.

GOD IS ALWAYS SEEKING MAN

Since the Garden of Eden way back when time began, God has been actively seeking to communicate with man. After forming him from the dust of the Earth, God breathed life into his nostrils, placed him in the garden, and gave him clear instructions on what he could and couldn't eat.

"The LORD God took the man and put him in the Garden of Eden to work it and take care of it. And the LORD God commanded the man, "You are free to eat from any tree in the garden; but you must not eat from the tree of the knowledge of good and evil, for when you eat of it you will surely die."
Genesis 2:15-17

God does not sit on His throne piously waiting for man to come to Him. He always meets man on his own level. The Bible is full of examples of God seeking to guide man.

- *God spoke to Noah instructing him to build an ark (Genesis 6:13-22)*
- *The Lord spoke to Abram to leave his home for an unknown destination (Genesis 12:1)*
- *The Lord spoke to Moses and Aaron with instructions to bring His people out of Egypt (Exodus 6:13)*
- *The Spirit of the Lord spoke to David (2 Samuel 23:2)*
- *The Lord spoke to Job (Job 40:6)*
- *The Lord spoke to the prophet Isaiah (Isaiah 8:5)*
- *The Lord spoke to the prophet Jeremiah (Jeremiah 46:13)*
- *The Lord spoke to Daniel granting him wisdom to interpret the king's dream (Daniel 2:18-23)*
- *The Lord spoke to Paul (Acts 18:9)*
- *The Lord spoke to John in the revelation of Christ (Revelation 1)*

Question and Reflect

Although many things change over time, God's desire to communicate with man has never changed. God still speaks to us today because of His great love and faithfulness toward us.

According to John 16:7,13-16, how does God communicate, guide, and direct us today in New Testament times?

_____

_____

THE TOWER OF BABEL

Before Christ in the time of the Old Testament, God spoke through priests, prophets, and kings who then relayed God's word to the people. Today God speaks to us individually through His Word, the Holy Scripture, and through the Holy Spirit dwelling in all who believe in His Son. God has never been far from His people and today He is closer than ever as He dwells in us, seeking to guide and direct our way.

Today's technology is a direct result of accumulated information that has been recorded, built upon, and passed down to each successive generation. Our modern conveniences of today did not come from the mind of one or even a few inventors. They spring from each generation's knowledge added to the previous. As each generation adds to the one before, man continues to advance. Technology today is progressing at the fastest rate in history.

Question and Reflect

Read Genesis 11:1-9.

What did one universal language give man (vs. 6)?

____ Insight   ____ Power

____ Wisdom   ____ Humility

The communication between men had never been better. However, man's communication with God was at its worst. What did God do as a result?

_____

_____

Man spoke one language before God confused his speech at the Tower of Babel. Without any barriers, this universal language gave man great power and unity, prompting God to say:

> *"If as one people speaking the same language they have begun to do this,*
> *then nothing they plan to do will be impossible for them."*
> Genesis 11:6

God knew this power of unity among men without Him would lead to their destruction. Man's heart easily becomes prideful. True to man's nature, their goal was to build a tower. A sort of stairway to heaven which allowed them to control and dominate the people.

Read Genesis 9:18-19.

After the flood, what did God do with Noah's descendants?

_____

_____

After the flood God desired to repopulate the Earth so he scattered Noah's descendants over the Earth. Over time, men became aware of the power they had when they united as one. With that power they decided to build the tower to heaven and take control. The pride in their hearts led them to rebel and would eventually have led to self-destruction if God had not intervened by confusing their speech.

> *"Pride goes before destruction and a haughty spirit before a fall."*
> Proverbs 16:18

The Tower of Babel is a prime example of the prideful hearts of men before a great fall. Never again in history has God allowed the Earth to have one universal language. Isn't it amazing how eagerly we learn from other people but how quickly we forget the lessons God has taught us?

With the exception of Noah and his family, God destroyed all of mankind due to their wickedness through the great flood. In no time at all, man again turned from God seeking their own desires to the point where God had to supernaturally intervene to keep them from their own destruction. Biblical records clearly show that physical advancement without spiritual advancement is a sure path to destruction. As powerful and vital as communication is to man and his physical advancements, spiritual growth and development are also dependent on the power that only communication with God provides.

So why do so many Christians today fail to tap into this power that lives inside of us? Why do we so often fail to communicate with God? These are very good questions and ones we will address soon but let's first look at three key communication principles:

1. Good communication is required for any relationship to grow.
2. Good communication involves both talking and listening.
3. Close proximity does not ensure good communication.

GOOD COMMUNICATION IS REQUIRED FOR ANY RELATIONSHIP TO GROW

Webster's Dictionary defines the word "relationship" as a state of being related, interrelated, or connected. For example, two cousins are related or connected through a bloodline giving them the relationship or connection as cousins. However, this alone does not ensure a close, intimate, relationship. They must communicate with one another to achieve a close bond. The degree and effort they put into communication with one another will determine the closeness of their relationship.

The same is true between God and His children. Though you and I may be His children and saved through the blood of Christ, we cannot achieve a close relationship with Him without good, regular, and ongoing communication.

GOOD COMMUNICATION INVOLVES BOTH TALKING AND LISTENING

Talking and listening are like a two-way road. Both are vital keys to good communication. One lane is used to talk to the other person, the other used for listening. So often we mistake this two-way road for a one-way highway. We have all been guilty of speeding down this road, talking a mile a minute, failing to realize there is another person who wishes to speak and needs our attention.

Often the biggest reason for our jump to speak and hesitation to listen is simply pride. Can't most of our problems be traced back to pride? We would much rather share our opinions than have to listen to and consider the opinions of others. Proverbs 18:2 addresses this when it says,

"A fool finds no pleasure in understanding but delights in airing his own opinions."

And often when we pray, we speed down the road in the same fashion. We beg, bargain, cry, and complain to God while rarely waiting to hear an answer. In our foolishness we list our requests and complaints as if God were a fast food drive-through. We quickly place our order and then pull up to the window expecting our answer. If our order isn't ready, or not what we expected, we drive off down the road still hungry and in need.

God has so much to say to us if we will take the time to listen to Him, the One who created us and knows us better than we know ourselves. He is our only source of wisdom and understanding; all we need to do is seek Him in prayer.

CLOSE PROXIMITY DOES NOT ENSURE GOOD COMMUNICATION

A husband and wife can live together for years under the same roof but not communicate effectively so that they know each other intimately. In fact, if good communication is lacking, they can be like complete strangers.

The same is true in our relationship with God. We often mistake going to church frequently for being close to Him. We can even teach Sunday school, help those in need, and be thought highly of by all who know us, and yet still never know God's heart. It's frightening to realize we can unknowingly settle for a distant relationship with God, or worse, settle for not knowing Him at all. Even those whom we admire and esteem as godly can fool themselves and others. The enemy is amazingly masterful in shifting our focus onto the things we do for God instead of the depth of our intimacy with Him.

CONCLUSION

As we close our first day's lesson, I hope you realize in a new way the important role communication plays in our physical and spiritual lives. It is absolutely vital for our growth and development.

Take time now to meet with God. Ask Him to reveal to you how He wants you to improve your communication with Him. List any new prayer needs He reveals to you and write down any answers to these prayers. Seek God. He is eagerly waiting to communicate with you!

_____

_____

_____

_____

_____

_____

_____

_____

_____

_____

_____

Week One

Day 2 - Communication Breakdown

"God looks down from heaven on the sons of men to see if there are any who understand, any who seek God."
Psalm 53:2

"In his pride the wicked does not seek him; in all his thoughts there is no room for God."
Psalm 10:4

REVIEW
Day 1 -The Power in Communication

THE MANY FORMS OF COMMUNICATION
Yesterday we focused on the power and importance communication has in our relationship with God and other people. List below all the different ways you can think of to communicate with others. Let me get you started by listing a few: our words, tone of voice, writing …

_____

_____

_____

     You may have listed body language, facial expressions, sign language, emails, TV, phone and more. Clearly we have devised many different ways to communicate. Even prisoners in solitary confinement develop ways to communicate with one another. God put within us this strong desire.

Question and Reflect

Think of a time when there was a breakdown in communication between you and another person. What was the result?

_____

_____

THE DEVASTATION OF POOR COMMUNICATION
     Communication breakdowns can result in anything from a minor inconvenience to devastating, lifelong consequences. My husband and I have learned first hand what these effects can have on a person when they are unable to communicate. Our daughter, now eighteen years old, was born Autistic and deaf. From the start, these two disabilities have rendered her unable to communicate with the world. The deafness keeps her from receiving incoming information and the

Autism keeps her from being able to respond back to the world.

Autism, in a nutshell, occurs when a person is walled off from the world. It "scrambles" the nervous system to the point where the person is a prisoner in his or her own body. All that they see, feel, hear, and smell enters in and gets scrambled so that little things boggle or agitate them. Commonly they will focus on little things leaving them unable to manage bigger, more important things. It is usually difficult or impossible for them to communicate their thoughts, feelings and needs. This leaves the Autistic person powerless and at the mercy of those caring for them.

"Normal" individuals, like you and I, have a nervous system that filters and organizes what our bodies see, feel, hear, and smell. As I write this lesson, I can hear the fan in my computer tower as it cools the system. I feel the ceiling fan blowing on my arms and my weight as I sit in the chair. I feel my sore thumb from a thorn prick each time I use the space bar on the keyboard and even taste the remainder of the morning coffee I finished several minutes ago. In spite of all the varied things I sense, my nervous system is able to prioritize them. They do not distract me so I am unable to concentrate. This filtering and organizing ability of the nervous system enables us to be functional and productive.

OUR PRIORITIES

Quality communication should be a top priority, especially when we understand the devastation that poor communication can cause. But what about our communication with God? How much effort do we give to building quality communication with Him compared with others?

Since prayer is the only way to communicate with God, you'd think we would seek Him with no problem. After all, we don't need a high level of education, money, or special equipment to pray. Anyone can pray: a child, the disabled, the uneducated, and even us non-theologians. We all have access to God through prayer. Communication with Him is easy, free, and available to us all.

Yet so many Christians today choose to be "Spiritually Autistic," walling themselves off from God by choosing to live a life apart from Him. And when we do this, it causes us to be spiritually disabled. Despite the ease and simplicity of communicating with God, we so often choose to ignore Him.

Think back to the list you made of all the different ways we communicate with others. There may be one way you overlooked because it's subtle and easy to miss. Let me guide you to the answer by asking a question (and please carefully answer the question before reading ahead.)

Question and Reflect

What message are you sending to a person when you refuse to communicate with them?

_____

_____

_____

_____

_____

We can send very powerful and painful messages by refusing to communicate with someone. Messages like:

    I don't like you

    I am irritated with you

    I am angry with you

    I am frustrated with you

    I don't care about you

    You are a low priority to me

    I don't want you in my life

       Our refusal to communicate with God also sends Him a strong message about our feelings toward Him and more importantly, the spiritual condition of our heart. Our action, or lack of, reflects the true condition of our heart.

Have you ever struggled to find time to be alone with God in prayer?
_____
_____

If so, try to describe how you think this makes Him feel.
_____
_____
_____
_____

Have you ever thought about how this reflects on your heart's condition?
_____
_____

How would you describe your heart's condition at this point in your life? Circle one.

                Heart Failure

                Weak Heart

                Healing Heart

                Strong Heart

Read the following verses and fill in the blanks:

> **Proverbs 27:19** "As _____ reflects a face, so a man's _____ reflects the _____."

> **Psalm 44:20-21** "If we had forgotten the name of our God or spread out our hands to a foreign god, would not God have discovered it, since he knows the _____ of the _____?"

> **1 Samuel 16:7b** "The Lord does not look at the things man looks at. Man looks at the _____ _____, but the Lord looks at the _____.

> **1 Chronicles 28:9** "And you my son Solomon, acknowledge the God of your father, and serve Him with whole hearted devotion and with a willing mind, for the Lord _____ every heart and _____ _____ _____ behind the thoughts. If you seek Him He will be found by you, but if you forsake Him, He will reject you forever."

We can hide our heart's true condition from those around us and frighteningly enough, we can even hide it from ourselves. But never from God. He created us and knows us better than we know ourselves. As Christ walked the Earth He knew the condition, intent, and motive of each individual heart. Just as He knew Nathanael's heart had nothing false in it, He knew that the heart of the rich young ruler could not follow Him because it held true to earthly possessions.

Christ always goes straight to the heart to perform on us what I call a "Holy Chest X-Ray." True freedom is found when we allow God to cleanse us from hidden sin that we may be completely unaware of ourselves. When we allow God into our hearts to remove this sin and cleanse us, we can then begin to draw nearer to Him in an intimate way. True freedom is found no other way. Either we are bound in our sinful nature or we allow Christ to set us free.

HOLY DIAGNOSIS

God has performed many "Holy Chest-X-Rays" on me and I've learned to ask for them daily. Through these, God has revealed motives in my heart that were dark and contrary to His will. Though I had them wrapped in pretty paper and stamped them with God's will, God knew my inner most thoughts and motives.

Question and Reflect

Can you think of a time when you allowed God to do His "Holy Chest X-Ray" on you? If so, what was your reaction to what God revealed?

_____

_____

Did you allow God to treat your "illness" or "sin"? Or did you leave against His medical advice, choosing to keep it hidden and allowing it to continue to grow?

_____
_____

CONCLUSION

Have you recently asked God for a "Holy Chest-Ray?" Remember, it's free, there is no co-pay and the Great Physician advises one daily. Write a prayer asking God to cleanse your heart and reveal and remove any cancerous spots that are hindering your intimacy with Him. Ask Him to reveal your heart's true motives and help you seek His will and way. Allow Him to do heart surgery. It may hurt for a time, but He will heal you and bring you to a stronger place that is closer to Him!

_____
_____
_____
_____
_____
_____
_____
_____
_____

Week One

Day 3 - The Danger of Self-Diagnosis

"He said to them, "You are the ones who justify yourselves in the eyes of men, but God knows your hearts. What is highly valued among men is detestable in God's sight."
Luke 16:15

REVIEW

Day 1 - The Power in Communication

Day 2 - Communication Breakdown

SELF-DIAGNOSIS

Have you ever felt sick and in need of a doctor but refused to go, choosing instead to self-diagnose and treat the problem yourself? Nurses like me are probably most often guilty of this. I know I'm guilty. It's not that I'm too proud to go to the doctor or that I think I know it all. I just like to try to figure it out on my own to save time and money. But when I do go to the doctor, you can bet there is a very good reason. If I need a prescription or can't figure out what's wrong, I'm eager to pass on the puzzle to my doctor. Perhaps my motives do have a hint of pride and a whole lot of independence in them, don't they?

It's dangerous when we attempt to diagnose ourselves because we are not objective. Let's face it; we are not good judges of ourselves. We may foolishly err on the side of hypochondria or dangerously dismiss a potentially deadly condition because we lack the objectivity needed to make an accurate diagnosis. We tend to remember facts in a way that enables us to manipulate the outcome. If we are convinced we are sick, we'll stack the deck in that direction and vice versa.

THE LAODICEAN CHURCH

The same is true when we attempt to diagnose our spiritual condition. So often we are not in touch with the true condition of our heart. The church of Laodicea was no different. Like all of us, they lacked the ability to see their true condition. They felt invincible in their wealth, choosing to ignore a deadly spiritual condition.

Question and Reflect

Read Revelation 3:14-22.

How did the church of Laodicea self-diagnose her condition? (verse 17a)

_____

_____

What diagnosis did Christ give the church? (verse 17b)

_____

_____

Their diagnosis was completely opposite of the one Christ gave them. They were blind to their own condition and didn't know it. They thought they were rich and in need of nothing when in fact, they were wretched, pitiful, poor, and blind.

What was it about this church that disgusted Christ? (v. 16)

_____

_____

THE CHURCH'S HISTORY

After the death of Christ, John the apostle founded six churches. According to Fox's Book of Martyrs, John founded the churches of Smyrna, Pergamos, Sardis, Philadelphia, Thyatira and Laodicea. These are six of the seven churches to which Christ wrote letters to in Revelation.

We can't fully imagine the love in which the church of Laodicea was founded. John, the disciple, whom Christ loved, was so struck by the love of Christ that he no doubt founded all his churches in the love and truth of Christ. The church of Laodicea was no exception.

John was an old man exiled on the island of Patmos when he wrote the book of Revelation and this letter to the wealthy city of Laodicea. The city was well known for its school of medicine and a special ointment for eye defects. Laodicea also had many banks and textile industries, clearly doing quite well in their own eyes and the eyes of man. Unfortunately in their wealth they drifted from God. Soon they began to worship a god associated with healing, and were lulled into a dangerous and false sense of security.

However, in spite of all their riches, they had a well-known problem they could not fix: their water supply. Their water that flowed was neither cold nor hot by the time it reached the city. It was a nauseating, lukewarm temperature that no one could enjoy.

Question and Reflect

In Revelation 3:19, Christ literally wrote a prescription to this renowned city of medicine to treat the failing condition of their hearts.

Fill in the prescription blanks:

"Those whom I love I rebuke and discipline. So be _____ and _____."

Does the Laodicean church remind you of some of the churches today? If so, in what way?

_____

_____

The church of Laodicea was unable to diagnose its own heart condition. They were dangerously far from the truth. If they had answered yesterday's question asking them to rate their heart's condition, they would have diagnosed themselves with a "Strong Heart" while Christ, knowing the truth, would have correctly diagnosed them with "Heart Failure."

There is a big difference between physical blindness and spiritual blindness. When a person is physically blind, he cannot deny its reality. He "sees" his blindness. But the person who is spiritually blind is nearly always unaware of his blindness. It's frightening to think we can have such a devastating condition and be totally unaware of it. We cannot fully or accurately self-diagnose our own spiritual condition.

God met the church of Laodicea at their point of need, just as He does with us. They were wretched, pitiful, poor and blind, and they didn't have a clue. They were not seeking Christ because they thought they were fine and not in need. But knowing the truth, He sought them to reveal their true heart condition and ask them to seek Him and all He has to offer.

Though God meets us right where we are, He shows no tolerance for the indifferent and lukewarm. Laodice's apathy disgusted Him. Though blind, they were still accountable for their condition. As a church founded on the gospel of Christ, they knew right from wrong. They had chosen to become lukewarm and independent from God. He would rather they had a passion one way or another than to be indifferent. The sedative effect of indifference caused the Laodicean church to neither seek God, nor fight the enemy, leaving them blind to their true condition.

Have you ever tried to help someone who was indifferent to their problem? What were the challenges you faced and were you able to help them?

_____

_____

Today, many believe we live in the Laodicean, or end times, when the hearts of men are sedated and indifferent to Christ. Blinded to this reality, men believe they are rich and sufficient when in reality; they are wretched, pitiful, poor, and blind. How Satan delights when God's people live in this false state of righteousness. While we have trusted Christ to save us eternally, we pose no threat to Satan by reaching others for the Kingdom of God. Remember, if he can't HAVE you for eternity, he'll USE you for now! Ironically, he masterfully uses Christians by making them useless.

THE SUBTLETY OF SPIRITUAL SEDATION

When an illness is very slow to develop, it is much harder to detect. Often it's not detected until the condition is severe. The same is true in the slow deterioration of our spiritual state. Perhaps you were once spiritually healthy and couldn't get enough of God. You had a passion for Him, read His Word, and shared Him with those around you. But over time you slowly became sedated. Your passion and zeal are now gone and if the truth were known you might not even care. Perhaps you even believe the lie that this is normal, that the natural progression of the spiritual life is to go from zeal to spiritual mediocrity. It could be that you have unconsciously listened to the enemy suggest that our spiritual life runs the same course as our physical life. Lots of energy when we're young and much less when older.

This is a lie straight from the mouth of the enemy. He wants you to believe that zeal and passion dissipate with spiritual maturity but it's quite the opposite. The disciples didn't become more sedate as they grew closer to Christ; they developed a stronger, more passionate love for Him. They testified to His truth and shared the gospel to the point of death. Their passion and love for Christ grew greatly and was clearly evident in their lives. We are to be alive in Christ like them, not sleeping with the enemy.

Question and Reflect

Read 1 Thessalonians 5:1-10, keeping in mind that "brothers" are believers, "darkness" is wickedness, and "light" represents God.

To whom were these passages written? Circle one.

Believers   Nonbelievers

What spiritual symptoms do those living in the darkness exhibit? (v. 6) Circle one.

They are alert
They are asleep
They are eager to work
They are watchful

What are believers instructed not to be like? (v. 6)

_____

_____

What are we as believers encouraged to do? (vs. 6 and 8) Check all that apply.

_____ Be alert

_____ Be self controlled

_____ Put on faith and love as a breastplate

_____ Put on salvation as a helmet

As children of God, we are to be spiritually alive, growing, active, and happy by remaining alert in Him. Faith and love are to cover our hearts and the joy of salvation is to cover our heads. We were never meant to be spiritually numb, stunted, or unproductive.

Remember, God has a perfect plan for good in our lives, while the enemy's plan is the complete opposite–total destruction. The enemy desires for us to miss the good God has for us and never taste of, or thirst for, God's Living Water. By keeping us ignorant and sedated he can steal our blessings and stunt our growth. There is no greater threat to him than a growing child of God!

CONCLUSION

Is your spiritual condition all you want it to be? Is it all Christ wants it to be? Perhaps Christ wants more for you than you do. We cannot earnestly hunger for something we have never tasted. Maybe you have been in a state of sedation so long that it feels normal. Maybe you have never experienced true intimacy with God. It is now time to ask Him for more and choose to come alive in Christ. God produces the passion we need – we can't do it ourselves. We all have more to learn about God. If we seek Him in prayer, He will do the rest. Write a prayer asking God to wake you up spiritually, accurately diagnose your spiritual condition, and bring you closer to His heart.

_____

_____

_____

_____

_____

_____

_____

_____

_____

_____

_____

_____

Week One

Day 4 - The Spiritual Infant

"And we pray this in order that you may live a life worthy of the Lord and may please him in every way: bearing fruit in every good work, growing in the knowledge of God."
Colossians 1:10

REVIEW

Day 1 - The Power in Communication

Day 2 - Communication Breakdown

Day 3 - The Danger of Self-Diagnosis

We ended yesterday by asking ourselves if our desire for spiritual intimacy with God matched His desire for intimacy with us. It's a sobering thought that He may want more than we want for ourselves. Although we have little trouble wanting to grow up physically into strong adults, many of us want to remain spiritual infants. We may not verbalize it and may even deny it but our actions prove it.

God always meets us where we are and is continually seeking to communicate with us. Communication breakdown is never on God's end. If we are spiritual infants, it is of our own choosing. The million-dollar question is why would anyone choose to remain a spiritual infant?

In my own life, I did just that until my mid-30's. Now that I understand why I chose to remain a spiritual infant and have experienced the joy of a deeper relationship with God, my passion is to expose the lies of the enemy that keep believers spiritually weak and immature.

THE ADULT INFANT

As far back as I can remember, I have always been aware of God. I clearly remember walking to the bus stop in the early mornings of my elementary years and seeing God in His creation. As the sun would rise and the dew glistened on the grass, I marveled at God's amazing beauty. We lived in the Midwest, which has four very distinct seasons. With each change of season, I never ceased to wonder how God's beauty seemed to outdo itself. After a cold hard winter, how could a tulip pop up through the snow so beautiful and alive? How could the dying leaves of summer be so colorful in the crisp fall air? It amazed me then and continues to amaze me to this day.

Although in awe of God's creation, I chose to live my life apart from Him. His work amazed me but for some strange reason, I kept my heart a certain distance from Him. While I was grateful our family went to church each Sunday, I always left God there, never inviting Him into my daily life. Occasionally I called on Him when I hadn't studied for a test and was in a panic. I would plead for Him to pull me through because deep down I knew that if He could bring a tulip up through the snow, He could surely grant me a passing grade.

But once the crisis was past, regardless of my grade, I would resume my life keeping God a certain distance away. Why in the world did I choose to keep this great God at arm's length? Although I knew God was real, all-powerful, good, and loving, I did not want to give my life over to

Him fully. It frustrates me even now to think of my absurdity. Not long ago, God began to reveal to me the reason for living my life apart from Him. Interestingly enough, this is the same reason most people keep God at arm's length.

HEALTHY FEAR VERSUS UNHEALTHY FEAR

Most people live their lives apart from God and keep Him at arm's length due to fear. This fear strikes many Christians today and either steers them away from God or paralyzes them spiritually. This fear and the shame of even having the fear can be so deeply suppressed and denied that it is usually not recognized.

Webster's Dictionary defines "fear" as:

1. An unpleasant, often strong emotion caused by anticipation or awareness of danger.
2. Anxious concern.
3. Reason for alarm, danger.
4. Profound reverence and awe, especially toward God.

The first three of the four definitions describes fear as a feeling that is negative or unpleasant and brings on anxiety and dread. The last definition speaks of a fear that evokes a sense of awe and wonder. When we have respect and reverence for God, this healthy fear will lead us to Him rather than away from Him.

These definitions help us to see how we can unintentionally develop an unhealthy fear of God. While God's Word instructs us to fear Him, fear does not come from God. This may initially sound like a contradiction but once we realize not all fear involves anxiety and dread, we can better understand the two different kinds.

2 Timothy 1:7 says God did not give us a spirit of timidity, apprehension or nervousness but a spirit of power, love, and self-discipline. There is a big difference in how we relate to God once we realize we are to fear Him with reverence and honor, not with anxious dread. When we are able to distinguish between these two types of fear, we can choose to fear Him with a healthy reverence and awe that will draw us closer to Him in an intimate way, rather than with a fear that paralyzes and pulls us away from Him. Since the enemy is the master at deception, he will take any command or word of God and twist it to work against you and God's plan. This misguided fear is a perfect example of Satan's attempt to distance us from God. He knows if he can get us to fear God in an unhealthy way, it leads us to pull away from God and distance ourselves.

Question and Reflect

There are many benefits we receive when we have a healthy fear of God, all of which Satan wants to steal from us. List some of these benefits described in the verses below:

Psalms 25:14 *"The LORD confides in those who fear him; he makes his covenant known to them."*

_____

_____

Psalms 33:18 *"But the eyes of the LORD are on those who fear him, on those whose hope is in his unfailing love."*

_____

_____

Psalms 34:9 *"Fear the LORD, you his saints for those who fear him lack nothing."*

_____

_____

Psalms 111:10 *" The fear of the LORD is the beginning of wisdom; all who follow his precepts have good understanding. To him belongs eternal praise."*

_____

_____

Psalms 147:11 *"The LORD delights in those who fear him, who put their hope in his unfailing love."*

_____

_____

Jeremiah 32:39-40 *"I will give them singleness of heart and action, so that they will always fear me for their own good and the good of their children after them. I will make an everlasting covenant with them: I will never stop doing good to them, and I will inspire them to fear me, so that they will never turn away from me."*

_____

_____

_____

Acts 9:31 *"Then the church throughout Judea, Galilee and Samaria enjoyed a time of peace. It was strengthened; and encouraged by the Holy Spirit, it grew in numbers, living in the fear of the Lord."*

_____

_____

Question and Reflect

What kind of fear of God do you have – healthy or unhealthy? Explain.

_____

_____

Perhaps you once feared and avoided God but have grown to revere Him in a healthy way. Or maybe you used to honor Him but now find that you have drifted from the closeness you once enjoyed with Him. Wherever we find ourselves, there is always room to move closer to God. Seeking a closer relationship with Him is a constant, never-ending process that will continue until the Lord calls us home.

The thought of having an unhealthy fear of God might create some anxiety in you, which is natural. Just because you have an unhealthy fear of God doesn't necessarily mean you don't have a heart that desires to know God. It may mean you've been deceived by the enemy who seeks to cloud the definitions of fear to cause you to view God in an unhealthy way.

It is now time to choose to fear God in a healthy way and seek Him with all your heart. Remember, sometimes an unhealthy fear of God may be deeply hidden in our hearts and subtly pulling us away from Him. How can we tell if it's there? Look for the signs and symptoms of this fear. Though Satan wants it to be deeply hidden, so we won't discover and overcome it, he knows how valuable unhealthy fear is in keeping us from God. Therefore, he will even use the symptoms that come from this unhealthy fear to achieve His desired goal.

Hang on with me now and don't stop or lose interest. The enemy, no doubt, is whispering a lie in your ear to keep you from moving forward. Let's venture deeper into our hearts to find the symptoms of any hidden and unhealthy fear of God. Think back again to Webster's four definitions of fear. The first three definitions provoke feelings of anxiety or dread while the last definition gives a feeling of comfort. An unhealthy fear of God also leads to feelings of anxiety and dread.

Now apply this unhealthy fear to your spiritual life and look for signs of anxiety, dread, or discomfort in your relationship with God. This may be very uncomfortable at first because this is usually an area of the heart that is uncharted territory. Be very honest with the next question, taking the time needed to fully answer it. Ask God to help you see your symptoms clearly and give you the words needed to write them down.

Question and Reflect

Describe signs and symptoms of an unhealthy fear of God that you currently have or have had in the past.

_____

_____

_____

_____

What signs and symptoms of unhealthy fear did you discover as you dug deeply? Maybe you identified a general apathy toward seeking God or perhaps no desire to seek Him at all. Maybe now you realize your true motive for attending church is not to worship God but a habit done to "do the right thing" or even to please someone else. Did you discover that you have kept God at a distance because deep down you really do not trust Him with your life and would rather run it yourself? Or maybe you found a sign of unhealthy fear as you noticed you have no fruit to show for the walk you claim to have in Christ.

As I think back on my past when my fear of God was unhealthy, I remember that it caused me to literally pull away from God. I knew little about Him and therefore did not trust Him. This led me to choose my own path in life and live independent of His will. When you mix lack of trust with independence from God, you get a person who plans her own life, focuses on her own goals, has a heart untouched by God, and exhibits virtually no spiritual fruit. This unhealthy fear of God leads to futility and emptiness.

CONCLUSION

Dig down deep in your heart and look for the fingerprints of God. His prints should be on every door of your heart. No door should be locked or kept from Him. Even the smallest room can hold hidden motives and desires that will be a wedge keeping you from that close, more intimate relationship with God. God knows all the rooms of your heart and what is in each one. He knows what doors are locked and what doors are open. He can enter any room at any time but He won't because He wants you to freely give Him access to all areas of your heart. He gave you free will and has ultimate respect for it, never overriding your choices. You decide what to keep under lock and key. But there is a price to pay for keeping parts of your heart from Him.

Write a prayer below asking God to show you any locked doors in your heart, including those of which you are currently unaware. Ask Him to give you a tour of your heart and show you the doors that lack His fingerprints.

_____

_____

_____

_____

_____

_____

_____

_____

_____

_____

_____

Week One

Day 5 - Seeking Spiritual Maturity

"Therefore let us leave the elementary teachings about Christ and go on to maturity"
Hebrews 6:1a

REVIEW

Day 1 - The Power in Communication

Day 2 - Communication Breakdown

Day 3 - The Danger of Self-Diagnosis

Day 4 - The Spiritual Infant

In our first week together we have identified the importance of good communication with God and others. Poor communication with God is always a result of a choice we have made and can completely disable us. Because we are unable to truly see our hearts as God can, we need His "Holy Chest X-Ray" to reveal what needs to be cleansed from our hearts. We also discovered how an unhealthy fear of God can exist without our awareness and keep us spiritual infants.

PAPER DRAGONS

Chronic spiritual immaturity is a very interesting and frightening thing. It is very subtle and dangerous yet a completely voluntary condition we allow. However, we often attempt to camouflage it by walking around like a Chinese paper dragon in a street parade. Deep down under all the colorful garb, there is almost nothing spiritually. We don't know how to use the power we have in Christ to defend ourselves from the enemy. We are like newborn babies with freshly cut umbilical cords, lying naked in a city street, vulnerable to the elements and predators of the world.

For a long time, I was a spiritual newborn playing games to hide my spiritual infancy and living vulnerably in enemy territory. My heart is burdened for other spiritual infants who feel a false sense of security as they foolishly hide in their paper dragon costumes. It's a dangerous place to be.

Recently I met a sweet sister in Christ who was trying to grow spiritually but frequently battling the enemy. At our first Bible Study meeting, she made it clear that she did not like Bible studies and did not like to study. Though I didn't like how she felt, I absolutely loved and admired her honesty, which created in me an immediate attraction to her. She didn't tell us what we wanted to hear and she wasn't disguising herself in a colorful costume - she just came as she was. And in spite of what she said, she was there! She bought a workbook and was attending the Bible study even though she "didn't like Bible studies" and "didn't like to study."

My admiration of her honesty prompted me to put my hand on her arm and encourage her to continue attending the weekly Bible study and just watch the videos with us. If she never wrote a word in her workbook, that would be fine.

Well, she did! This sweet honest sister came for 5 weeks straight while faithfully doing her workbook each day. It seemed as if a miracle had occurred. She was happy, growing, and making a complete turn around when suddenly the warfare began again. It seemed to come out of the blue and was constant and intense, causing her great fear and confusion. Then something else happened….she quit attending Bible Study. Her friends said she thought if she quit studying the Bible and attending Bible study, the warfare would stop.

Question and Reflect

Stop here for a moment and let me ask: Have you ever felt like my friend? Have you ever felt like going belly up and crying "uncle" to the enemy? Describe your situation.

_____

_____

Once again, I didn't like what this sister said. Her logic was dangerous but I understood her actions and greatly admired her honesty. She actually told her friends, "If I quit Bible study, the spiritual warfare will stop."

Ladies, half of the spiritual battle is being able to verbalize our thoughts even if we are off track. My friend's logic and plan were wrong when she entered the study and when she stopped in the middle, but her honesty was superb. This exemplary display of honesty is precisely how we should relate with God. He already knows what is in our hearts better than we do, so doesn't that free us to be completely honest with Him, the One who knows us best? He created us and knows every fiber of our being. Trust me-He can handle our thoughts even if they are off track a bit.

THE SINCERE HEART

Honesty with God is a major key to spiritual growth. We are all sinners and God knows it. He loves us all but deals differently with honest hearts than He does with dishonest hearts. God is much harsher with a prideful, dishonest heart than He is with an honest heart that is slightly off track. We will find His mercy is bountiful and endless when we go to Him with the honest truth.

Why do we need to confess the truth about ourselves if He already knows it? When we are willing to bring the truth to the surface and confess it to Him, we are fearing God in a healthy way and giving Him permission to correct and redirect us. If you, like my friend, don't like Bible studies and don't like to study, tell Him! It is healing to bring the truth out in the open and into God's light so we see it for what it is. Once we are willing to speak the truth to God, our hearts will be willing to hear and accept His words of truth in return. Then…. spiritual intimacy begins!

Maybe you believe that confessing your true heart to God sounds right in theory but you still have trouble being brutally honest with God. The enemy may be telling you how disrespectful it is to tell your Lord that you have no interest in Him and want to live your own life. Satan may be whispering that God will heap His wrath on you if you dare put into words your true struggle in getting intimate with Him. May the following verse from Hebrews free you from the bondage of these lies.

"Let us draw near to God with a sincere heart in full assurance of faith,
having our hearts sprinkled to cleanse us from a guilty conscience
and having our bodies washed with pure water."
Hebrews 10: 22

Question and Reflect

According to this verse, what kind of heart are we responsible to have as we draw near to God?

_____ A clean heart

_____ A sincere heart

     This verse clearly reveals what is needed for spiritual maturity: a sincere heart. While salvation can only be obtained through Christ, our spiritual growth and development hinge solely on the sincerity of our heart. Don't skim over this and miss the fairness and love of God. He will never ask us to do what we are unable to do. We cannot save ourselves and He knows it. This is why He allows our filthy, sinful hearts to come to Him. He knows we are unable to come any other way, which is why He sent His Son Jesus Christ. He does, however, hold us responsible for that which only we can do - come to Him with a sincere heart that confesses its sin, turns, and walks with God. These are qualities of a heart that draw Him closer to us.

How sincere is your heart at this point in your spiritual walk with God? Circle a number between one and ten (and be truthful.)

    Insincere   Moderate   Very Sincere

        1......2......3......4......5......6......7......8......9......10

If you ranked your heart as less sincere than you would like, why do you think you are not?

_____

_____

_____

_____

_____

_____

There are many reasons we fail to be genuine, honest, and true with God. Circle some of the following reasons that apply to you:

Pride	Control	Fleshly Desires	Shame
Denial	Fear	Defiance	Selfishness

At one time or another in my life, I could have circled all of the above AND filled up all the lines. Maybe you also included more than you would like. If you did, I commend you for your honesty. Don't let the enemy condemn you for your willingness to see your problem for what it is. How can you confess and give something to God if you refuse to admit it in the first place?

Remember, God asks us to have a sincere heart as we confess our sins. When we approach God, He takes care of the filthiness of our sin, freeing us to focus on the sincerity of our hearts. God is able to handle our lack of zeal, anger, or pride. Not only can He handle it, He can also change it! But sister, ya gotta be honest with Him!

CONCLUSION

As we end our first week's study together, write a prayer asking God to draw you nearer to Him. If your heart lacks sincerity or a desire to seek Him, ask Him to give it to you and He will. Confess your sins and ask Him to reveal any hidden sin in your life.

_____
_____
_____
_____
_____
_____
_____
_____
_____
_____

_____

_____

Now I would like to pray for you.

"Dear Heavenly Father,

    How I praise You for this opportunity to pray for my fellow sister in Christ. As we finish our first week of study, I pray that You will draw closer to your dear one, giving her the desire to draw closer to You in a new and intimate way. May your Holy Spirit bring her into Your presence, cleansing and refreshing her with Your power. Help her to hear Your truth over the lies of the enemy, and be with us as we journey through this study of your Word together.

In Jesus' precious name and Holy blood,

Amen"

Week Two

Day 1 - Sin and Sincerity

"If we claim to be without sin, we deceive ourselves and the truth is not in us."
1 John 1:8

SIN AND SINCERITY

At the end of week one, we found comfort in God's great love and fairness as we learned He will never ask anything of us that we are not able to do. He will never ask us to come to Him clean and free from sin because that would be impossible for us. He only asks us to do what we are able to do and interestingly enough, what He asks us to do is something only we ourselves can do ----- come to Him with a sincere heart.

Sometimes when we do one thing it consistently leads to another and there is no way around it. For example, whenever I go out to get the mail, I invariably see a weed or two that needs to be pulled, the newspaper that needs to be picked up, or I run into a neighbor and wind up talking for several minutes. One simple task can lead to many more. So it is with sin and sincerity. When we allow our hearts to be sincere with God, our eyes are opened to the truth about our sin. There is no way around how these two things go hand in hand.

You may be thinking, "Wow, it's hard enough getting sincere and honest with God-now I'm going to find even more sin in my life?" Well, yes. You hit the nail right on the head. But it's a good thing. Though this may sound like one painful act leading to another, this is truly where freedom and intimacy with God begins. A sincere heart that allows God to reveal and remove sin is a heart that is drawing nearer to God.

THE "WEDGES" OF SIN

God is a perfect and holy God. He cannot be part of, mix with, or be near sin. Sin has separated man from God since Adam and Eve were sent out of the Garden of Eden when time began. Sin is the wedge that keeps us from God unless we are first cleansed by the blood of Christ. When we accept Jesus as our Savior, all of our sins are forgiven and we receive eternal life. When Christ died on the cross, His death paid for the entire sin debt of the world - past, present and future. This eternal life through Christ is permanent and cannot be lost or taken away (see John 10:27-29). However, salvation alone does not bring us into a close, intimate relationship with God. If it did, every Christian would experience intimacy with God instead of so few. Although Christ paid the sin debt we could not pay, we are ultimately responsible for the intimacy we have with God because it comes as a result of the condition of our heart.

Through Christ we are God's adopted children, but on Earth, we still sin. These sins are wedges that come between God and us. We commit them consciously and unconsciously, a few today and a few tomorrow. Though these wedges cannot permanently separate us from God, they do create a barrier. As time goes by and we fail to confess our sins, the wedges accumulate and the distance widens between God and us. Intimacy with God isn't possible if we allow the wedges of sin to remain.

But there are some nagging questions, which, if left unanswered, can become major stumbling blocks in achieving intimacy with God:

- If Christ died for my sins, why do I have to confess my sins?
- Do I really have to confess my sins every day?
- How can there be any wedges between God and I if Christ's death gives me access to the throne of God?
- If Christ forgave all my sins at the time of my salvation, why do I need to keep confessing them?

These are legitimate questions that many of us have had at one time or another. Let's look at the Lord's model prayer and see if we can find some answers to these questions.

The Lord's Prayer

Our Father in heaven, hallowed be Your name.
Your kingdom come, Your will be done, on Earth as it is in heaven.
Give us today our daily bread,
and forgive us our debts, as we also have forgiven our debtors.
And lead us not into temptation, but deliver us from the evil one."
Matthew 6:9-13

Question and Reflect

From Matthew 6:9-13, write the verse in the Lord's Prayer that indicates we should pray on a "daily" basis.

_____

_____

Matthew 6:11 instructs us to ask for our "daily" bread. Since we all must eat each day, yet are instructed to ask only for that day's bread, it stands to reason that this model prayer is meant to be prayed daily. However, prayers were never meant to be memorized and prayed in a rote fashion. God always wants our prayers to come from the heart - a sincere heart.

When Jesus walked on the Earth, they did not have ways to write and carry things with them to help them remember. Instead they were given topics to memorize that would help them remember a scripture, in this case, a prayer. When Christ gave them this model prayer, they were to identify the important topics and implement them into their own personal prayers.

When you break down the Lord's Prayer, you'll find the following basic topics, which the Lord instructed us to include in our daily prayers:

Worship

"Our Father in heaven, hallowed be Your name
Your kingdom come, Your will be done on Earth as it is in heaven."

Provision

"give us today our daily bread."

Confession

"forgive us our debts, as we also have forgiven our debtors."

Guidance/Protection

"and lead us not into temptation,
but deliver us from the evil one."

What topic did Jesus include in Matthew 6:12a that we are to include in our daily prayers?

_____

_____

Remember that Christ was giving this model prayer to the very ones who would become the foundation of the New Testament church. Christ was teaching and grooming His apostles to prepare them to usher in the new church age, the age in which we live today. We are New Testament believers who believe in Christ's teachings and those of His apostles who witnessed His death and resurrection. Therefore, His instructions to them are for us as well.

Does it seem like a contradiction for Christ to die for our sins yet instruct us to ask for forgiveness daily? If it does, take heart, because God never contradicts Himself. There is a very good reason why we are to ask God daily for forgiveness of our sins.

Question and Reflect

Read 1 John 1:8-9 and 2:1-2 below:

1 John 1:8-9 "If we claim to be without sin, we deceive ourselves and the truth is not in us. If we confess our sins, he is faithful and just and will forgive us our sins and purify us from all unrighteousness. If we claim we have not sinned, we make him out to be a liar and his word has no place in our lives."

1 John 2:1-2 "My dear children, I write this to you so that you will not sin. But if anybody does sin, we have one who speaks to the Father in our defense--Jesus Christ, the Righteous One. He is the atoning sacrifice for our sins, and not only for ours but also for the sins of the whole world."

What happens when we confess our sins according to 1 John 1:9?

_____

_____

Now read Hebrews 3:13 below:

*"But encourage one another daily,
as long as it is called Today,
so that none of you may be hardened by sin's deceitfulness."*

In Hebrews 3:13, sin is described how?

_____

_____

What happens to our hearts when we allow sin to deceive us?

_____

_____

Sin is deceitful and if left unchecked, it will harden our hearts. These verses were written to believers to warn us that we can be deceived into believing we are either without sin or in no need of confession (1 John 1:8). According to Hebrews 3:13, this deceit hardens our hearts causing us to become spiritually blind to our sin. This blindness is a harbor for the wedges that distance us from God. Instead we are instructed in 1 John 1:9 to daily seek the purification we receive through confession of sin.

But why do we need to confess sins that have already been forgiven through Christ? The answer is relatively simple. It all comes back to our heart. Everything in our Christian walk boils down to our hearts. As we discussed last week, we can easily misdiagnose our own heart's condition. Our daily confession of sin is not for God's benefit or to get us into heaven. It's not even to uncover anything we think we've successfully hidden from God. Our daily confession of sin is for our own sake, especially for our hearts.

The opposite of confession is denial. Look at each path below and how it affects our hearts and our ability to draw closer to God.

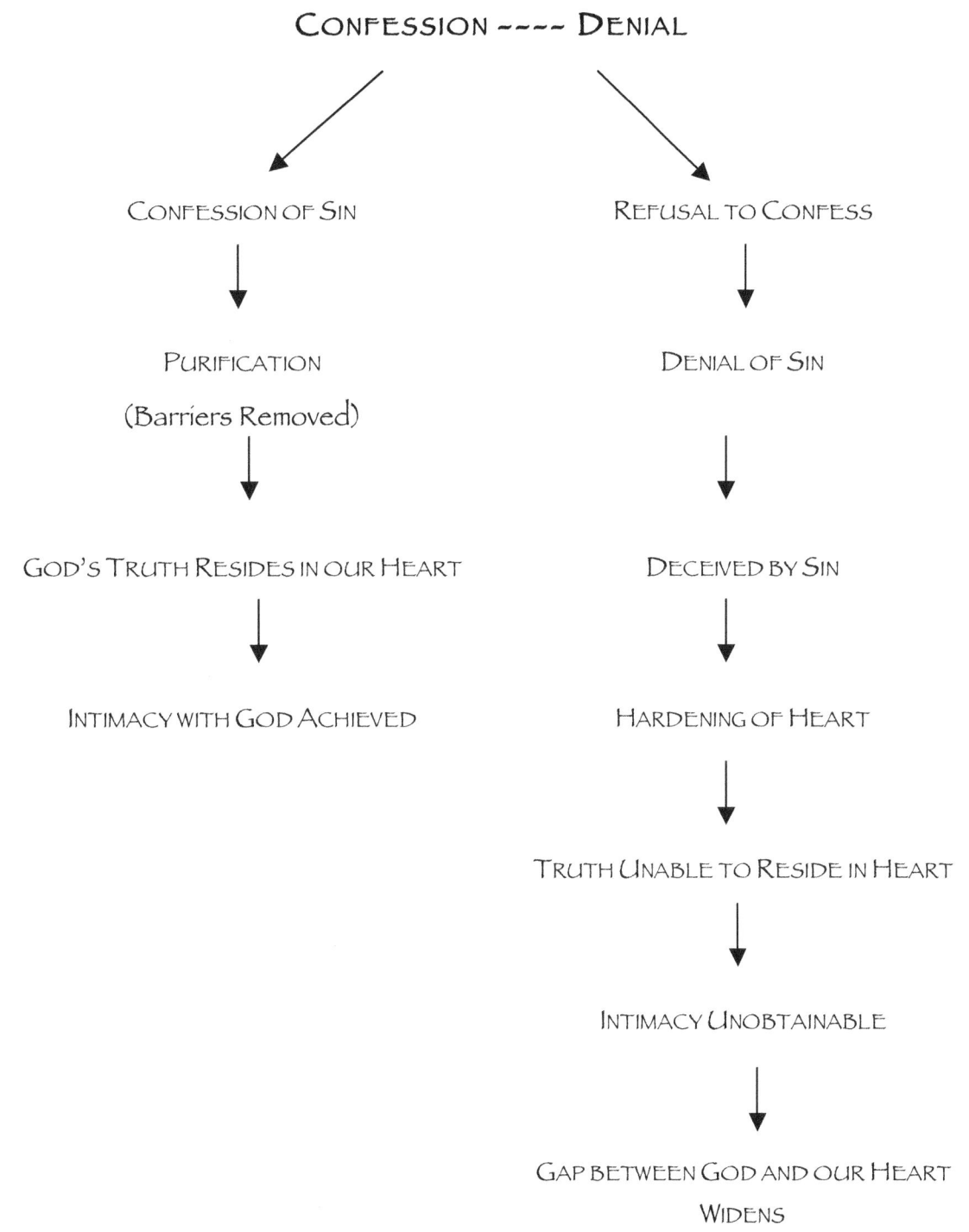

CONCLUSION

Yes, Christ died for all the sins of the world. But He will not do for us what we need to do for ourselves. Write a prayer below confessing your sins, asking God to remove these barriers that prevent intimacy with Him. Ask Him to purify you from all unrighteousness so your heart will be able to receive His instruction and truth.

_____
_____
_____
_____
_____
_____
_____
_____
_____
_____
_____

Week Two

Day 2 – The Fork in the Road

"For I know the plans I have for you," declares the LORD, "plans to prosper you and not to harm you, plans to give you hope and a future."
Jeremiah 29:11

REVIEW

Day 1 – Sin and Sincerity

"I DON'T KNOW YOU GOD"

Many times in my life when God called me to follow Him, I never did more than hear Him, wave, and go my own way. He continued to call me through the years but it wasn't until my thirties that He finally got my attention. He called loudly when He gave us our Autistic daughter, Dani. He used her to begin breaking my extreme independence of Him. He and I both knew I wanted to give Him my life and follow Him, but my desire for independence always prevailed. Even after Dani's birth, I fought for years to gain control of a situation that could not be controlled. Her extreme disabilities were something no doctor could fix. Once I realized this, I began to pester God to heal her. I coaxed, bargained, and screamed my case to Him.

After years of fighting this one-sided battle, I finally began to break. My independent heart learned to submit and I began to lean on Him and hear Him speak to my heart. In my exhaustion I finally stopped long enough and got close enough to hear Him tell me the most simple, yet life changing fact: "Nancy, you don't follow me because you don't know me." He went on to say that if I knew Him better, I would then love and trust Him enough to follow wherever He led me.

When He pointed this out, I remember thinking, "God is right. I really don't know Him and further more, I really don't trust Him either. No wonder I won't give control to Him." Once aware of this, I began to seek to know Him better because then I would be able to trust and follow Him fully. As I searched for Him, He began to open my eyes to the many facets of His wonderful character. Though we can never fully know God and all His majesty, He was faithful to give me a glimpse of His glory, just enough to be amazed. And just as He said, when I got to know Him, I fell in love and fully committed myself to Him.

Question and Reflect

Read Jeremiah 29:13 and Proverbs 8:17. What do these verses say will happen when we love the Lord and seek Him with all our hearts?

_____

_____

_____

GOD HAS A PLAN

As God revealed more of Himself to me, my desire for independence slowly began to wane. One day in particular a great deal of independence fell away. I had just taken our daughter Dani, who was 3 ½ years old at the time, to her special school. Although I felt like a mouse on a wheel driving her forty minutes round trip, twice a day to and from school each day, I knew it was the right thing to do for her. But there was little reward in it, as her progress was agonizingly slow. She still couldn't walk, lacked eye contact, didn't like being held, and never cried for my husband or me. She choked on all her food, wasn't potty trained and the list goes on. It was so painful to never feel like her mother, instead, only her nurse and caregiver. I wasn't anyone special to her, or so it seemed.

For some reason, as I arrived home on that beautiful sunny fall day, I had had enough. Talk about being honest with God. That session with Him either earned me a blue ribbon or knocked a few jewels out of my crown in heaven! Right in the middle of my living room, I took off the gloves and got completely honest with God. I told Him how tired I was with Dani's lack of progress, reminding Him of how many times I had begged Him to heal her while He remained seemingly unmoved. I told Him how the cat gave me more attention than Dani did and I was sick and tired of not knowing how to help her or what to do for her. Holding nothing back, I aired every grievance I had with Him. I finished by pointing my finger to the heavens and asking Him, "Why won't you heal her?"

Just as clear as a bell, God suddenly spoke to my heart and said, "Nancy, I won't heal her for two reasons. First, you want her healed for you! You don't want her to be healed so much for her sake as you want it for you. You want out! Second, I can do more through not healing her than I can by healing her."

God had spoken and His answer was clear. Although I have since asked Him to heal Dani, I have never questioned Him again on the "why" issue. I feel privileged to have received an answer, which was a "two-point" answer to boot! While He didn't reveal His plan to me, He did reveal that He has a plan that is not only specific for Dani but for our family. It's amazing that the God, who created and named the stars and galaxies, has taken the time to plan the life of a little disabled girl. He chose the year, day, hour and place she would be born, and He chose me to be her mom. She can't speak and she can hardly hear but He watches and protects His little lamb. He knows the thoughts she can't convey to us and in spite of her limitations, He has a mighty plan just for her. God truly works in mysterious ways.

Question and Reflect

Oh, sweet sister, if He has a plan for our little disabled lamb, you can know for certain that He has a mighty plan for you!

Read Jeremiah 29:11 below:

"For I know the plans I have for you,
declares the LORD,
plans to prosper you and not to harm you,
plans to give you hope and a future."

According to Jeremiah 29:11, does God have a plan for you?

_____

_____

What does His plan for you include according to this verse?

_____

_____

Do you truly believe it or do you believe you are an exception? Explain.

_____

_____

Isn't it interesting that in our daughter's case, God's plan does not involve healing? He specifically told me He could do more through not healing her. And it was this very revelation that put me on the road that led closer to Him. For years it seemed God and I were at a fork in the road. I kept saying, "Let's go left toward healing" and He kept saying, "No, we need to go right toward no healing." He never abandoned me and I didn't want to abandon Him, so I just kept trying to talk Him into turning left down the easier road.

But, all those years of coaxing God to turn left came to an end one day when God met with me again in that same living room. On this day, I wasn't angry with Him, just very sad. I was finally beginning to absorb the finality of having a disabled child for the rest of my life. I grieved the loss of not having a normal child or a normal life. The reality of never being free to do as I wished, as my children flew from the nest, descended on me bringing with it great sadness. Quite honestly, I felt cheated.

God again met me in my living room and spoke clear words to my heart that ended the debate at the fork in the road. As I stood there grieving the loss of the life I had wanted, the God of the universe paid me a visit. His words of truth literally saved me from a life of bitter sadness. He said, "Nancy, you have grieved long enough and it's now time to move on. Today you are at a difficult but crucial fork in the road and the choice you make will determine the rest of your life. You can choose to remain sad and grow to be a bitter old woman, or you can choose to be happy and make the best of your situation. The path you choose today will be yours for good."

The choice wasn't hard for me. I love to have fun and I missed being happy. I didn't like the thought of being a bitter old woman - it didn't fit my personality. So that day, I finally chose to walk with God on the "right" path and it's been a great trip. Has it been hard? Oh, yes! While He hasn't healed our daughter, He has healed me of ailments I never knew I had. To give my life up to care for His little disabled lamb has instilled Christ-like qualities in me I would never have obtained if God had healed her. The more purifying and refining He does with me, the more I see how badly I need it.

Turning "right" and accepting Dani's condition as permanent didn't look like a pretty or easy path, and honestly, it hasn't been. God's purification is painful but perfect and permanent. Let me encourage you to not fight His purification in your life, even though it may involve a lot of blood, sweat, and tears on your part. Turning "right" isn't easy and it isn't for the weak, but if your heart is sincere and you really want to follow Him, He will never leave or forsake you. He will strengthen you and sustain you as you walk this road together with Him at your side.

CONCLUSION

Have you been fighting with God at a fork in the road of your life? Is He inviting you to the right while you keep trying to persuade Him to go left? When we don't want to go God's way, it is usually because we do not know and trust Him. Our pride tells us we know what is best and that what we see on the left is better for us. But we can't see all that this path has in store. What we see as best may not be what God plans to use to heal and purify us.

Drop your pride and let God lead you down His path. Trust Him when He says He has a special plan for you. One that will prosper you and never harm you. His plan will give you hope and a future. Living in His plan will also give you His peace that passes all understanding - guaranteed!

Write a prayer telling God you wish to turn right. Tell Him you choose to follow Him this day and for all the days of your life. And if that seems impossible to ask for at this point in your life, ask Him to first fill your heart with a desire to follow Him. He will do the rest.

Week Two

Day 3 - Knowing God

"You shall have no other gods before me."
Exodus 20:3

REVIEW

Day 1 - Sin and Sincerity

Day 2 - The Fork in the Road

WHO IS GOD?

Since time began, man has been asking, "Who is God?" There are endless choices of gods to follow and we have complete freedom to choose which one we will worship. As Christians, we know there is only one true and living God, yet there are still many gods worshipped today.

As we read through the Bible we see the words "God" and "god" used in two distinctly different ways. When the word "God" is written with a capital "G" it refers to the one true living God, the God of the Bible, the God of Israel, our Creator, and Father. When the word "god" is written using a lower case "g" it refers to inferior, worthless, man-made gods. These gods are not living; they are temporal and will pass away. They are worthless tools that the enemy uses to shift our focus and devotion from God.

It is often said that it really doesn't matter what you believe, just that you believe something. I recently heard this from my uncle who is currently caught up in the New Age movement. This man, who was raised in a Christian home on a Kansas farm, has heard the truth of the living God. But through the years he has allowed his belief system to be fogged by the enemy. Now he thinks that just believing in anything will get him to heaven. The enemy has stroked and nurtured his pride, encouraging him to create his own truth and turn from the only real truth, Jesus Christ.

When my husband and I visited with him recently, it was clear that he believed in everything and yet in nothing. He believed a little of this and a little of that, but he had no solid foundation. The only thing he emphatically believed was that God was not the only true God. It was as if he used twigs and twine to build a car. What he believes isn't solid and doesn't work. He can call it a car all he wants but it will never run. He is completely unable to defend his faith because it has no substance. His foundation is based on lies from the enemy.

I walked away from this visit with my uncle realizing that God is the only firm foundation. We have one Bible and one God who never change. He isn't a little of this or a little of that. The Bible clearly states that He is the great "I AM." He is perfection and the only One we can confide in and trust.

Question and Reflect

Read the following verses and write down how the "gods" of these verses are described:

Genesis 35:2 _____

Exodus 12:12 _____

Exodus 20:23 _____

Exodus 32:4 _____

Leviticus 19:4 _____

Deuteronomy 4:28 _____

Now let's look at how the Bible describes "God". Since the descriptions of God are so many, let's zero in on one man, Noah, and how he might describe God given the special relationship they shared. Noah was a righteous man who was blameless and walked closely with God. In spite of the wickedness of all of mankind, Noah knew God and faithfully served Him.

Let's look in Genesis to see how he would describe his Lord. Fill in the blanks:

Genesis 6:6 "The Lord was _____ that he had made man on the Earth, and his heart was filled with _____."

Genesis 6:9 "This is the account of Noah. Noah was a righteous man, blameless among the people of his time, and he _____ with the Lord."

Genesis 6:12 "God _____ how corrupt the Earth had become, for all the people on Earth had corrupted their ways."

Genesis 6:13 "So God _____ to Noah, "I am going to put an end to all the people, for the Earth is filled with violence because of them."

Genesis 6:17 *"I am going to bring floodwaters on the Earth to _____ all life under the heavens, every creature that has the breath of life in it. Everything on Earth will perish."*

Genesis 6:22 *"Noah did everything just as God _____ him."*

Genesis 8:1a *"But God _____ Noah and all the wild animals and the livestock that were with him in the ark."*

Genesis 8:21a *"The Lord _____ the pleasing aroma and said in His _____: Never again will I curse the ground because of man, even though every inclination of his heart is evil from childhood."*

Genesis 9:1 *"Then God _____ Noah and his sons, saying to them 'Be fruitful and increase in number and fill the Earth.'"*

Genesis 9:8-9 *"Then God said to Noah and to his sons with him: I now establish my _____ with you and with your descendants after you."*

Compare the verses that describe "God" and the other "gods". What is the major difference between the two?

_____

_____

GOD VERSUS god

Our God is a living God. There may be many "gods" but they are worthless and man-made from silver, gold, wood, and stone. They can be any shape and come from anywhere. In a nutshell, they are a little of this and a little of that. They have no foundation and no ultimate control. They cannot see, hear, smell, speak, instruct, bless, or walk with man. They are worthless and their only value is to Satan who uses them to distract us from the one true God.

What a comfort to see that our God is living and eternal. He created all the heavens and the Earth and is in complete control. God created man and can destroy the wicked. He is involved in each of our lives and seeks to bless us. He has a heart full of compassion. God speaks to those who love Him and knows the righteous heart that seeks Him. No one can compare to His glory.

Question and Reflect

Although the terms "God" and "god" are distinctly different, they do have one common denominator as indicated in the following verses:

"While Israel was staying in Shittim, the men began to indulge in sexual immorality with Moabite women, who invited them to the sacrifices to their gods. The people ate and bowed down before these gods."
Numbers 25:1-2

*"Jehoshaphat bowed with his face to the ground,
and all the people of Judah and Jerusalem fell down in worship before the LORD."*
2 Chronicles 20:18

What common thread did you find in the relationship between man and his god in these two verses?

_____

_____

In both verses, man was worshipping his god but in only one case was the worship beneficial to man. It is a lie that the only thing that matters is that we believe. It is crucial to our salvation that we believe in Jesus, the only One who can save us. It <u>does</u> matter what and in whom we believe!

We were created to worship and therefore we all believe in, and worship something. The object of our worship is what we devote ourselves to and adore, love, and respect. Where we place our time and money is where our hearts can be found. If our worship isn't given to the true and living God, it will be given to any variety of worthless substitutes.

What are some "gods" we worship and trust in today?

_____

_____

Satan will tempt us to worship anything and anyone, as long as it isn't God. He hates God and His goodness and wants no one to follow Him. His goal is to thwart God's kingdom plan, which is to bring all men to Him. The enemy will stop at nothing to prevent a lost soul from coming to Jesus. If you have already accepted Christ, he cannot have you but may still tempt you to worship another god.

Christ was tempted in all the ways that we are. Matthew tells us that just before Jesus began His ministry, He fasted in the desert where the enemy came and tempted Him to worship another god other than His Father God.

*"Again, the devil took him to a very high mountain and
showed him all the kingdoms of the world and their splendor.
"All this I will give you" he said "if you will bow down and worship me."*
Matthew 4:8-9

Oh sister, being tempted isn't a sin – even Jesus was tempted and He was sinless. We sin when we give into the temptation, take our eyes off God, and substitute Him for another god. Satan isn't intimidated by our salvation. If he tempted Christ, the Son of God, he will surely tempt us. It is so easy to trust in and worship the most worthless things. Absolutely anything can become a god: money, status, children, appearance, food, or cleanliness-you name it and it can be a god. If it takes your time and focus away from God, it is a worthless god. While none of these things are bad in and of themselves, Satan desires to take any normal and healthy thing, and twist it into something that you will place before God.

CONCLUSION

Is there a god you have placed above the only true and living God? As we close for today, write a prayer to God confessing any gods you have placed before Him. Name each god and ask Him to help you place Him first in your life. Don't allow anything to keep you from being honest with Him. He is waiting for you and asks you to come!

_____

_____

_____

_____

_____

_____

_____

_____

_____

Week Two

Day 4 - The Age Old Tool

"You shall have no other gods before me."
Exodus 20:3

"You shall not make for yourself an idol…"
Exodus 20:4a

REVIEW

Day 1 - Sin and Sincerity

Day 2 - The Fork in the Road

Day 3 - Knowing God

On day three we learned the difference between "god" and "God." We learned that anything exalted above God is a worthless god and only He is worthy of all glory, honor, and praise.

Since the beginning of time, Satan has tempted man to substitute other gods for the only true God. In the Garden of Eden (Genesis 3:5), Satan tempted Adam and Eve to seek the level of God, which led to sin and the fall of man. He used this tool on Christ in the desert (Matthew 4) just before He began His ministry in an attempt to thwart God's plan. Satan uses the same tool on each one of us today to steer us in any direction other than toward God. Christ did not give in to this temptation and remained submitted to the Father's will, but men and women throughout history have fallen into this trap with disastrous results. This trap is very real and very common. It is vital that we learn to identify this tool of the enemy in order to draw closer to God in an intimate way.

WHY DO WE CHOOSE OTHER GODS?

It isn't much of a mystery why an unbeliever would follow a false god because we understand that they probably don't know any better. What's more of a mystery is why a believer would choose to place anything or anyone before her Savior. How can anyone who has the presence of the Holy One living inside her choose to place anything above He who is so holy and true?

But it's a fact - Christians frequently place other gods before their holy God. It is a battle we all face, and when this battle is continually lost, it prevents us from drawing nearer to God. God is a jealous God who will not take second place in our lives. He loves us with an everlasting love and wants more for us than to follow worthless idols that lead to destruction.

Why has the enemy used the same tool over and over throughout history on everyone, including Christ Himself? Well, you've heard the saying, "If it ain't broke, don't fix it." Satan knows first-hand how effective this tool is, and he uses it because it works. Satan is evil, but he's no fool. Let's go back before time began and see this effective tool in action.

Question and Reflect

Many believe the Ezekiel 28 account of the King of Tyre is really the story of Satan's fall from heaven. This passage helps us understand what led up to his fall and the tools he uses to cause us to fall. Read the following verses keeping in mind that the king of Tyre represents Satan.

Read Ezekiel 28:1-2, 11-17.

Before Satan's fall, how did God describe him according to verses 12-15?

_____

_____

What was the cause of his fall according to verse 17?

_____

_____

In verses 1-2, what did Satan's pride convince his heart to believe?

_____

_____

Did you catch it? Do you see the tool he uses? Let's not move another step forward until we understand that pride is the universal tool Satan uses on every single one of us. Pride caused Satan and 1/3 of the angels to fall from heaven. Our pride prevents us from drawing near to and following God.

Look up Proverbs 16:18 and fill in the blanks.

"_____ goes before _____

and a haughty spirit before a _____."

Satan uses the tool of pride over and over because it is highly effective in meeting his goal of destroying us. His pride caused him to fall, and although he lost the battle, he desires to bring down as many with him as possible. He doesn't care if you are saved by the blood of Christ. He will still use you by making you useless or by tempting you to be mastered by your own pride. Either way you are not seeking God, which meets his primary objective.

Pride is such a subtle sin and the enemy uses it to tempt us to elevate ourselves. Pride itself is a god because when we place ourselves first, we are dethroning God in our lives. When we remove God from the position of honor, we are rebelling and following our own path just as Satan did. As we rebel (even though it may be unconscious), we choose to take over God's role of authority, thus removing Him from the number one position in our lives.

God knows how destructive pride is and how easily it puffs us up. When our God-given free will is mixed with pride, it can be a fast path to destruction. But God hasn't passively watched man fight this battle throughout history. He addressed this very issue of pride in the first two commandments He gave to Moses, clearly indicating their importance to us and to God.

Read Exodus 20:3-4 and write below the first two commandments we are instructed to follow:

1. _____

2. _____

On day three you were asked to confess any gods that you have placed before God. My prayer is that you took the time to prayerfully evaluate your priorities because pride is so subtle that we cannot take care of it on our own. We need God and His holy chest X-ray once again and we need it daily. We cannot get rid of pride on our own or all at once. Because we are often unaware of hidden pride in our own lives, we must ask God to remove it daily to prevent it from becoming an overpowering monster.

HIDDEN GODS

As you'll recall, God told me that He would not heal my daughter because my request was more for me than for her. This was my first lesson in the frightening subtly of pride and is the most memorable awakening I have ever received regarding hidden pride in my heart.

Our inability to be honest with ourselves is a serious problem and affects our walk with Christ. So often we walk along the Christian path crippled with the terrible disease of pride. Christ offers to help us as He sees our suffering, but due to the nature of our disease, we say, "I'm okay. I can make it on my own." when in reality, we are so disabled that we are nearly useless to Him.

That is precisely what I did when my daughter was born. The humiliation of having a disabled child was something I was so ashamed of that I hid it to the point I couldn't find it if I tried. The mind-boggling thing is I didn't know I was stuffing anything and I was certainly unaware I had a pride problem. I only knew I was fighting something deep within me because I wasn't happy and I didn't want the life I had. The blessed thing about God knowing our hearts is that when we suffer the crippling disease of pride and are unable to detect it ourselves, we have the great physician who is waiting to help and heal.

We naturally seek human counsel when in painful situations. Although there are times when this is good and right, we should seek God first in all things. A good friend or family member cannot know, or be expected to know, the hidden things of our heart. In my case, the pain I experienced held a deeper element than even I understood. Everyone who knew me could clearly see I was grieving over having a disabled child, and they all felt my grief was valid and reasonable. I can't think of anyone who didn't understand my desire for Dani to be healed. Rest assured, if I had been on the outside looking in, I would have diagnosed my grief as evidence of a mother's greatest love for her child. But God knew my pain went much deeper and was caused by more than a mother's love. Although I hurt as a mother who loved her child, I hurt most deeply because I was filled with pride. While I have always greatly loved our daughter and want nothing but the best for her, there was a hidden and much deeper issue of pride that God knew had to be dealt with.

For years, God has been stripping away the layers of sin and He isn't finished yet. Now I see what God was doing then when He so lovingly revealed my deep sin of pride and I am forever grateful for His faithfulness to teach and heal me. My hidden pride may seem like a little god, but it was a huge wedge between God and me. It had all the signs and symptoms of a god. It was temporal, it made me self-centered, it took my eyes off God, and it distracted me from His will.

Dear sister, please know that not all gods are visible to the eye or even our hearts. They can be so deeply hidden that we are completely unaware of their presence. We can mask and hide them with labels like grief or good intentions, but since God knows what they really are, we need to humbly ask Him to reveal the gods we have placed before Him. Once we allow Him to help us recognize the truth about our misplaced priorities and move Him back into His rightful place of honor, He will be free to perform a mighty work in our lives.

CONCLUSION

Pride is a subtle god that leads to profound destruction. When we allow God to strip away our layers of sin, we are then free to grow. In Him we find the hope and strength needed to follow and obey His commands. And as we do, He promises to bless us. Take a moment to write a prayer asking God to reveal any areas of pride in your life. If you fear what He might reveal to you, confess the fear. Ask Him to show you your path toward healing.

_____
_____
_____
_____
_____
_____
_____
_____
_____
_____
_____
_____

Week Two

Day 5 - The Danger of Role Reversal

"So God created man in His own image, in the image of God He created him; male and female He created them."
Genesis 1:27

"God saw all that He had made, and it was very good. And there was evening, and there was morning—the sixth day."
Genesis 1:31

REVIEW

Day 1 - Sin and Sincerity

Day 2 - The Fork in the Road

Day 3 - Knowing God

Day 4 - The Age Old Tool

THE GREAT PLAY OF HISTORY

To me, God's kingdom plan seems like one big play being acted out throughout history. There is one holy script, and as with all good dramas, there are the good guys (God, His angels and the people who choose to follow Him) and the bad guys (Satan, his evil angels and the people who choose to follow him). In this grand play, God is the director, writer, producer, casting agent, studio owner, caterer, and set supplier. Everything in the production is His and everything that occurs must receive His approval before being carried out.

The problem in this kingdom play is that many players, the bad guys, are rebellious and do not want the play to go as planned. They want the good players to forget their roles and lose their focus. They seek to destroy the set and create chaos every chance they get. In a nutshell, they want to bring the curtain down. But in the midst of what appears to be chaos, we can rest in knowing that the curtain is already down.

When Christ died on the cross, the curtain separating us from God was torn in two giving us full and complete access to Him. As God's children, we can never be snatched from His hand. Our salvation is final and sure through Christ. The great play of history is being carried out according to God's will, and the enemy and his followers will be destroyed in the end. For now, our job is to keep our eyes on God and know the role we play in His kingdom plan. We must not allow the enemy to distract or confuse us, but instead choose to be loyal and committed to God and His mighty work in progress.

DISRUPTIONS AND DISTRACTIONS

Unlike plays here on Earth, God's kingdom plan contains a very unusual component that appears to detour, distract, and complicate it and any attempts to carry it out. This unusual component is man's free will. With the free will of man thrown in the mix, things can seem quite unpredictable from our perspective here on Earth. Sometimes it seems as though God is not in control, or is choosing to give up control to the enemy. Right when things are going well for the good guys, it seems like a hurricane comes and knocks us to the ground. It seems we are fighting a constant battle to accomplish God's will and the truth is, we are! However, it's comforting to know that God sees the entire play from beginning to end. Though His ultimate plan is complicated by man's free will, God is still in perfect control according to His word. In Scripture, God reveals how it all began and how it will end.

As good guys in this seemingly unpredictable play, we often feel tossed about as parts of the set coming crashing down as bad guys seek to attack and distract us. Life can be quite difficult and just plain exhausting. In times like this, we must choose to trust in the One who is in complete control. All we have to do is learn what our part is in His kingdom plan then seek His direction and guidance. We don't have to worry about the ultimate plan because that is God's job, and He has it under control. Nothing in the world happens that He is not aware of and does not allow. Although man has free will, he does not have free reign and the bad guys are not controlling the world. Only God has complete reign, power, and control over all of His creation. Therefore, we can rest in Him, focus on doing our job for the kingdom, and leave the rest to Him. (Hopefully this makes you feel much better– I sure do!)

TACTICS OF THE ENEMY

Satan attempts to weaken God's people by confusing them about their role in this great play. Throughout history, he has been quite successful in convincing well-meaning good guys that they deserve a better part in this play. He is always ready to encourage God's children to pridefully exalt themselves above God. The enemy doesn't care how he dethrones God in each of our lives nor does he care with what he dethrones Him. His only goal is to replace God with another god.

Remember, God and Satan are enemies, and we are the ones caught in the middle of this battle. Satan doesn't want you; He just doesn't want God to have you. So in the subtlest fashion, the enemy methodically works to keep us ignorant, or cause us to question our role in God's kingdom plan. And of course he doesn't stop there but leads us on to question God's role as well. He knows from there we will move on to question God's motive and plan. Once we start questioning God, we are a breath away from removing Him as Lord of our lives. Our lack of trust leads us to leave God out of our decision-making, to cease talking with Him and finally, to literally walk our own path apart from Him. When we do this, we dethrone Him and exalt ourselves.

Though Satan knows we can never actually be God, he knows that the process of trying is all it takes to bring us to a fall. When we place ourselves above God, it is absolutely no threat to Him and His position as Lord for He will always be Lord. However, we suffer because when we walk away from God, we remove ourselves from under His umbrella of protection and guidance.

THE ACCOUNT OF CREATION

Read Genesis 1:1 through 2:3 for the complete account of creation.

Today many people find it difficult to believe the world was created as described in the book of Genesis. If they aren't struggling to believe there is only one true God, they battle to comprehend how God could create the world in six days. Throughout history, man has theorized and attempted to explain God and His wonders as if that were possible. But there is no explaining God. If we could explain Him, He wouldn't be God, and we would be able to understand the "un-understandable" and be gods ourselves. Though God does not discourage us from asking questions and seeking to know more of Him, it is prideful to attempt to explain God in areas we cannot begin to comprehend.

God is God, and we are mere mortals, so there are going to be a lot of things we simply do not understand. If it isn't the account of creation that causes us to question, it will be the puzzling concept of predestination, or any other host of topics. The enemy loves to use our legitimate questions to cause confusion and lead us to doubt God. He knows that once we begin to doubt, it is easier to tempt us to seek our own answers by "filling in the blanks."

Some of us are very meticulous and thorough so blanks left unfilled can drive us crazy. Others who are intellectual by nature also find it difficult to accept things without good reason and will try to fill in the blanks simply to acquire an answer. The enemy loves it when we focus and dwell on the unexplainable things. When we hesitate or pause spiritually, it tickles the enemy pink because that's precisely his goal. He knows if he can get us into a spiritual lull by focusing on what we don't understand, we will begin to lose ground spiritually as he steals from us the wonderful work God has for each of us.

While it is fine to ask God questions, we are not to lose stride in our spiritual walk with Him. We are to diligently walk with Him on a daily basis, pestering Him with questions all the way if needed, but we must never quit talking with Him. The enemy often tells us it is wrong to ask God questions but it isn't – it's the pauses that come as we wait for answers that can grind our spiritual walk to a halt.

Question and Reflect

Do you find it difficult to believe in creation as it is stated in the book of Genesis?

_____

_____

Do you have other questions about God or His word that have caused you to pause or grind to a halt spiritually? Explain.

_____

_____

_____

_____

_____

_____

If you answered yes to either question, I commend you for your honesty. God loves an honest heart. If you have questions that have slowed or halted your walk with God, now is the time to choose to believe His word by faith and begin to walk closer with Him today.

QUESTIONING GOD VERSUS ASKING GOD QUESTIONS

While the enemy is a master at causing us to question God, he will never encourage us to ask God questions, for when we do, we are in communion with Him. Questioning God versus asking God questions are two totally different heart conditions and Satan knows it. The enemy wants you to distrust and drift from God as opposed to walking by His side asking questions. The goal is to not allow our questions to lead to doubt that can develop into a canyon between our Creator and us. So how can we remain close to God without drifting in the midst of unanswered questions?

Read Isaiah 7:9b and fill in the blanks:

" If you do not _____ _____ in your _____,

you will not_____ _____ _____. " (NIV)

When we doubt, we lack the faith needed to please God. When we try to answer questions ourselves, we are in danger of creating our own theology. Remember my uncle who believed a little of this and a little of that? Asking questions is not a bad thing. Our questions and doubts are a protective mechanism given to us by God Himself. We are not expected to believe everything that comes our way. In fact, we are instructed in His word, to test all things to determine what is of God and what is of evil (1 John 4:1.) We not only have the right to question things, but God encourages us to do so.

We must realize, however, that God isn't the only one who hears the questions we ask. The enemy is always present and listening. As he listens to our questions, he is planning to tempt us to take our questions further, leading us into doubt. This is where faith becomes our saving grace and why God is so pleased when we believe by faith. How it blesses Him when we are sure of what we hope for and certain of what we do not see! (Hebrews 11:1)

OUR ROLES IN GOD'S KINGDOM

Question and Reflect

So what exactly is our role in God's kingdom plan?

Read Genesis 1:1 and write down God's role.

_____

_____

As we see in this account of creation, God's role is Creator. He was in existence before creation and He created all things. His role will never change and He will never abandon His role. He is forever solid, firm, and unchanging.

Read Genesis 1: 26 and write down the role of man.

_____

_____

As God began to reveal this lesson to me, one of the most fascinating things He brought to my attention was the sixth day of creation. It is different from the others because God clearly seemed to save His best for last. At the end of all the other days of creating, Scripture states, "God saw that it was good". But when man was created on the last day, God said, "it was very good". With all other creation, He saw that it was good but as He gazed on man, his prized possession, He spoke words of complete pleasure and delight!

Along with saving His best for last, it was on this day that scripture states that the Trinity, the Father, Son, and Holy Spirit, came together to create man (Genesis 1:26.) As in collective agreement, the three-in-one made man in their own likeness. It is here at creation that God assigned man's role in the kingdom plan: to rule and tend the Earth and all that He created. The enemy seeks to twist creation in our minds, for when we believe in the literal account of creation, we understand our role under God and trust His role as Creator and Lord.

Does man's creation on the last half of the last day have any other significance to you?
_____
_____

Perhaps man's creation on the sixth day doesn't strike you as particularly significant. It is something many of us believe by faith, which is good, but if we look deeper, it will shine a new beam of light on God's sovereignty, which will help us keep Him in His rightful place in our lives.

It was not a fluke or random choice of God to create man last but rather His divine plan. While it does indeed show He saved His best for last, it also shows something we all need to keep in the forefront of our minds. It has always been man's tendency to take control and live independent from God. Therefore, we need to understand that because we were created last, we were completely uninvolved with the creation of anything. Just because man takes control doesn't mean he has control. In fact, as we look deeper into this account of creation, we see that man has never had any say in any creation whatsoever. When Eve was created, God put Adam into a deep sleep (Genesis 2:21), took one of his ribs and then went away to privately create the woman. Genesis 2:22 states that God later "brought" the woman to the man. Adam had no active part in Eve's creation, or the creation of anything else in the world. We must never forget that we were created by and for God with the purpose to know and fellowship with Him. We have no power or authority to place anything before God, who created all things.

When kept in proper order and allowed to work in tandem, these distinctly different roles of God and man are a very rich and powerful combination. When we choose to do our part and work with God rather than against Him, mighty things will happen in our lives. But we must keep these roles in proper order to enable us to be involved in His perfect will and plan.

CONCLUSION

As we close our week of study together, let's take time to give God all glory and honor. I pray that you will trust and believe He has a mighty plan for you. The God of the universe made you alone and in private, later presenting you to the Earth as His prized possession. You are a unique and special creation of the Creator, intended for His divine purposes.

Write a prayer of dedication putting God in the place of honor in your life today. If you have placed other gods before Him, remove them now. Ask Him to take over and be Lord once again. There is no security or peace that compares to hiding under the shadow of His wings.

_____
_____

Week Three

Day 1 - The Throne of Your Heart

"As water reflects a face, so a man's heart reflects the man."
Proverbs 27:19

We ended our last study learning the importance of keeping our role and God's role in proper order. We learned how the enemy is always ready and waiting to tempt us to switch roles with God. Dethroning God is something we've all done and battle daily. Although it's human tendency, it's not something we do intentionally. We don't wake up on a given day and literally say to ourselves, "Today I am dethroning God and taking over." It tends to be more subtle as the enemy tempts us gradually.

I HAVE A THRONE?

I always knew that God had a throne but it never occurred to me that I did too. In spite of the fact I live an obscure life as a wife and mother, I too have a throne… and so do you. It's not something we'll get later when we go to heaven; it's something we actually have now.

Perhaps you didn't know you have a throne. If not, I can help you find it, for I know exactly where it is. Let's start by asking: What is the most important thing in your life right now? You are not allowed to list two or three things; it can only be one thing that is most important to you. If you find it hard to pinpoint, then answer these three questions: What dominates your thoughts? What do you pour your energy into? And what do you spend your money on?

Write below the name of what comes first in your life.

_____

To find your throne, you simply look beneath what you just named. There is your throne – the one you've had all your life. We were all born with this little throne. God gave it to us so we can elevate and hold high that which we prize most in our life. You may call it the desire of your heart, or your life's ambition, but it's a throne just the same and we all have one. Even the homeless man on the street has one, placing what is most important to him on it. Because our throne is "high and lifted up", what we place there is what we see first and foremost. It ultimately becomes part of our life's landscape.

WHAT'S ON MY THRONE?

Because God has given us free will, we are free to place whatever we choose on our throne, yet God is our perfect fit. He wants us to place Him on our throne so that in all we do, He becomes our landscape. God doesn't want to be on our throne to force or control us in any way. Instead He wants to guide and protect us.

God has His throne in heaven and we each have a throne in our lives. Who else has a throne according to Revelation 2:13?

_____

_____

Isn't it interesting that God gives free will to all His created beings, even Satan? In His unselfish love, God gives all His angels and people personal thrones and the freedom to choose what they place on them. He also gives us the free will to follow Him or not. We are not robots but cherished individuals who are treated with respect and honor. Even more astounding is that our salvation is not dependent on whether we keep God on our throne. We can place Him there just long enough to ask Him into our heart then replace Him with another god. We can be saved for many years with full assurance of salvation and yet not keep God on our throne much of that time.

Oh my! Does this sound right? Can a person be a Christian for so long and not put God on her throne? You bet and it happens all the time. Christians all over the world, who will one day go to Heaven, live their lives without God on their throne. They have accepted Christ, go to church (maybe even faithfully), and like all that God represents, yet still have not given Him complete control of their lives. God may be a close second but something or someone else is on the seat, and many of His children simply can't resist the temptation to sit on the throne themselves!

TEARS IN HEAVEN

There is always a price to pay when we put God second. We will not lose our salvation as we dethrone God, but we sacrifice any chance of intimacy with Him. For many Christians, the first real intimacy they have with God will come when they arrive in Heaven. Having missed out on fellowship and friendship with Him here on Earth, they will enter heaven and meet God for the first time as if on a blind date.

Revelation 21:4 tells us that in heaven, Christ will wipe every tear from our eyes. We tend to equate no more tears with no more suffering. Yes, heaven will be paradise where God the Father and Jesus the Son will reign forever. But let's look a little closer at this passage and make sure we aren't missing God's real meaning.

Question and Reflect

"He will wipe every tear from their eyes.
There will be no more death or mourning or crying or pain,
for the old order of things has passed away."
Revelation 21:4

Chapter 21 of Revelation tells us what it will be like in heaven, the New Jerusalem. This is the place Jesus said He was going away to prepare for us (John 14:2). The New Jerusalem is where we will dwell forever with God and all His saints (other believers.) This verse says that in the New Jerusalem, there will be no more death, mourning, crying, or pain.

When we read this passage we tend to think only of our Earthly pain and suffering. But as we look closer at verse 4, we see that Jesus will "wipe every tear" while we are in heaven. This means there will be tears in heaven. Will they be tears of joy? Yes, probably so as saints of the Lord who have waited so long to see His face, finally meet their Savior. But not all who enter heaven will have tears of joy in their eyes. Many of God's children who never put Him on the throne of their lives and therefore chose to forfeit an intimate friendship with Him, will enter heaven with tears of regret and sadness as they gaze upon the Holy One.

Most Christians don't intentionally dethrone God or intentionally set themselves up for such regret upon entering heaven. It is a choice, yes, but so many do not realize the full impact of their choice. The enemy tempts us all to wait until later to learn and grow closer to God. Satan feeds us lies telling us we can't get to know God well, or we already know all we need to know about Him. He persuades many well-meaning Christians to believe that having God near their throne is as good as having Him on their throne. All of these lies hinder us from having that close relationship with God while we are here on Earth.

So let us evaluate our lives. If you were to die today, would you go to heaven? Have you accepted Jesus as your personal Savior and asked Him into your heart? If not, invite Him into your heart right now. Then write today's date in the cover of your Bible so you'll be forever reminded of the date you made this incredible decision. Writing this date down will also reassure you of the security of your salvation the next time the enemy tempts you to doubt. And if, by chance, you are not sure of your salvation, confirm it with God today. Once you are saved, you are secure in the hands of God---forever!

"I give them eternal life, and they shall never perish;
no one can snatch them out of my hand."
John 10:28

If you have already invited Jesus into your heart and you died today, would you have tears of joy or sadness upon entering into the presence of God? Would you have any regrets?

_____

_____

CONCLUSION

As we close today, I wonder if God has spoken to your heart as He has to mine about what it will be like when we enter into His presence. It won't start off joyous for some of His children. I have many regrets, especially the 30 some years I wasted putting worthless idols on my throne. In pride, I sat on the throne most of the time. How I regret the years I failed to honor Him, pushing away the One who loved and cared for me most. Countless times I have asked the Father of time to "double my speed" to make up for the time I wasted. I'm eager to catch up for all those years when I turned my back on Him.

Do you have regrets? If you went to heaven today, would God seem like a stranger to you? If so, it's not too late to get to know Him. Although He may feel like a stranger to you, He has been at your side all along and you are certainly no stranger to Him! Ask God to introduce Himself to you so that you can know Him in a new and special way.

Week Three

Day 2 - The Image of God

"So God created man in his own image, in the image of God he created him; male and female he created them."
Genesis 1:27

REVIEW
Day 1 - The Throne of Your Heart

Yesterday's daily verse was Proverbs 27:19: "As water reflects a face, so a man's heart reflects the man." We learned that God has His throne in heaven, Satan has his throne here on Earth and we each are given a throne on which to place that which we value most in life. What we choose to place on our throne clearly reflects the spiritual condition of our heart. We also read in Revelation 21:4 that there will initially be tears in heaven that Christ will wipe from our eyes. Some tears will be tears of joy when God's children finally meet the One they have longed to see. But many of God's children will have tears of sadness when they see the Holy One for the very first time. Many life-long believers who have never allowed God to be first in their lives will shed tears of regret and remorse for the intimacy they missed and the honor they failed to give God while on Earth.

We were challenged to not be deceived by the enemy who tells us that God is far away and unobtainable. We asked God to reveal Himself to us in a new and special way. As we begin today's lesson, let's pray this prayer again asking God for a fresh revelation of Himself. This is a lesson I cannot begin to teach. God must be your teacher so allow Him full control.

Please take a moment now to ask God to reveal a new facet of Himself to you. Ask Him to plant His nuggets of truth deep in your soul to enable you to draw closer to Him in an intimate way.

NO WORDS CAN DESCRIBE

As I approached these lessons for week three, I sensed God leading me to describe Him and His character. My first thought was, "Yes, this is good. We need to know Him before we commit to Him. This is logical and will be quite effective. But how can any human describe on paper the greatness of God. The great I AM?"

There was no doubt this was God's plan for this lesson but the thought of starting to write it literally reduced me to tears. Crying to God, I humbly asked how I could possibly begin to describe all that He is, having only seen glimpses of Him. As my tears flowed, He gently and lovingly spoke to my heart saying, "It isn't words on a page that teach. It is the Holy Spirit that teaches, guides, and directs."

It was a gentle but profound reminder I hope to never forget. It lifted the weight off my shoulders; a weight I was never intended to carry. What God has to teach you in these particular lessons is something only He can teach. Look to Him for every answer and He will reveal His truths to you.

As I more calmly asked God to show me how to begin to describe Him, He reminded me of a particular verse. It seemed to put a more tangible view of Him in my mind. Although it does not fully encompass all that He is, it does make Him more personal and concrete. This verse helped solidify in my head a concept of God that will provide a good springboard for all us "simple folk" who seek to know and fall in love with Him more.

IN HIS IMAGE

Let's begin by rereading today's Bible verse:

"So God created man in his own image,
in the image of God he created him; male and female he created them."
Genesis 1:27

Question and Reflect

Pretend for a moment that you have been asked by someone to describe your Lord. In the space below, write your description.

_____

_____

_____

_____

Was it difficult to describe God? Any words we attempt to use to describe God seem sketchy and inadequate because we simply cannot fully describe Him. If we were to attempt to describe our God to someone who believes in another god, and they described their god to us, we would probably both sound much the same, using descriptions such as "great power", "great knowledge", "great strength", etc.

But our God is unlike all other gods. It is crucial that this become more than factual head knowledge to us. We need to know it based on a deep conviction in our hearts so that we fall in love with and completely follow God. We must believe and know God is the only true and living God. Today's verse reveals the difference between our God and other gods.

In your own words, what does Genesis 1:27 say?

_____

_____

When we read this verse, we see that God created man in His own image. At first glance, the focus is on man and how he is created in the image of God. This is one way of looking at it; however, to know God, we need to look at the same verse from another angle. We must shift our focus from man to God.

Take a moment to re-read Genesis 1:27, looking at it from this new angle. In your own words, how does this verse describe God?

_____

_____

      You may be a little frustrated at this point. Often, when I see something one way and then try to look at it from a different angle, I simply can't. If you still see nothing in this verse but that "man was made in the image of God," trust me, I understand. Don't get frustrated and quit. Bear with me as I try to move you to a slightly different perspective.

      Because we are made in God's image, we share some of His attributes and abilities. The more we seek Him, the more clearly we see these attributes in Him and in ourselves. This doesn't mean we are gods in any way, nor does it imply that He is limited as we are in strength, power, wisdom, and knowledge. Instead, it means we are a reflection of Him much like a child is a reflection of his parents. He is not a far off foreign God, but someone we have already seen in many respects. If we recognize some attributes of God, it's because we are made like Him. This familiarity should cause us to feel free to draw near to Him.

      This idea may be foreign, even repelling, to some because we never want to think of God as being like man. After all, God does not sin and fall short as man does. God does not envy, betray, and kill to get His way. He is not selfish and does not disobey, causing others to stumble as men throughout history have repeatedly done. But when we look at this verse closely, we see that it does not say God is like us, but rather that we are His likeness. Therefore, any good attributes and qualities we possess are clear reflections of the God who created us in His image.

THE FRUIT OF THE SPIRIT

Read Galatians 5:22-23 below:

> *"The fruit of the Spirit is love,*
> *joy, peace, patience, kindness, goodness,*
> *faithfulness, gentleness, and self-control."*

      Because of our sin, we cannot be a full and complete reflection of God. But scripture states we are still created in His image; therefore, we reflect some of His character. To better relate to Him and draw near to Him, we need to see how we were made in His image. As we become more familiar with the One whose image we reflect, we will in turn seek to know Him in a deeper, more intimate way.

Galatians 5:22-23 is a beautiful description of God. When we allow the Holy Spirit to live inside us and have control, these characteristics (fruit) will reflect His image through us.

Question and Reflect

List the <u>nine</u> fruit of the Spirit from Galatians 5:22-23:

    1. _____

2. _____

3. _____

4. _____

5. _____

6. _____

7. _____

8. _____

9. _____

List <u>three</u> fruit of the Spirit that you exhibit on a regular basis.

1. _____

2. _____

3. _____

Was it difficult to come up with three fruit you exhibit on a regular basis?
_____
_____

No one can say they exhibit all nine fruit on a regular basis. The only human who ever consistently possessed all nine fruit of the Spirit throughout His life was Jesus. The rest of us are weak in some areas while having more strength in others. You may have the "patience of Job" but lack faithfulness. Another individual may be full of love but clearly not the gentlest soul who ever walked the Earth.

Look again at the list of nine fruit of the Spirit and list the <u>three</u> you display least often:

1. _____

2. _____

3. _____

MURPHY'S LAW IN REVERSE

Patience is my number one withered fruit on the vine. I am one of the most impatient people God ever created. Although it is much more controlled now, when I was younger I wanted to run over, past, or through anyone who was in my way or couldn't keep up with me. When God revealed to me this withered fruit of impatience, He also revealed how this one bad fruit affects other fruit on my vine.

One bad fruit contaminates another one, or two, or three. For instance, my lack of patience always went on to challenge me in the area of self-control, which invariably stole my peace and robbed me of any joy. That's four fruit! It's like Murphy's Law: one bad thing invariably leads to another. But (and this is big), when we allow the Holy Spirit to freely dwell in us, we will experience Murphy's Law in reverse. Just as one bad fruit spreads its cancer to another, the presence of the Holy Spirit can produce good fruit in our lives. This good fruit will inevitably drop seeds that germinate into more good, healthy, and healing fruit. When I allowed the Holy Spirit to reside unrestricted in me, I began to naturally possess a greater degree of patience. This in turn gave me more self-control along with the added gift of peace followed by inevitable joy!

If just one of God's character qualities can affect you and me in such deep and profound ways, imagine what God is like – He who possesses all nine fruit! Can you imagine having a close and intimate friend who doesn't just possess these fruit but IS the fruit? Do you desire to have a close and intimate friend, one who has all these wondrous qualities that rub off on you, filling your life with peace and joy? That, my friend, describes God whom we have the choice to serve. He is the One to whom we want to draw closer. Never distant and non-caring, He possesses all these fruit!

CONCLUSION

Doesn't it comfort you to know God isn't a far-off distant God? To know that I was made in His image makes me warmly familiar with Him and curiously eager to get to know Him more. He possesses qualities that are not only familiar to me as a human being, but qualities I can understand as I grow closer to Him. Getting to know and trust God is much like getting to know and trust a special friend - only it's a million times better! While having close friends is a good thing, having God as your best friend far surpasses any human friendship because He will never let you down and can only build you up.

As we end our lesson today, ask God to remove any cancerous fruit from your vine and fill you with His Spirit. Ask Him to plant His good fruit in you so that your life can be a clearer reflection of His true image.

Week Three

Day 3 – Christ - The Pure Reflection

(Part 1)

"The Son is the radiance of God's glory and the exact representation of his being, sustaining all things by his powerful word. After he had provided purification for sins, he sat down at the right hand of the Majesty in heaven."

Hebrews 1:3

REVIEW

Day 1 - The Throne of Your Heart

Day 2 - The Image of God

The nine fruit of the Spirit are love, joy, peace, patience, kindness, goodness, faithfulness, gentleness and self-control. Yesterday we searched our "vine" for both healthy and unhealthy fruit. We learned how these nine fruit are images, or reflections, of the character of God. And when we allow His Spirit to dwell in us, we become a more clear reflection of Him.

As with any crop, one bad fruit can contaminate another much like a cancer. Like "Murphy's Law," a single bad fruit can invariably lead to more. But true to God's nature, He can take what is bad and make it good. No crop or condition is too bad for Him to restore. The Great Physician can heal us far beyond our wildest dreams; we need only to seek and ask. Our great Lord defies all dynamics of nature by taking "Murphy's Law" and setting it in reverse. Just one of His good fruit will inevitably lead to the growth of more if we let Him freely reside in us.

THE PURE REFLECTION

Because of sin, no man can fully reflect the image of God. Although we are made in His likeness, our sin is much like dirt, mud, or soot that blurs His true image. The impurities of sin act as a veil making it difficult, if not impossible, to see His reflection in us. But in some people we see God's reflection with amazing clarity.

For example, Mother Theresa's faithful, lifelong, selfless service to the orphans in India gives a clear image of the unconditional love and compassion God has for His children. In contrast, the diabolical atrocities of Adolph Hitler reflect how sin severs us from all that is good and holy. Somewhere in the life of one of history's most evil men, the image in which Hitler was originally created was obscured by the darkness of his sin. These two lives vividly illustrate the contrast between a life full of, and flourishing with, the Spirit of God, versus a life completely void of any light and truth.

Question and Reflect

Read Hebrews 1:1-3.

In the past, how did God speak to His people and through whom? (vs.1)

_____

_____

How does God choose to speak to His people in these "last days"? (vs. 2)

_____

_____

Who is the only one who has ever been a "pure representation" or reflection of God? (vs. 3)

_____

_____

In your own words, how is Christ able to be a "pure" representation of God? What makes Him different from all the prophets sent before Him?

_____

_____

_____

_____

There are three key phrases in verse 3 that we need to absorb into our spirit. In the NIV Bible, Christ is described as "the radiance of God's glory", the "exact representation of His (God's) being", and one who "provided purification for sins." Oh, the power in these three statements. Any desire to see the true image of God is fulfilled in His Son, Jesus Christ. God knows we tend to walk by sight and we struggle to follow a God whom we have never fully seen. In His great compassion and understanding, He sent His Son to live and walk among His people. God sent His pure reflection in human form so that we would have a clear and tangible image of Him.

THE DEITY OF CHRIST

> *"Jesus answered, "I am the way and the truth and the life.*
> *No one comes to the Father except through me."*
> *John 14:6*

Have you ever wondered why we must come to God through Christ (Be honest)?

_____

_____

I was raised to believe in the Holy Trinity and in the church I grew up in, there was a beautiful symbol of the Trinity. In the front of the sanctuary, on a huge white wall, was a light blue pastel design. It was three circles and a triangle similar to the drawing below, although the one in my church was far more beautiful.

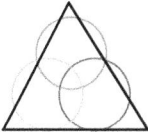

Each Sunday, I stared at it, marveling at what a great visual depiction it was of the Father, Son, and Holy Spirit. I would look at how they were separate parts, yet connected as one. On the design in my church, each circle was painted the same light pastel blue but as the circles overlapped, the color of blue darkened. The darkest blue was in the very center of the design where all three circles and the triangle overlapped. I remember looking into the inner most part of the design, the deepest blue, and thinking how wonderfully it represented the deep power of the Three in One as they work together as the Godhead.

Amazingly, after sitting before this wonderful visual of the Trinity throughout my childhood, I found myself asking questions about the deity of Christ in my early 40's. After years of being a "sleeping" Christian, I finally began to wake up. As if emerging from a coma, I awoke asking questions. It hurt to ask them because they seemed to question the very foundation of my faith. I felt like an idiot questioning facts that I knew to be true deep in my heart.

But there was something about waking up from this Christian coma that also awakened a new boldness in my spirit. Somehow I knew that if I didn't ask God these seemingly dumb questions and didn't get them resolved and nailed down solidly in my heart, I would again slip back into that coma. So I frankly and humbly asked God questions like: "Why do we have to go through Christ to get to you?" "Can't a person believe in only one of You and still get to heaven?" and "Can't either of You let us in?"

While curling my hair (of all things) each Sunday morning, I would ask God to nail down these issues in my heart. Knowing them as mere superficial facts, or head knowledge, was not cutting it for my spiritual growth. As dumb as these questions may have seemed to anyone else, and certainly were to me, they were in no way foolish to God. He honored my honesty with His gentle guidance and teaching. He never told me I should already know this. He didn't tell me my faith was weak. And He didn't reprimand me for wasting His time. Rather, I think He smiled a Holy smile as He thought, "She is coming to me with her most intimate questions. She finally trusts me enough to tell me her inner most thoughts."

Along with being so gentle and understanding with me as I questioned His precious Son's deity, God faithfully responded with the answers I needed to put this issue to rest in my heart. Sister, I can assure you that He is more than happy to answer any questions you may have. He doesn't want you to be spiritually sedated or comatose. He wants us to be awake, alert, and walking with Him. He doesn't want us lying in a bed, saved but useless. If it takes the divine answer to a seemingly silly question to help you "wake up and smell the coffee," then ask it. No question is too dumb to ask. Asking questions is how we learn. Some of the simplest questions left unanswered can become major stumbling blocks. Trust me, I know. I have grown oodles since going straight to the Father with questions about His Son.

CONCLUSION

Unfortunately we must end our lesson for today. Some of you hear your children waking, many of you need to go to work, and a few of you need to go to bed. But this issue of unanswered questions is much too important to leave incomplete, so tomorrow we will pick up where we left off. I will share with you what God revealed to me about His Son. His answer awakened me and I can't wait to tell you how. God not only helped me see Himself more clearly, but for the first time in my life, I began to see Christ and His deity with marvelous clarity. And all because I asked Him a seemingly silly question.

If you aren't where you want to be in your relationship with God, chances are you have some unanswered questions. The enemy has most likely urged you to skim over some questions that need to be nailed down. Don't let the enemy tell you that you should already know the answers. His goal is to keep you quiet, sedated, and far from God.

I challenge you to wake, speak and stand up! Go to God in prayer and ask all the questions you need to ask. Write and date your questions in a journal if you have one and keep praying through them until He answers. He may answer you directly through His Word or through another of His children (pastor, speaker, friend, etc.) Be patient as you wait for His answer and don't give up. When the answer comes---you'll know it! And as these little questions get nailed down, the foundation of your faith will become increasingly firm and strong, leading you closer to your Lord!

On the lines below, ask God all your unanswered questions. No question is too small or insignificant and you can trust in knowing He is faithful to hear and answer you in His perfect time and way.

_____

_____

_____

_____

_____

_____

_____

_____

_____

_____

_____

Week Three

Day 4 – Christ - The Pure Reflection

(Part 2)

"The Son is the radiance of God's glory and the exact representation of his being, sustaining all things by his powerful word. After he had provided purification for sins, he sat down at the right hand of the Majesty in heaven."
Hebrews 1:3

REVIEW

Day 1 - The Throne of Your Heart

Day 2 - The Image of God

Day 3 - Christ - The Pure Reflection (Part 1)

Today we continue with the deity of Christ. This concept is simply too important to skim over or condense into just one lesson since it is vital to the foundation of our Christian faith. You may have noticed that each daily lesson is a certain length. I have found that chewing on a little of God's word each day is the best way to savor and fully digest what He has to teach us. We are more likely to remember each nugget of truth if we take a little at a time and meditate on it throughout the day. Let His living water gradually ooze into your soul like a soaker hose. Turning the faucet on "full blast" will result in most of it running off. Therefore, we'll spread this lesson out over three days.

THE DEITY OF CHRIST (continued)

The deity of Christ is an issue that was hotly debated when Christ was alive and is still debated today. While some religions deny His deity all together, many lukewarm Christians also have questions or doubts about it. Many Christians know Christ is Lord out of head knowledge but have never allowed it to take root in their hearts. It is simply a fact floating around in their heads. The questions I shared with you yesterday are prime examples of a saved person on her way to heaven who does not have Christ on the throne of her heart. It's called the "Christian game" and unfortunately, we are all guilty of playing it at one time or another. We dress up like a Christian, we talk like a Christian, and we walk the halls of a church building with other Christians, but our hearts do not have Christ on our throne. It's a scary masquerade and often only God knows what truly lies deep in the heart of those who claim His name.

AN AERIAL VIEW

When I asked God to show me why His Son was the only key to salvation, He chose to reveal it to me in an "aerial view." He took me from a pinpoint view of Christ to an aerial view as if being taken up on a hot air balloon ride. As He pulled me back, He literally had me look at Christ from Genesis to Revelation. (It is important to mention here that His answer to me was not a quick, one-time answer. It took time and work on my part. I had to study His Word and meet with Him daily over many months for all the pieces of this puzzle to fall into place. But when they did, they were solid!)

As I looked at Christ from this new view, I saw His life in three segments or parts:

- Christ before His birth
- Christ while He walked on the Earth
- Christ in Heaven now

Circle the segment of Christ's life you feel you know the most about.

We generally hear and learn most about Christ's ministry here on Earth. We study very little about Him before and after His time on Earth. With this new view of Christ, I desired to learn more about Christ before His birth and after His death. God showed me that I would never see Christ in all His glory until I examined all three parts of His life. I was missing two major building blocks that kept me from seeing Christ for who He really is. Consequently, I wasn't able to grow closer to His Father. My prayer is that you will also take this aerial view and see Christ Jesus as you have never before seen Him ---in all His glory and majesty!

CHRIST BEFORE HIS BIRTH

Look up the verses below and match them to their correlating statement.

a. John 1:14   Christ was in glory with the Father before creation.

b. John 1:3   Christ was present at the creation of man

c. John 1:1-2   Christ made the world

d. John 17:5   Christ became man

Of the four gospels, John is my favorite. Although God inspired the entire Bible and all four Gospels are vital accounts of the life of Christ, John writes with an astounding degree of love, revealing Christ's majesty and deity. You can turn to the book of John for help in clarifying any questions you might have about the deity of Christ and should you need more help, you can read John's last writing, the book of Revelation. These books never fail to bring me to tears as they teach me more about Jesus.

WE ARE CHRIST'S SPECIAL CREATION

In week two, we covered the account of creation. We read in Genesis 1:26 that when man was created on the sixth day, the Trinity gathered collectively for the special event. It reads, "Let Us make man in our own image." While the Holy Spirit is mentioned in Genesis 1:3 as "hovering over the waters" and God is mentioned throughout each day of creation as Creator of all things, the first mention of Christ is here in Genesis 1:26 where we see He was personally and specifically involved in the creation of man. The Trinity was involved in all creation, but specific persons are mentioned at different times as they took on a more specific role.

Question and Reflect

Read John 1:10-11 below, keeping in mind that "He" is Christ.

10 "He was in the world, and though the world was made through him,
the world did not recognize him.
11 He came to that which was his own,
but his own did not receive him."

According to verse 10a, what role did Christ have in creation?

_____

_____

According to verse 11a, what was Christ's role in the creation of man?

_____

_____

Again John's writings clearly bring out the deity of Christ and His love for His people. Verse 10 refers to the world being made "through" Jesus so we know He was present at creation. Verse 11 then refers to Christ and His relationship to man saying, "He came to that, which was his own". Do you see this personal connection Christ has with man? He was involved with the creation of the world but, He also had a special hand in the creation of man. I wonder if on the sixth day, God stood back and smiled as He let His Son take over. God entrusted man's creation and eventual redemption to His Son. Even at this moment in time, the Holy Trinity knew the future of man and that one day, Christ would step into the world to sacrifice Himself for His own special creation.

As I write these words, I cry as I picture the Son as He created man. His very fingerprints are on each of us as He formed us in His own image. It touches my heart to think that the hands that created us are the same hands that were nailed to the cross for our salvation.

Do you see our value in God's eyes? Can you feel the special love Christ has for you? Oh, how the enemy loves to hide the love of Christ from us. He knows that when we are unaware of Jesus' love for us, and fail to see His fingerprints on our lives, we will not seek Him. The enemy desires to keep us ignorant and indifferent to God's love for us. Unfortunately, Satan is successful too much of the time. John 1:11 begins by telling us of Jesus' love for His own creation. But the end of the verse says, "…but His own did not receive Him," warning us how the enemy pulls a veil over the eyes of many people.

According to John 1:10b, why did the world not receive Christ as their Creator and Lord?

_____

_____

The enemy seeks to decieve us by feeding us lies, distracting us, and puffing up our pride. He does anything to prevent us from recognizing Jesus as our Creator and Lord. Do you recognize Christ for who He is? Is He on your throne or just near it? Is His deity a fact floating in your head, or has it taken root in your heart? It doesn't matter how old you are, or how long you have been a Christian, as long as you have breath, it is not too late to place Christ on your throne and exalt Him as your Creator and Lord. Whether you realize it or not, His fingerprints are all over you! You were hand-made, in private, by the Son of God. He has also redeemed you and you are very special to Him.

Today I pray that you have seen Christ in a new light---in His light. He is the Son of God and it is only through Him that we can go to the Father. He made us and He died for us granting us access to His Father. He is the only Way, the only Truth, and the only Life.

CONCLUSION

As we close today's lesson, write a prayer to Christ acknowledging Him as your personal Creator and Savior. You may need to get things right with Him. Maybe you've had doubts or questions about His deity like I did for so many years. If so, ask Him your questions and tell Him your doubts for He has known them all along. Remember, He is the pure reflection of the Father and encompasses all fruit of the Spirit. He IS love, joy, peace, patience, kindness, goodness, faithfulness, gentleness, and self-control. He understands that you have questions, and He wants you to bring them to Him!

_____

_____

_____

_____

_____

_____

_____

_____

Week Three

Day 5 – Christ - The Pure Reflection

(Part 3)

"The Son is the radiance of God's glory and the exact representation of his being, sustaining all things by his powerful word. After he had provided purification for sins, he sat down at the right hand of the Majesty in heaven."

Hebrews 1:3

REVIEW

Day 1 - The Throne of Your Heart

Day 2 - The Image of God

Day 3 - Christ - The Pure Reflection (Part 1)

Day 4 - Christ - The Pure Reflection (Part 2)

THE DEITY OF CHRIST (continued)

Today we will resume our "balloon ride" high into the sky to take an aerial view of the life of Christ. This aerial view is how God chose to show me the majesty of His Son. If you struggle understanding why Jesus is the only Way, Truth, and Life, I believe today will be the "aha moment" for you.

In yesterday's lesson, we stepped back to get a new perspective of Christ's life before His birth. We saw how He personally created man and therefore has a special love for each of us. We saw with clarity how the hands that created us were also the hands that were nailed to the cross to restore our relationship with Him. Today we are going to look at Christ's life after His death. I want to cry already because today's lesson is so visual. The Holy Scripture vividly speaks of Christ after His resurrection and it brings to life that which we cannot see at the present.

When I think of Christ, I usually have an image of Him as flesh and blood in the context of His earthly ministry. This isn't all bad because one reason God sent His Son was to show us God's true reflection in a form to which we could relate. But there is so much more to Him. Stop and think about what we miss when we limit our knowledge of Him to the 33 years He lived here on Earth. Imagine how much greater God would be in our hearts and minds if we learned more about Jesus in eternity before and after His life on Earth. Imagine knowing Christ in a fresh new way, one that is not limited by flesh or time.

For me, learning about Christ beyond His ministry on Earth has had a tremendous impact on my faith. It absolutely turned my Christian life upside down and infused it with amazing power. My prayer is that this new view of Christ will do the same for you!

Question and Reflect

Describe what you picture Christ will look like when you get to heaven.

_____

_____

What do you think you will do when you see Him for the first time (Cry, bow, sing, lift your hands)?

_____

_____

_____

_____

Earlier this week, we read in Revelation 21:4 that Christ will "wipe every tear from our eyes." When we get to heaven, many will have tears of joy in their eyes while others will have tears of sadness and regret for having missed a close relationship with the One who loves them so much.

No matter what kind of relationship we have with Christ here on Earth, nothing can prepare us for the day when we will see the Son of God for the first time. He will not be like the image we have in our minds of a man with a beard and white robe. His image will be both breathtakingly glorious and indescribably heartbreaking. At the very sight of Him, we will all fall to our knees.

> *"At the name of Jesus every knee should bow,*
> *in heaven and on Earth and under the Earth,*
> *and every tongue confess that Jesus Christ is Lord,*
> *to the glory of God the Father."*
> *Philippians 2:10-11*

What exactly will we see in heaven that will cause us to drop to our knees? Let's read scripture to find out.

Read Isaiah 52:14 and describe Christ's appearance after He suffered at the hands of men just before His death.

_____

_____

Read Revelation 5:6a. Describe Jesus as He stands in the center of the throne in heaven.

_____

_____

Read Zechariah 12:10b. Describe how we will react when we see Christ in heaven.

_____

_____

SCARS IN HEAVEN

When we get to heaven, along with shedding tears of joy and sadness, we will also be in a state of shock and awe at the first sight of Christ. Though heaven will be paradise, the price Christ paid for our sin debt will not be withheld from us. Throughout eternity, we will see the constant reminder of how we got to heaven. The trauma that Christ endured will be forever evident as we gaze on the "Lamb that was slain."

In heaven, all our earthly scars will be healed forever. There will be no more death, no more disease, and no more disabilities. The blind will see, the deaf will hear, and the mute will sing praises to the God of heaven. We will be healed of all pain and suffering and we will live forever with God the Father, God the Son, and God the Spirit. We will all be healed but there will still be scars in heaven. There will be One who will forever bear the marks of our sin as a constant reminder of Christ's love for His own.

Imagine gazing for eternity on the Lamb that looks as if it had been slain, but is standing in the center of the throne. This slain (slaughtered) Lamb will not be a grotesque sight however. Rather, it will overwhelm us as we come to the full realization of Jesus' love for us. While thousands upon thousands of slain lambs lay dead on the altars of history, our Lord is the only living sacrifice who "stands" in the center of the throne of heaven for all to see. His very scars will be our eternal reminder of the cost He paid on our behalf. For that, He is lifted high on the throne in heaven.

Can you now see why there will be tears in heaven? Everyone one will cry these tears. And Christ, who personally created us and personally died for us, will also personally tend to each of us by wiping away our tears. How it touches my heart to envision our Lord approach each of His children individually. The very hands that created us and were nailed to the cross will be the hands that wipe every tear from every eye. I can see Him now as He comes to each of us to lift our lowered head, cup our face in His hands, and draw our eyes to His. At this moment, for the first time in our lives, we will look into the eyes of our Creator. For the first time, no matter where we look, we will see nothing but the evidence of His love. If we look down, we'll see the nail marks in His feet. If we look forward we'll see the scars in His hands, and if we look up, we'll see His wounded and disfigured His face.

As I think of this moment in the future, it causes me to cry. I have such regret for wasting so much time in a "Christian coma." I had no idea He loved me so much, I had no idea I meant that much to anyone, and certainly had no idea He suffered so greatly out of love for all mankind. Maybe you have regrets too, and they have been magnified at this new insight to Christ. What a waste it would be for us to just fall into a heap of regrets and stay there. I challenge you to not stand still and focus on your regrets. God can take anything bad and turn it around for His good and glory. While our regrets should not to be forgotten (for they serve as reminders of where we don't want to return), we should use them to spur us on toward Christ.

Sister, if you are in a Christian coma, I can relate! I awoke from a 20-year coma with horrible bedsores, spiritually weak as a kitten, and missing out on a lot of what God had planned for me to do. But in spite of my self-induced coma, God has graciously turned my life around. Once I opened my eyes, looked around, and started asking God questions, He began to heal me, strengthen me, and I believe is now "doubling my speed." I am finally getting caught up with what His original plan was for me in His kingdom. He can do the same for you!

CONCLUSION

As we end our week of study together, I'm sorry to say our aerial ride is now over. The view was awesome and I have to tell you it is awesome every time I take it! I love this ride high in the sky with God to see the breathtaking view of the life of Christ. I love to meditate on His eternal presence with the Father before He came to Earth. To imagine Him creating us with His own hands as His Father looked on, to see His humble descent to Earth to walk among His own. And finally, to look into the future to see my King of kings and Lord of lords! These rides bless me greatly and I am glad to have taken another one along with you. My prayer is that you will regularly go up with God and take this view of Christ to clarify and strengthen your love for His Son.

If God has revealed a new facet of Himself or His Son to you this week, write what you have learned in the space below. Acknowledge what He has revealed to you and thank Him for His faithful guidance and teaching.

_____

_____

_____

_____

_____

_____

_____

_____

_____

_____

_____

Week Four

Day 1 - The Committed Life

"So then, those who suffer according to God's will should commit themselves to their faithful Creator and continue to do good."
1 Peter 4:19

Last week we stepped back to look at Christ from a new and different perspective. We saw His great majesty and deity in greater depth as we looked at His life before and after His earthly ministry. It is vital that we see Him and who He is in a broader way so we're able to dedicate our lives to Him completely. Having only head knowledge of God will never lead us to spiritual growth.

Did you catch that? Don't let the enemy grease up this nugget so it slips away for it is too important to miss. Let me say it again: Having only head knowledge of God will never lead to spiritual growth. In other words, spiritual growth does not occur in the head. Our heads aren't fertile soil for the Word of God to take root in. Our heads simply house the eyes and ears with which to take in the Word. God's truth was never meant to rattle around in the caverns of our minds. It was meant to be breathed in and absorbed into our heart where the soil is rich and fertile. While our minds and hearts are very closely connected, it is in our heart that God plants and nourishes the fruit of His Spirit. All of our actions, motives, and desires are rooted and derived from the heart; therefore, we need God's Word to be firmly planted in our inner most being.

GOING BELLY-UP!

Have you ever fully committed yourself to God? Not just received His salvation, but given Him all your days? Have you truly gone "belly up" and given Him everything in your life - your ambitions, your will, your desires, your hopes, your dreams, your problems and your failures? When I awoke from my Christian coma, one of the first things I did was hand everything over to God. I finally released all the little things I kept from Him and had tried to control over the years. They seemed like little things and were relatively few in number, but little did I know they were the very things that kept me in that coma.

The million-dollar question is why didn't I give everything to Him way back when I was saved? If not then, why not when Dani was born with all her disabilities? Well, although I'm a slow learner, I can now see that the real reason was my lack of trust in God. Other people (and yes, even God) must prove to me that I can trust them. I never consciously decided to be this way - it's just the way I am. I keep company with few friends and am close to even fewer, tending to observe people closely over time before I allow them into my personal life. As one who knew of God for many years but didn't know Him on a personal level, I unknowingly kept Him at a distance because I hadn't yet seen the proof I needed to fully trust in Him.

How did God ever "prove" to me Himself to be trustworthy? It began as my eyes slowly opened from this long sleep. What woke me up was the excruciating pain of having a disabled child and the grief of knowing I would never be free again. I felt so trapped I couldn't bear it anymore. It seemed that I had been sent to prison to serve a life sentence and would never see the light of day again. As my eyes began to open, something stood out like a sore thumb, something I had always heard about but had never actually seen with my own eyes. The faithfulness of God! In that moment, I finally realized how faithful He had been to me throughout my life. Though I had taken

Him off the throne of my heart and sat in His place, He patiently and faithfully waited for me with the greatest love and dedication. He knew I was desperately seeking happiness but looking for it in all the wrong places. As a wise, dedicated and loving Father, He simply sat at my bedside waiting for the day I would wake up.

You know, there are some things we learn by our mistakes that cannot be taught any other way. I wouldn't advise a Christian coma to anyone, but if you are in one, see where you are and seek to leave and never return. Use it as a reference point. Mark where you are now and head toward God. Don't avoid, ignore, or deny where you are---look at it for what it is and dedicate it to memory. Let God discharge you from this hopeless hospital bed and go experience real life with Him!

Question and Reflect

Do you have a situation in your life that you need to hand over to God? Do you feel like you are trapped in a prison of sorts? If so, explain.

_____

_____

Dear Sister, I know what it's like to feel trapped and have your life ripped out from under you. I understand the anger, the frustration, and the utter confusion that results when life takes an unfair turn, but I want to encourage you that keeping it to yourself is not the answer. Putting on a Christian costume and holding back a part of your heart from God is going to catch up with you sooner or later. They say time heals, but I say time reveals. Where you are now spiritually is a direct result of how much of your heart you have given God.

After eighteen years of pain and frustration, I can now look back and see that God has used our daughter's disabilities to strip down the old selfish, worthless, shallow me in order to rebuild a new creature that reflects more of Him. In other words, He has been refining me. Is it painful? Yes. Is it worth it? A thousand times yes! I wouldn't change a thing. The privilege of getting to know the God of the universe through this pain has been worth it all. If you take God's hand and allow Him to walk you through your situation, you too will come out a new creature that reflects His image. But remember, you can't hold back part of your heart. You must determine to give it all to Him - the good, the bad, and the ugly.

DANIEL - COMMITTED FOR LIFE

I love the prophet Daniel. He is a great example to those of us who are in a prison. While we may not be in a physical prison, Daniel was literally taken into exile at the age of 15. Yet, even at his tender young age, he was completely committed to God. Most likely born and raised in Jerusalem, he was clearly taught to know the Law and had great dedication to God even as a teen. When King Nebuchadnezzar of Babylon came to take all the healthy, strong young men of Jerusalem for his court, Daniel encouraged others to keep the faith and remain dedicated to God. In spite of being taken from His home and family to live and serve a pagan king, he never wavered in his faith. Even though they changed his name to Belteshazzar, which means "prince of the pagan god Baal", Daniel chose to stand firm with his God.

Imagine being 15 years old and suddenly taken, without your consent, from all you know and love to be placed in a detestable foreign land. Your identity is changed and you are sent to serve and live in a land that opposes your God. Imagine pondering that the only wrong you had committed was being healthy and strong. What must this young man have thought? Did he question his God? Did he ever get angry with his Lord for allowing this event that changed his life forever?

Daniel chapter 6 gives us great insight into how he survived in this foreign land. Perhaps you've heard the story of Daniel in the lion's den and imagined him as a young man when this occurred. However, Daniel was probably in his 90's when he was thrown in with the lions. As you answer questions and reflect in the next section, keep in mind Daniel's old age. And remember that for nearly 75 years, Daniel has been held captive in a pagan land with only God to help him survive.

Question and Reflect

Read Daniel chapter 6.

What was Daniel's position in the kingdom in which he lived? (vs. 1-2)

_____

_____

What was his reputation? (vs. 3-4)

_____

_____

According to verse 10, how would you rank Daniel's level of dedication to the God of his youth?

_____

_____

What were Daniel's first words to the king after spending the night in the den with hungry lions? To whom did he give credit for being alive? (vs. 22)

_____

_____

After 75 years of living a life he had never planned, Daniel remained faithful to his God. Astounding, isn't it? And it doesn't stop there. We must never fail to see the faithfulness of God in all things. Although Daniel was taken where he would have never chosen to go, he kept God in his heart and as a result, God performed a mighty work in his life.

One of the first faithful acts we see God perform was when He preserved Daniel's name. Some 2,500 years after Daniel's death, we still know him as Daniel, his original birth name, not his pagan name, Belteshazzar, that he had been called his adult life. God also showed Daniel great faithfulness by granting him favor in this land of exile. Placed among pagans as a witness to the God of Abraham, Daniel lived and worked with the highest officials of the land. His work was exemplary and God blessed him faithfully all his years.

Did God prevent bad things from happening to Daniel? No. Daniel remained a minority in the land, was persecuted for not bowing down to their god and was eventually thrown into the lion's den. But God never left his side. In fact, it was through these very acts of persecution that Daniel's faith grew greater and God's glory shone brighter!

However, God's greatest blessing in Daniel's life was giving him prophetic visions. God took this 15-year-old Jewish boy who was exiled to Babylon, and turned him into one of only four Major Prophets of the Old Testament. Like John the beloved disciple, Daniel was given a glimpse into the eternal kingdom. Far beyond the time he lived on Earth, Daniel saw the vision of the hope of Christ. This vision gave his life on Earth an entirely new perspective as he realized its brevity. These visions were Daniel's balloon ride that gave him a greater focus on, and dedication to, His Lord. God took him high into the heavens giving him the same "aerial view" we took last week. This look into the future gave him a new, powerful, and encouraging perspective of Christ!

Because of the prophetic insights given to Daniel and John, we too can take aerial rides with God. Through these visions, God blesses us by revealing His plan and purpose, which in turn helps us gain a new perspective of our own earthly problems. We then realize that our troubles here on Earth are temporary and our only true hope lies in our future with God and His Son, Jesus Christ!

CONCLUSION

Is God refining you through a trial? Is your life exactly what you never wanted? If you are in a painful situation, I assure you the hand of God is refining you and I pray you won't stop Him. Let Him perfect you. If you are weary, I encourage you to take a moment to thank God, not for the situation, but for the cleansing it is doing in your life. Painful as it may be, you are being transformed. Focus on the purification, not the discomfort. When we focus on the pain, we often pull away from God, accusing Him of inflicting it or not caring about us. But when we focus on the refining process and the blessings that come as a result, we focus on God and His ultimate plan. Don't let the enemy tell you God doesn't care because He does! He will never leave or forsake you, and He has a mighty plan in store for all who keep their eyes on Him.

Let's allow Daniel to be our example. Let's choose to put God first in our life regardless of our circumstance. Even if you feel like a prisoner in a pagan land with lions nipping at your heels, determine to keep God on the throne of your heart every day of your life. Give your situation to the Lord and thank Him for His faithfulness. If you are in so much pain that you cannot genuinely thank Him, start by asking Him to help you get to the point where you can give thanks. Don't let yourself drift from God, but instead cling to the fact that He cares for you and has a mighty plan for your life. Be like Daniel – take it to God in prayer!

_____
_____
_____
_____
_____
_____
_____
_____
_____

Week Four

Day 2 – Setting Your Heart on God

"Daniel resolved not to defile himself with the royal food and wine, and he asked the chief official for permission not to defile himself this way. Now God had caused the official to show favor and sympathy to Daniel."

Daniel 1:8-9

REVIEW

Day 1 - The Committed Heart

Yesterday we learned about Daniel and his amazing life-long commitment to God. At the young age of fifteen, he was taken from all he knew and loved and forced to live a life he never chose. But astonishingly enough, although removed from all his family and security, Daniel kept his faith in God. We also observed God's faithfulness to Daniel as He blessed him throughout his life in Babylon. No doubt the greatest blessing God gave Daniel was his prophetic visions. Daniel was given an "aerial view" of the future and was greatly blessed to see the glory of the future kingdom of God.

BLOOMING IN A DESERT

How did Daniel live alone in a pagan culture for all those years and not become a pagan himself? What did this fifteen year-old boy's parents teach him that sustained him for the next seventy plus years? Even if they had known he would be taken away to a pagan land, how could they have prepared their son to be the only light in a dark land? How could they have readied him to become a prophet of God?

Although Daniel's parents were used by God to point him in the right direction, they were not the source of Daniel's great strength and dedication to God. Nor was his environment. Since most of his life was spent in a land that did not believe in God. It also wasn't due to any support system, for he had virtually no one the majority of his life. The source of Daniel's supreme dedication and faith in God is found in his heart. Daniel's heart was so firmly set on following God, that he could be stripped of everything and still remain faithful and steadfast. In fact, his heart was so dedicated to God that his faith grew without any outside spiritual nourishment at all.

Question and Reflect

How does your life compare to Daniel's? Describe how similar or different your physical life and spiritual life are to Daniel's.

_____

_____

_____

Your physical life: (similarities/differences)

_____

_____

Your spiritual life: (similarities/differences)

_____

_____

PHYSICAL SIMILARITIES

In many respects, our physical lives are very different from Daniel's in that we have not been abducted to a foreign land. We have family members with whom we can talk and visit with. If we don't have family, we most likely have friends or some sort of support system. And all of us in America have easy access to God's word.

But for some of us, our physical situations are strikingly similar to Daniel's. Maybe you have a health problem that restricts you and has stolen much of your freedom. You may have a job that requires you to work with unbelievers, leaving you to be the only "light" shining in a pagan land. Maybe you feel all alone as you raise your young children and the isolation is almost more than you can bear. Perhaps your children are grown and gone, leaving you to feel lonely and worthless. Or maybe some of you are like me, called to serve and minister to one of God's disabled lambs for the rest of your life. All your plans are forever set aside, most likely never to be accomplished. Your future holds many challenges and even more unknowns. There are times when you feel as though you have been robbed of your life, much as Daniel must have felt when his life so radically changed.

All of these situations can make us feel as though a straight jacket has been placed on us. I have literally had moments where I physically panicked from feeling so permanently trapped. There have been times when the reality of my situation began to sink into my heart, soul, and mind causing my heart to race and the adrenaline to pump. I have felt so trapped I've wanted to bolt. One day this anxiety erupted uncontrollably while dropping my daughter off at my mother's home. I was in such distress when I left that I burst out the door hearing myself say, "I cannot believe this is my life!" The fear of what my life had become had come to a head at that desperate moment.

Sister, if this is how you feel, I want to encourage you to turn to God. Ask Him to give you His perspective on your situation and help you hear His truth. These feelings of panic and anxiety are from the enemy. God is a God of peace, not fear. He is in full control and He knows exactly where you are and what you are going through. I can't tell you how many times the enemy had told me I am trapped. He repeatedly tells me I will never be free and that God does not love me enough to set me free. When I hear these lies, it is imperative I turn to God to hear His truth.

I remember one day in particular, when the straight jacket felt the tightest ever. I went to God in a crying heap of tears. He saw my distress and in great love gently spoke to my heart in a way that will forever bless me. He revealed to me that the tightness I felt was not my imagination and in fact was very real; it just wasn't coming from where I thought. He said, "The tightness you feel is not a straight jacket that binds you in isolation but rather it is my hands that are holding you secure. You can get out if you really want to but I am protecting you and molding you in my grip."

Since then, I've never been the same. The blessing of hearing His truth absolutely turned me around. His truth put things in proper perspective giving me greater faith, hope, and trust in Him. Do you see how the lies of the enemy can lead us to make wrong moves? I am not tied up and left forgotten by God. I am safe and secure in His holy hands. If I had bolted during my panic,

I would not have been escaping from a straight jacket, but rather from the hands of God. This is why we need His word and Spirit dwelling deep in our hearts so that when the lies of the enemy enter our heads, they will not take root in our hearts.

SPIRITUAL SIMILARITIES

How did you compare your spiritual life to Daniel's? In spite of the access we have to churches, Bibles, and Bible studies, America's spiritual health continues to drastically decline. While some of us can relate to Daniel's physical life, sadly few can relate to his spiritual life. Though totally deprived of a Godly environment, somehow Daniel thrived spiritually. How did he do it?

As we begin to look into how Daniel flourished in a spiritual desert, let's first stop and acknowledge that what Daniel had was not something meant just for him. His spiritual growth and maturity were not unique gifts reserved for only a few, but are available to all of God's children. That includes you! You too can grow close to God. The question is, do you want to?

Question and Reflect

Read Daniel 1:8 and describe Daniel's determination to not defile himself or his God. What words best describe this determination?

_____

_____

_____

_____

The NIV Bible states that Daniel "resolved" not to defile himself with the royal food and wine. Other translations say he "set his heart" or "determined." When we look up the words "resolve" and "determine" in the Webster's dictionary, we find the key that helped Daniel thrive spiritually alone in a pagan land. Let's look at these definitions to see what helped Daniel's spiritual growth even while in a spiritual desert.

Webster's definitions:

"Resolve"

- To break up/separate
- To reduce by analysis a problem into simple elements
- To distinguish between parts
- To separate into two components

"Determine"

- To fix conclusively or authoritatively
- To settle or decide by choice of alternatives or possibilities

Question and Reflect

Based on the above definitions, list two ways Daniel grew spiritually while living in a pagan land.

_____

_____

     Clearly one key was Daniel's conscious and deliberate decision not to defile himself or his God. That alone, however, was not what sustained him for over seventy years. What sustained and strengthened his faith was not only "what" he decided but also "where" he decided it - in his heart! It wasn't a "head" decision but a "heart" decision. We must learn to make the distinction between the two because any decision made in the head will not last since we are driven by our hearts. Here is another nugget we can't let slip away so let me say it again: <u>Any decision made in the head will not last since we are driven by our hearts.</u> If our heart insists on holding things back from God and dethroning Him, decisions will be made in the head that eventually cause us to weaken and falter in our faith and walk with God. Satan loves to persuade us to make only "head" decisions because he knows they will not lead to spiritual growth. He knows God looks at the heart and promises to strengthen and bless those whose hearts are set on Him. If Satan can get us to keep all our knowledge, decisions, and commitments in our heads, we will eventually fail in our commitment to the Lord.

> *"For the eyes of the LORD range throughout the Earth*
> *to strengthen those whose <u>hearts</u> are fully committed to him."*
> *2 Chronicles 16:9a*

     Notice in the verse above how God seeks to bless those who have already fully committed their hearts to Him. What Daniel had spiritually is not something unique to him, or reserved for only a few, and here is our proof. Scripture doesn't state that God searches only for the specially chosen, the anointed, or even the strong. It says He searches for those whose hearts are fully committed to Him. They are not perfect people and may not even be spiritually mature. They have simply set their hearts to seek God faithfully. Spiritual maturity and intimacy with God always come after, not before, this decision of the heart.

Question and Reflect

Read Daniel 1:9 and 17.

After Daniel resolved in his heart not to defile himself or his Lord, how did God bless Daniel and his three friends?

_____

_____

_____

CONCLUSION

Is your heart fully committed to God, or are you first waiting for Him to bless you? God will not bait you with a bribe in order to have your allegiance. Jesus has provided us salvation and granted us access to God. The rest is up to us. God wants us to come to Him with fully committed hearts. The degree of our commitment will determine the degree of our spiritual growth.

Regardless of whether you have lots of head knowledge about God or know very little, if your heart isn't fully committed, you will not achieve a close intimate relationship with God. Take a moment now to ask God to search your heart for any area you have not given to Him and ask Him to help you hand it over. Ask Him to take any head knowledge that you have and plant it deep in your heart where it can flourish and grow.

Week Four

Day 3 - Expectations of a Heart

"Many are the plans in a man's heart, but it is the Lord's purpose that prevails."
Proverbs 19:21

REVIEW

Day 1 - The Committed Heart

Day 2 - Setting Your Heart on God

This week we have read about Daniel's life-long commitment to God. In spite of being forced to live a life he would never have chosen, he determined in his heart to remain faithful to God. Though most likely never freed from his captivity in Babylon, God was faithful to bless Daniel far beyond what he could have ever anticipated.

It's hard to imagine how difficult it must have been for Daniel to realize that all his boyhood plans would most likely never come to be. As the years passed and the captivity continued, his expectations most likely dwindled and faded away. He must have wondered why God allowed this event in his life and what exactly He was doing. Amazingly enough, in spite of any disappointment he may have had, there is absolutely no record of Daniel ever being angry with God or failing in his faith. He kept his eyes and heart on God in complete obedience and never allowed this painful event to veer him off course.

Has there been an event in your life that has dashed your hopes and dreams?
_____
_____

How has this event affected your relationship with God?
_____
_____
_____
_____

ISRAEL ANTICIPATES THE MESSIAH

What dreams might have been dashed for Daniel? Surely he had them, for everyone ponders their future in their heart. And, what do we do when life doesn't turn out as we anticipated?

Question and Reflect

Read Daniel 1:3.

What kind of family did Daniel come from?

_____

_____

What kind of expectations might Daniel have had for his life as a young boy being born into this family?

_____

_____

      It must have been traumatizing for Daniel to be abducted from his home and family and taken to a foreign land at such a young age. But Daniel suffered an additional trauma by being taken from a family of royalty and nobility. His hopes were dashed and they were probably high ones too. As a Jewish boy born into an affluent family line, Daniel and his family waited for the coming Messiah and quite possibly dreamt He would be born into a royal family like theirs. Over the years, the Jewish people had developed an expectation of the coming Messiah that involved His being a great earthly king, who would come from a line of kings to redeem and restore the nation Israel. By the time Christ came, He was not at all what the Jewish people were expecting.

Read Isaiah 11:1-5 below foretelling the coming Messiah. Circle or highlight all the words describing the One the Jews were to anticipate.

> *"A shoot will come up from the stump of Jesse;*
> *from his roots a Branch will bear fruit.*
> *The Spirit of the LORD will rest on him--*
> *the Spirit of wisdom and of understanding,*
> *the Spirit of counsel and of power,*
> *the Spirit of knowledge and of the fear of the LORD--*
> *and he will delight in the fear of the LORD.*
> *He will not judge by what he sees with his eyes,*
> *or decide by what he hears with his ears;*
> *but with righteousness he will judge the needy,*
> *with justice he will give decisions for the poor of the Earth.*
> *He will strike the Earth with the rod of his mouth;*
> *with the breath of his lips he will slay the wicked.*
> *Righteousness will be his belt*
> *and faithfulness the sash around his waist."*

Now read Micah 5:2-5 below circling the same descriptions of the coming Messiah. Although Micah appears after the book of Daniel in your Bible, it was written before Daniel was born, so he would likely have been taught this passage as a boy.

> "But you, Bethlehem Ephrathah,
> though you are small among the clans of Judah,
> out of you will come for me
> one who will be ruler over Israel,
> whose origins are from of old,
> from ancient times. "
> Therefore Israel will be abandoned
> until the time when she who is in labor gives birth
> and the rest of his brothers return
> to join the Israelites.
> He will stand and shepherd his flock
> in the strength of the LORD,
> in the majesty of the name of the LORD his God.
> And they will live securely, for then his greatness
> will reach to the ends of the Earth.
> And he will be their peace."

Place yourself in Daniel's shoes and describe what you would expect in a coming Messiah given these verses from Isaiah and Micah.

_____
_____
_____
_____
_____
_____

    Surely Daniel, along with all the Jewish people throughout history, awaited a great and powerful Messiah. No doubt the more desperate the situation became for the Jews, the greater their anticipation of the One who would come and restore the people. He would come from the line of David and as a result, they expected a similar earthly king. And how disappointed, and eventually angry, the Jews became when Jesus didn't come as the much-anticipated, powerful, earthly king sent to free them. Similarly, Daniel must have been disappointed to find his life taking a completely different path than the one he had hoped for as a boy.

How do you think your spiritual walk would have fared if you, like Daniel, had been seized and brought to live in a foreign pagan land?

_____

_____

_____

_____

_____

Disappointments are part of life, and how we respond to them is critical to our spiritual growth and development. Some people grow closer to God in desperate times as Daniel did, while others stray far away, some never returning. Even a heart that is fully committed to God can be thrown for a loop when circumstances become too confusing or unsettling.

It boggles the mind that God greatly blessed Daniel throughout his life, but never chose to release him from captivity. Wouldn't it seem right that the greatest blessing would be freedom? Well apparently not, and as one who will probably be in a type of captivity all of her life, I can attest to the fact that God does bless those in confinement. In fact, often confinement IS the blessing, as it serves to tether us closer to God.

God richly blessed many great men of the Bible while in confinement. The apostle John was blessed with the revelation of Christ while on the isle of Patmos. Moses was prepared to bring Israel out of captivity while in the desert alone with God for forty years, and Paul wrote many of his New Testament letters from prison. Daniel is in good company with many great men of God who, while confined, allowed their captivity to become their solace with God. They didn't waste time mourning their loss, trying to talk God into freeing them or planning an escape. Instead, they remained steadfast where God planted them and as a result, they grew immensely.

CONCLUSION

Has God disappointed you in some way? Has He failed to rescue you from a painful situation? Is your primary goal to be removed from your situation or are you willing to learn what God has to teach you right where you are? Could it be that God is preparing you for a mighty work in this painful place?

Take a moment now to confess any disappointments you've had with God. Your honesty is vital, so put all your thoughts and feelings out on the table. Even if the disappointment seems small, or was from long ago, give it to God now. Commit to growing and blooming right where you are and trust that He has a plan for you and will bless you greatly!

_____

_____

_____

_____

Week Four

Day 4 - Hidden Agendas of the Heart

"Then Judas, the one who would betray him, said, "Surely not I, Rabbi?" Jesus answered, "Yes, it is you."
Matthew 26:25

REVIEW

Day 1 - The Committed Heart

Day 2 - Setting Your Heart on God

Day 3 - Expectations of a Heart

Yesterday we learned about Israel's expectant heart. God's people eagerly anticipated the coming Messiah, one who would redeem and restore the people as a nation. They anticipated a man much like King David. In the time of Christ, the Jewish people were living in oppression under the Roman Empire. Though allowed to worship their God, they were subject to the Roman government. Although the people of Israel had long since been a powerful and independent nation, their trust remained in the coming Messiah and the deliverance He would bring them.

Instead of taking a balloon ride high in the sky to get an aerial view, today we are going to dive deep to the bottom of the ocean floor of our hearts. You may be thinking, "Haven't we already dug deep into our hearts?" Yes, but God desires to dig deeper because our hearts are masters at manipulation. All of us are very skilled at projecting an image that does not truly reflect what lies deepest within us. Therefore, God seeks to methodically take us through each of these heart issues through this study. He desires that we see what is truly in our hearts so that we will be able to abide in Him and He in us.

BEYOND COMMITMENT

Having a committed heart like Daniel is vital to living a life dedicated to God. However, there is a "speed bump" in the road of life that can catch any genuinely committed and well-meaning Christian off guard. It can alter the path Christ intends for us to follow, and we must be very careful to either avoid this bump or at least keep in control if we hit it. It can be hard to see, since we tend to think that commitment to God equals faith, but this is not always true. It may not sound right or logical, but God's Word reveals this to be true. The Bible is full of examples of real people who appeared committed to God but deep in their hearts lacked faith. Why? Because they were thrown off course by the speed bump of unmet expectations. God wasn't what they expected, and His plan didn't match their own plan.

SO CLOSE TO CHRIST

Let's take a look at a man who was as close to Jesus as anyone could get during His walk on this Earth. He was one of the twelve disciples. The one always listed last, the one no one suspected, and the one who did the unpardonable when he betrayed our Lord…Judas. He may seem an unlikely person to learn from, but in reality, he is not so different from you and I.

Judas was a human being created by God who faced all the same feelings, thoughts, and temptations we face today. He walked and talked with Christ. He ate, traveled, and prayed with Him. Judas was closer to Christ physically than any of us will ever get while here on Earth, yet in spite of all the miracles and teachings he witnessed, his heart was never fully committed to Jesus.

Judas is a prime example of how we can project an outward image that in no way reflects what truly lies in our heart. On the outside Judas appeared more refined than the other disciples. He was the only non-Galilean, having come from Jerusalem. He of all people knew what to expect in a coming Messiah. When called by Christ, he like the others left everything to follow, but when times got tough, his true heart was revealed. And as with things of the heart, it shocked everyone.

HIDDEN AGENDAS

Earlier this week, we talked about how Daniel first committed his heart to God and then received blessings. Although Daniel was right to place his commitment before his expectations, it is more common for us to want God's blessings before we commit ourselves to Him. This subtle and frightening way of thinking is a symptom of a heart that holds a "hidden agenda." It is also the primary difference between Daniel, the eleven disciples, and Judas. While all their hearts were fully committed, only Judas' heart had a hidden agenda that kept him from submitting himself fully to Christ. It was so deep in Judas' heart that perhaps even he didn't recognize or acknowledge it.

What was Judas' hidden agenda? If he was evil from the start, why did Jesus choose him as one of the twelve disciples and allow him so close to Himself? If he wasn't evil from the start, what went so terribly wrong?

There are several theories why Judas betrayed Jesus:

1. Greed
2. Jealousy of the other apostles
3. Bitterness from unmet expectations that Christ was not the Messiah he expected
4. Fear of political persecution
5. He was a pawn of Satan

Question and Reflect

Of these five theories, which one do you think might explain Judas' actions?

_____

_____

_____

No one truly knows what motivated Judas to betray Jesus. It could be any one, or a little of all these theories. However, one stands out as foundational to the others. It's the true hidden agenda buried deep in Judas' heart, which cultivated and nurtured what came to be his most disastrous and regrettable action. Let it serve as a warning to us since all our hearts have the capacity to hide agendas that run counter to the will of God. The crux of all these theories is theory #3, the one snuggled in the very middle. Judas' faith was shattered because Jesus wasn't the Messiah he had hoped for and the bitterness of his broken dreams consumed him.

Since the time of King David, God's people eagerly anticipated the coming Messiah. Each generation taught the next that a savior would come to restore their nation and people. During these years of longing, the Jews gradually developed hidden expectations. They didn't intend to do this, but they did it just the same. Conscious or otherwise, the Jews expected a Messiah who would be a visibly strong king, like David, who would restore them as a people here on Earth.

After hundreds of years of persecution, captivity, waiting, and expecting, God's chosen people finally heard the voice of John the Baptist saying, "Look, the Lamb of God who takes away the sin of the world!" (John 1:29) Word spread quickly that the Messiah had finally come, and as Christ called each of His disciples, one by one they willing and eagerly followed. John 1 gives the account of Phillip and Nathanael's response to the news that the Messiah had come. In spite of their eager anticipation of the arrival of the Messiah, Jesus didn't fit their expectations even from the beginning,

Read John 1: 43-46.

When Nathanael heard about Jesus, what was his first response?

_____

_____

What does this tell us about the Jews' expectations about the coming Messiah?

_____

_____

_____

_____

Nathanael's response was the beginning of countless unmet expectations. As Christ lived out His ministry, he wasn't what many expected, which put a big speed bump in the lives of those who sought Him fervently.

Are we any different today? Once we begin to realize God's plan is not what we expected, our walk is challenged and tested. All the disciples hit the same speed bump, but only Judas allowed it to permanently detour him. Christ was not what any of them expected, which is why it took more than a commitment to follow Him. They each had to surrender and submit their deepest hopes and dreams by giving every inch of their hearts.

But many Jews rejected Jesus because He did not fit into their agenda, proving that commitment alone does not bring us into close fellowship with God. The unmet expectations that were planted deep in their hearts had been nurtured to the point where they were on the throne of their hearts above God Himself. Those who rejected Jesus chose not to submit their unmet expectations to God, and as a result, they missed the Messiah!

CONCLUSION

This, dear sister, this is the ocean floor of our hearts. This is where the rubber meets the road. We cannot go to God with preconceived ideas on how He should look, act, respond, or carry out His will. We must come giving Him everything because if we don't, like Judas, we will ultimately be driven by what lies deepest in our hearts. Like an undercurrent in the ocean, we will eventually be swept away by these deepest desires.

Is your life not what you had expected or hoped for? Have you sought God only to find His agenda does not match your own? If so, I know the heart ache. My life is nothing like I had originally planned. For years after hitting my speed bump, I lay stunned by the side of the road. But let me testify to you that though your life may not be what you had always hoped for, if you give it to God, it will become more that you ever expected. As with Daniel, God can take a life of broken dreams and turn it into something grand.

Tomorrow we are going to dive to the ocean floor of our hearts again. In the space below, ask God to prepare your heart for this journey. Ask Him to help you see clearly while at your heart's floor. It is normally pitch black down there but if you ask God to shine His light, He will reveal to you things that are often hidden to all but Him. Great healing and spiritual growth are at stake so get plenty of rest tonight-----you will need it for your dive tomorrow!

_____
_____
_____
_____
_____
_____
_____
_____
_____
_____

Week Four

Day 5 - Finding Our Heart's Hidden Agenda

"All a man's ways seem innocent to him but motives are weighed by the LORD. Commit to the LORD whatever you do, and your plans will succeed."
Proverbs 16:2-3

REVIEW

Day 1 - The Committed Heart

Day 2 - Setting Your Heart on God

Day 3 - Expectations of a Heart

Day 4 - Hidden Agendas of the Heart

Are you rested and ready for our journey today? Some of you will be going to deep places that you have never before allowed yourself to venture. Some of you don't want to take the dive out of fear of the unknown. Others of you are honestly eager to take the plunge. Regardless of how you feel, we all need to take this dive.

If it's fear that is overtaking you, remember God will always be at your side. If you are anxious about the unknown, remember God is never lost and He will guide your way. If you have been looking forward to this dive but are beginning to feel like a lamb being led to slaughter, remember God will protect you and He will never lead you to harm. Just as flying high above the ground in a hot air balloon can feel scary, so can diving deep into the ocean floor of our hearts. But in both cases, God is not only there to guide and protect us, but He is there to reveal and heal things that only He can reveal and heal.

STARTING AT THE BEGINNING

As Julie Andrews would sing, "Let's start at the very beginning….a very good place to start." The beginning is a very good place to start because we are dealing with the heart and its ability to manipulate, hide, and suppress. Many things are hidden deep in the heart for very good reasons. They have often been there for a long time and have since been forgotten. Broken dreams from long ago often act as debris in our hearts. We may be totally unaware of their presence, but God knows all about it and wants to gather them and make them into something new. His desire is to give us a bright future that involves Him, but we need to be willing to view this wreckage we hold deep inside.

Question and Reflect

Let's begin by thinking back on our childhood and teenage years. What do you remember being your life's dream regarding your career, personal accomplishments, husband, children, family or spiritual growth?

_____

_____

_____

_____

Now think about your dreams of today. How do they compare with those you had earlier in your life? Have your expectations changed? Have any come true? Have any been crushed? Take a moment to explain how you feel as you compare the dreams of the past with the reality of your life today.

_____

_____

_____

_____

While I hope you were able to write about things that have indeed come true, many of you probably wrote heartbreaking experiences of unmet expectations. Some of you may have found a deeply hidden dream you never knew existed and discovered it will most likely never come to pass. Maybe marriage isn't what you thought it would be or is yet to come true. Perhaps your children have brought great heartache and you feel as if there is no hope. Maybe you or your spouse's health is declining at a time in your life when you thought you would finally have the freedom to travel. Perhaps your spouse has died and your grief is more than you can bear. Some of you have had a lifetime of unresolved family conflict, and you wonder if things will ever change. Others of you have health problems that threaten your very life.

Oh sister, you are not alone. We all have problems and pain that come in different forms. We all have fantasies that never come true. Even those who appear to have a perfect life, struggle with unmet expectations. The question we must answer is how do we handle these things in life that haven't yet, and may never, come to pass?

HIDDEN HOPES AND DREAMS

We all have plans, many of which we are aware of and some we are not. For example, when I was a teen I had the tangible dream that I would finish college, find the perfect man, and start a family. I didn't realize however, that right on the heals of this conscious plan was an unconscious one as well. I could have never verbalized it at the time but there was another dream planted deep in my heart.

My unconscious dream was the assumption that my children would grow up to be independent adults. Concealed within me was the expectation of eventual freedom. This dream was hidden so deeply within my heart that I was completely unaware of its presence until our daughter was born. Once we began to realize the severity and permanence of her disabilities, the pain of this hidden, but very real shattered hope, began to surface.

Surprisingly enough, I was unable to identify the source of my pain because I was grieving over an expectation I had not yet identified. I felt and reacted to the pain of losing my anticipated freedom long before I was conscious of the dream itself. It took me years to realize how much I resented losing my freedom and still longer before I was able to put it into words and submit it to God. I spent many years grieving the loss of a dream I never knew I had. It wasn't until I allowed God to bring it to the surface that I could fully heal and move on.

WHAT DOES SCRIPTURE SAY ABOUT HOPE?

How can we clean up the wreckage that lies in our hearts? How can we prevent litter from developing in the future? Once again, the answers can be found in God's handbook of life—His Word!

Read Psalm 62:5. From where does our hope come?

_____

_____

Read Colossians 1:23. Where is our hope held?

_____

_____

Read Colossians 1:3-6. Where is our hope stored?

_____

_____

Read Isaiah 40:31. What four things are promised to those who hope in the Lord?

_____

_____

_____

_____

Read Isaiah 49:23. What is promised to those who hope in the Lord?

_____

_____

These verses teach us to place our hope in God to obtain strength, endurance, and guaranteed satisfaction. All hope comes from Him and is stored in heaven. We must read His word and seek Him in order to tap into this great source for the strength needed to get us through any trial. When we place our hope in God, we will never be disappointed!

Please don't misunderstand - there is nothing wrong with wanting good health, strong Christian children, a godly husband, and a life that is satisfying and pleasurable. But true intimacy with God and ultimate happiness will not be found in any of these things. They are only found in God! My hope of regaining freedom as my children leave the nest is forever dashed, but God has faithfully shown me that He has a better plan that happens to include my shattered dream. He and I have taken many dives into the depths of my heart to collect every broken shard, which my Creator has taken to form a new purpose before my very eyes. The very dream I so desperately wanted to come true was indeed broken down only for God to rebuild it into a new and greater dream, one custom built just for me.

It isn't wrong for you and I to have plans. God created us to have them, but we are never to place anything above His will and plan. We are called to submit everything to Him.

Question and Reflect

Do you have a broken dream you need to give to God? If so, what is it?

___

___

___

___

Do you trust Him to rebuild your dream into one greater than the original?

___

___

CONCLUSION

Unmet hopes can become scattered wreckage in our hearts. Do you see how very real, hidden, and corrosive these dreams can be to our hearts? It is so important that we ask God to examine our heart so that we can see for ourselves what lies deep in the depths of our soul. In so doing, we will find many answers to why we do what we do. We can also discover why we keep God at a distance, why we are not in God's will, why we are not receiving His blessings and quite simply, why we are miserable.

Scripture says that all of our motives and actions originate in the heart. If our hearts hurt, it will reflect in our actions, feelings, and spiritual development. This is why God has meticulously taken us through these lessons on the heart. While we may project a calm outward appearance for all to see, it only takes one storm to dredge up the filthiest litter from the deep waters of our hearts. And what lies deepest in our hearts is always what comes out when we are put to the test.

If your dive wasn't deep or long enough today, ask God to take you on another journey. Ask Him to reveal any unmet expectations from the past that are affecting your walk with Him today. If your self-esteem is low, or you feel bitter or depressed---take a dive. If you don't feel close to God and sense you are holding back from Him, take the time to examine what lies deepest in your heart. Be honest with Him so that when He is honest with you, you will hear Him clearly. Honesty is His language!

___

___

Week Five

Day 1 - Fearfully and Wonderfully Made

"I praise you because I am fearfully and wonderfully made; your works are wonderful, I know that full well."
Psalm 139:14

When I was a little girl, I wanted to follow God but feared where He might lead me. I learned of missionaries going off to Africa to live in the jungle and I thought that was what it meant to "follow God." I knew there was absolutely no hint of a desire in my heart to live in a buggy jungle without electricity, so I withheld my heart from God early on. This fear led me to choose my own path in life and never fully submit myself to Him. Like so many comfortable Christians, I had a love for God, but was only willing to follow Him if it meant I could stay in the United States with my luxuries.

I have since discovered that I had another misconception of God. I believed that if I followed God 100 percent, not only would I have to go where I didn't want to go, but I would have to become someone I didn't want to be. I assumed I wouldn't have as much fun and would require a complete overhaul to the core. Basically, I thought that if I submitted my life to God, I would lose my personality, personal goals, and all the things I loved and aspired to do. Naturally, the thought of becoming someone I wasn't born to be not only didn't sound good but also scared me. As a result I steered clear of the road that would take me closest to God.

Question and Reflect

Have you ever had (or still have) any misconceptions of what following God would do to your life? Even if you can't describe it by name, are you at least able to sense a hesitance in your spirit when thinking of completely following God? Explain (and be honest.)

_____

_____

_____

_____

_____

When I finally got to know God on a more personal level, I realized I couldn't have been more wrong about following Him. I had no idea that following the very One who created me would be the most rewarding path I could ever choose. Following God has indeed taken me through places I would never have wanted to go, but the ultimate destination is wonderful. Though I have not yet reached my final destination (since I am still breathing), just being on His path has given me a glimpse of what He has in store for us all. His path is so much more peaceful—even in the midst of life's storms. He is indeed the faithful and true One who will never steal our personality and ambitions to replace them with a life sentence to boring religious duties.

Oh sister, don't believe this lie like I did - it couldn't be further from the truth! God created us all as unique individuals with unique personalities, character traits, talents, ambitions, and goals. His intent is for them to be used to their fullest, not replaced with anything less. The truth is, when we give our all to Him, He takes that which He gave us originally and develops it into an even greater gift used to do His mighty work.

But how can we know for sure that following God is the most rewarding path? How can we know that when we give our all to Him, we won't end up feeling as though a great part of us has been taken away and we won't end up with regrets? How can we trust that we won't miss our old life once we turn and follow God?

In this week's study we will look at four men of the Bible and see how God uses our natural born talents, ambitions, and character traits to do a mighty work for His kingdom. Their example will bring great comfort by showing us we will never feel cheated or dissatisfied when following Him. We will, in fact, be totally fulfilled.

YOU ARE A UNIQUE AND TREASURED INDIVIDUAL!

All that we are, God has made us to be. As today's Bible verse says, we are fearfully and wonderfully made. We are a great workmanship of God, and we are to know it and praise Him for it. You are the only you, and you have been placed at this point in time on God's kingdom calendar to do a great work for Him. He has a special and unique purpose just for you that involves your very personality, talents, ambitions, and situation. The goal and purpose of our lessons this week is to reassure us that when we give ourselves to God, we will never have regrets. God will never take anything away from us that He will not replace in full measure, and it is imperative we trust in this truth. When we trust and know that God is always looking out for our best interests, we will then choose not to veer away from Him, but seek Him and all the blessings He has that are custom-built just for us.

Look up each verse below and list the talents and abilities that God gave.

Exodus 35:30-31 _____

Exodus 35:34 _____

Exodus 35:35 _____

Deuteronomy 8:18 _____

Daniel 5:12 _____

Read Romans 12:6-7.

According to verse 6, who has God blessed with gifts?

_____

_____

According to verse 7, what various gifts does God bless His people with?

_____

_____

_____

_____

What talents has God given you? (Don't leave this blank. Remember, when God created you, He blessed you with your own talents. Just think of things you enjoy doing or things that give you pleasure.)

_____

_____

According to Hebrews 2:4, who determined the abilities that God gave you?

_____

_____

These verses are such wonderful news. God has gifted each and every one of us with certain abilities, all according to His will. I was so comforted when I learned this truth. I can't tell you how many years I spent trying to be someone I wasn't. I focused on all that I wasn't and believed the lie that I was completely inadequate. The enemy had me so focused on my weaknesses that I couldn't see any of my strengths. It wasn't until I decided to head to God that He began to lift me up. He showed me my unique character qualities geared especially for His will and plan. How satisfying it is to finally live out what I was always meant to do. Isn't it funny how I always feared God would change me if I followed Him, yet I spent most of my youth trying to be something I wasn't? We can be such puzzling creatures.

THE FOUR "VARIED" GOSPEL WRITERS

The four Gospel writers are superb examples of how God not only gives, but also uses our personality, talents, ambitions, and goals. It is interesting to note how different each Gospel writer was individually and even more interesting how God used their unique differences to do His will. Remarkably, He was able to orchestrate His plan into being while never tampering with their personalities.

The lives of these men are excellent examples of how God can accomplish His will through an individual, while also allowing them to fulfill their own personal goals and dreams. With great honor and respect, God uses us just as He created us to be in order to accomplish His will. As a result, we both win. Now that's something only God can do!

> **Question and Reflect**

Look up each passage below and describe each Gospel writer.

Matthew (Matthew 9:9)

_____

_____

Mark (Acts 12:25, Colossians 4:10)

_____

_____

Luke (Colossians 4:14)

_____

_____

John (Matthew 4:21-22)

_____

_____

What a conglomerate group of authors: a tax collector, a friend, a doctor, and a fisherman called by God to testify to the life of His Son. These four ordinary, yet unique, individuals were called to do a mighty work and their diversity fit precisely into God's plan.

CONCLUSION

I find great comfort in knowing that following God doesn't require a personality transplant. You can still be you, and I can still be me. We are simply more fulfilled when we follow Him. Giving ourselves fully to Christ weeds out the bad and magnifies the good. Like a Holy sifter, He removes things that hold us back; leaving only what serves Him best. How exciting to know that God never seeks to steal anything from us, but rather always desires to bless us to the fullest extent.

This week as we look at each Gospel writer, my prayer is that you'll see the unique plan God has for you, which involves your distinct personality and character traits. I hope you will begin to see how God seeks to use all His children, just as we are, never desiring to turn us into "religious robots." Because of this there is nothing to fear and everything to look forward when following Him.

Ask God to reveal to you any hesitation you may have toward fully following Him. Thank Him for creating you as a unique one-of-a-kind individual, and ask Him to reveal to you His specific plan that involves you and your personal gifts.

_____

_____

Week Five

Day 2 - Matthew

"As Jesus went on from there, he saw a man named Matthew sitting at the tax collector's booth. " Follow me," he told him, and Matthew got up and followed him."

Matthew 9:9

REVIEW

Day 1-Fearfully and Wonderfully Made

Remember our lessons in week three when we took a balloon ride to get an aerial view of Christ? Taking this ride enabled us to get a new view of Christ and His majesty and deity. Much like that ride gave us a new perspective, the four Gospel writers give us four different perspectives of Christ and His ministry on Earth. Their views, though not aerial, are simply different, because each writer viewed the same person from a different angle.

To best understand these different views, imagine Christ standing on a rock preaching to a mass of people that are all around him in every direction. Now picture each Gospel writer standing next to Him, one on each of His four sides. Let's place Matthew on the north side, Mark on the south, Luke on the east, and John on the west. Each Gospel writer is listening to Jesus preach the same message, but their views are from four different angles. Not only is each man's literal perspective different, but each is also different in his personality, history, occupation, talents, abilities, and nationalities. As each man views Christ from his perspective, he then processes that view using his own distinct make up. With these four different people and their own personal perspectives, we get a compilation of writing that gives us all a full picture of Christ and His ministry while on Earth.

Not only does each Gospel writer have a different view of Christ, but each also possesses one of the four basic personality types. One writer has a dominant personality, one is an extrovert, one is patient, and one is a conformist. No matter who you are or what personality type you have, each of us can relate to, and learn from, one of these writers. This allows us to better understand at least one Gospel writer while seeing new perspectives through the others. Through it all we gain a more clear view of Christ.

God is so good! He is so comprehensive and works with such perfection. He knows just what we need, and He thinks of everything! And how considerate for Him to give us writings that we can each relate to on a personal level in order to learn and grow closer to Him. The more I learn about Him, the more I love Him.

MATTHEW THE CONFORMIST

We learned yesterday that Matthew was a tax collector. From the four personality types, this man of numbers definitely possessed the personality of a conformist. Knowing his occupation and reading his subsequent writing, it is clear his focus was on details and accuracy. As a conformist, he approached his work systematically. Because he enjoyed what he did, he was willing to endure persecution from all sides.

Along with being a tax collector for the Roman government, Matthew was a Jew. This was quite a volatile combination. Imagine the inner and outer battles that occurred with being a Jewish man living under Roman (pagan) rule and choosing an occupation that involves collecting taxes for the very government that oppressed your people. Matthew couldn't possibly have been favored in any man's eyes. To the Romans, he was looked down upon as a Jew. To the Jewish people, he worked for the enemy. If that wasn't enough, he worked in a profession that was widely known for its dishonesty. Everyone looked down on tax collectors with disdain and Matthew was no exception. Given these facts, I think it's safe to say that Matthew was a very strong individual. He dealt with many people in his job, and in spite of persecution from both sides, he managed to do his job, get along with people, believe in his God, and most of all, recognize the Messiah when he saw Him.

Question and Reflect

Read Luke 5:27-30.

When Jesus called Matthew (Levi) to follow Him, what two things do these verses say Matthew did?
_____
_____

Here we see the heart of Matthew. Unlike many Jews of that day, he immediately recognized the long awaited Messiah. Not only did he recognize Christ as the Son of God, but he also desired to share Him with his unsaved friends. He knew he had found something very special and he wanted to share it with his fellow tax collectors, i.e. sinners. Regardless of his occupation, his friends, and what people thought of him, Christ called Matthew and he immediately followed. Whether Matthew was a man of honesty or not didn't matter; when called---Matthew responded. From this act of obedience, God eventually used him as a conduit to reach the Jewish people.

As a Jewish man, Matthew knew the Jewish lifestyle, traditions, and beliefs. He knew the inner most workings of his people, and he knew the stumbling blocks that would cause many to reject their own Messiah. His writings clearly target the Jewish people as he repeatedly points them toward their Savior.

Remember our visual of Matthew on the north side of Jesus as He preaches to the masses all around Him? Imagine all the Jewish people of that day standing on the north side of Jesus behind Matthew. As Jesus speaks, Matthew takes in the teachings and interprets it for the Jewish people so they can best understand it. He speaks to them in their language. He is able to do so because he himself was a Jew. He reaches them by referring to more Old Testament prophecies than any other Gospel writer. He knew these prophecies were always in the forefront of the Jewish mind as they awaited the coming Messiah. His God-given interest in detail and meticulous record keeping honed through his occupation was used by God to record the genealogy of Christ (Matthew 1). This provided proof for the Jewish people that Jesus came from the line of David, the greatest Jewish king. He even went on to trace the lineage of Christ back to Abraham, the father of the entire Jewish nation.

MATTHEW ENHANCED

Isn't it wonderful to see God use Matthew's own gifts, talents and abilities? Matthew's interest in detail and accuracy, which was strong enough to override any persecution as a tax collector, was not extinguished when he followed Christ but rather enhanced and used by God. All that Matthew was before he followed Jesus was improved, amplified, and used by God. Matthew was greatly blessed as he used his skills for the kingdom of God.

I would have worked well with Matthew, because I am also a conformist. I cannot approach any project without a preset plan of some sort. Even if the system proves not to work, it helps me get started. I ponder every angle before I even begin to start. I chart and trend all sorts of things such as answered prayers, calories burnt in a workout, and my own menstrual cycle. I love to document things, and my profession as nurse only served to hone this skill more extensively.

If I could go back in time and visit Matthew in his day, I would love to present him with a huge care package. It would be full of sticky notes, pens, and spiral notebooks. As one conformist to another, I know he would love them! He could document and trend all the pertinent information that came his way. I can just envision his eyes lighting up with delight as he would gaze on all the items that would fulfill his heart's desire to obtain and maintain accuracy. He would be in hog heaven as he began to organize all the items in the package. I think the icing on the cake would be to present it all to him in a briefcase. Wow, something to actually carry all his prized possessions in wherever he went. Bless his heart---I love the guy!

Matthew, this great disciple of Jesus who possessed such a strong sense of detail, lived a life fully dedicated to Christ to the very end. He used every ounce of his God-given talent to reach his and God's own people----the Jewish nation. Matthew eventually translated his own Gospel writings from Greek into the Hebrew (Jewish) language. He went on to spread the Gospel in Parthia and Ethiopia, and was eventually fatally stabbed with a 6-foot sword. This sinner so looked down upon by the Jewish religious elite, was a unique and cherished individual whom God honored by using all his natural abilities to become an author of one of the books in His Holy Word.

CONCLUSION

Can you relate to Matthew as a detail oriented person? Or maybe you know of, or live with, such a personality. We conformists can drive people nutty, but our gifts come from the Lord and are meant to be used for His plan and purpose. Matthew used the skills he had and did what he loved to do right up to the point of his calling. When called to follow, he could never have known the great vision in store for him when he left his booth that day. This detail-oriented man was taken from being a tax collector sitting at a booth, to a Gospel writer whose name is now written on the walls in the New Jerusalem for all of God's children to see for eternity (Revelation 21:14). Matthew could never have imagined.

Is God calling you to leave your "booth" and follow Him?

_____

_____

Do you trust that He has great things in store for you beyond where you sit right now?

_____

_____

Write a prayer asking God to help you trust and follow Him today. If you doubt your talents, or feel hesitant to follow, confess it, He understands.

_____

Week Five

Day 3 - Mark

"He gives strength to the weary and increases the power of the weak."
Isaiah 40:29

REVIEW

Day 1 - Fearfully and Wonderfully Made

Day 2 - Matthew

Yesterday we learned about Matthew, the tax collector-turned-Gospel writer. We learned how God used Matthew's gifts as a detail oriented person to do His will while blessing him as an individual to the very end. Matthew's immediate obedience to follow Jesus that day at the tax collecting booth led to blessings far beyond what Matthew could have ever imagined. His submission to Christ that day is not only a testimony to how we should follow our Lord without hesitation, but it is also a testimony to the faithfulness of God to all who seek Him with a true heart!

MARK, THE EXTROVERT

Today we are going to learn about Mark, the second Gospel writer. But before we do, let me ask: Have you ever noticed that not all four Gospel books were authored by a disciple? It's easy to assume each writer was one of the twelve, but Mark and Luke were not. In fact, Mark is only mentioned four times in scripture, and his mention is meager at best. Let's get started by first reading what the Bible does say about Mark and go from there.

Read the following passages and write what you learn about Mark.

Acts 12:12-17

_____

_____

Acts 13:13

_____

_____

Acts 15:36-39

_____

_____

Colossians 4:10

_____

_____

From these verses, you probably gathered the fact that Mark (also called John Mark) was a friend of the apostle Peter, one of the twelve disciples. It was Mark's mother's home where Peter went first when he was miraculously released from prison by an angel. The household was fervently praying that night for Peter and was gathered together at the time of Peter's release. Mark's mother had a maid named Rhoda who answered the door, leading us to believe Mark came not only from a godly family, but a fairly well off one as well.

We see in Acts 13 that Mark left on a missionary journey with two of God's great men, Paul and Barnabas (Mark's cousin). Unfortunately, he prematurely returned to Jerusalem for a reason that clearly did not meet the approval of Paul. In Acts 15, Paul stated his extreme disapproval of Barnabas' suggestion to once again bring Mark on another missionary journey. The two men had such a dispute that they parted ways for good (Acts 15:39). Colossians 4:10 brings us great comfort that when all was said and done, Mark grew to be a faithful man of God, and Paul learned to trust and love him as well.

Though mentioned only four times, the scripture paints a clear picture that Mark had very close connections with some of the greatest men of the Bible. He knew Peter well and the two were close companions. Much of Mark's writings came from his friend Peter. Remember, Peter himself was quite the extrovert, and Mark's writing paints a full reflection of Peter's own personality. Perhaps Mark wrote for Peter because Peter couldn't sit still long enough to write down all that was in his mind. It wasn't until Peter's later years that he actually penned the books of First and Second Peter. Prior to that, Mark wrote as he spent time with his friend.

A "MARK" OF MATURITY

I am so happy to see, in Acts 15:39, that Mark was given a second chance, aren't you? Paul was a pistol and had no tolerance for anything less than 110 percent. When Paul had written Mark off as too weak to complete a missionary journey, Barnabas kept the faith. It was Barnabas who gave Mark his second chance, and it cost Barnabas any future missionary journeys with Paul. Mark and Barnabas were raised in a great godly family. They prayed together, they supported one another, and they forgave one another. Because of Mark's godly upbringing and support from his family and cousin, he was able to grow spiritually and eventually write one of the four Gospels.

Question and Reflect

Have you ever needed a second chance?

_____

_____

Have you ever had to give someone who disappointed you a second chance?

_____

_____

Our God is a God of second, third, and fourth chances, and for that He deserves our praise. Like Barnabas, God saw great potential in Mark. He knew that in spite of great failure, the heart of this weak young man eagerly wanted to do His will. Mark originally set out to do a good work but had to return home. He wasn't ready for the mission, but God continued to nurture him through his godly mother and family who warmly received him back. They took him in, allowing him more time to grow, so the next time he flew from the nest, he would soar to new heights.

We can be so unforgiving as Christians. How tempting it is to sit on our high horse, like Paul, as we weed out the weak that get in the way of our mission. I have perched on this high horse many times myself. Our daughter is very weak and often impedes my mission. God has gone to great lengths to teach me that my mission is not exclusive from those who can't keep up with me. In fact my mission involves those who are slower, and it's not for their sake that I should slow, but rather it is for my own, so that Christ may hone His qualities in me.

Riding a high horse leads to a painful fall for any who ride it. I often can't resist mounting this horse and when I do, it is by stepping onto a ladder made with rungs of pride, impatience, narrow-mindedness, hypocrisy, and selfishness. This ladder is sure to lead to a fall as it diverts us from the heart of God. I am not to run ahead of my daughter or drag her along side me at my preferred pace, because this is not a reflection of God. Our Lord never leaves us behind, nor does He skin our knees dragging us along side Him. He meets us right where we are as He lovingly tutors us along. As He does for us, we too should do for all His children.

Is there someone who is impeding your mission?
_____
_____

Could that someone be a Mark in the making?
_____
_____

Wouldn't you rather be a Barnabas to the weaker brother? It's so easy to be a pistol like Paul and misfire, shooting the weak that quite possibly hold in them great potential. What if God shot us down every time we failed? We'd all be lying on the side of the road dead. Encouragement is a gift that lasts a lifetime, giving the weak just what they need to fly in the right direction. And when they soar, it is an awesome sight to behold! This very workbook is an example of my husband's words of encouragement saying, "You can write your own workbook. You don't need anyone else to do it for you." How I thank him for saying those few simple words. They set me on the right course, and now I am finally off the ground, flying in the direction God has destined for me.

THE PEOPLE "SOUTH" OF JESUS

We used the analogy yesterday of Matthew and the Jewish people being on the "north side" of Jesus as He preached to the masses all around Him. Matthew was used by God to interpret the message to the Jews in their own language and culture. We envisioned Mark on the "south side" of Jesus. Mark was half Jew and half Gentile, so his writings were used to reach the Gentile people. This Gospel was penned in Rome, the center of world power of that day, and specifically written to the Roman Christians.

Mark does not go into detail as Matthew did with the genealogy of Christ. It also does not include as many of the Old Testament prophecies. It gets right to the point of Christ and what He did. Mark's writing reflected the actions of Christ and how He was always on the move. His extrovert personality mixed with his half Gentile nationality fit perfectly into writing to and reaching the Roman (Gentile) citizens. Matthew's approach would have bored them silly, and all the details would have gone over their heads. Mark's writings reflected his self in every way and fit his audience perfectly.

Here is yet another example of God's perfection. Matthew was given his niche in God's workforce, and so was Mark. Two very different men, one methodical, the other always on the go, and God found a perfect place for each of them. One followed Christ immediately. The other failed in his first mission trip. But God nurtured and strengthened this weaker one into an even more powerful state.

Can you relate to Mark? Does the enemy tell you that you should be more like Matthew in order to be effective in the work of God? Or maybe you started gung ho on a project only to fizzle out, feeling like a failure. Let me be like Barnabas and encourage you to be who you are, just as God created you. If you have failed in doing a work for God, even though you tried your hardest, don't be discouraged by believing God will never use you again. Simply go back home like Mark did, and let God nurture you into a stronger state. We are strengthened through our failures, and they are part of our precious history that God will use in the future. Remember, God uses all of us just the way we are, but He can only use those who let Him.

Question and Reflect

Read Romans 15:1.

From reading this verse, do you think Paul ever learned how he misfired when he shot down the chance for Mark to join him and Barnabas on the missionary journey?

_____

Praise God, Paul did learn. He also made mistakes, and thankfully he learned from them. Did you happen catch to whom Paul was writing in this verse? Yes, the very group Mark was called to reach - the Romans. Paul was called to a great work, but so was Mark. I cry as I read Paul's words in this verse because I understand his battle of dealing with the weaker. I struggle daily to deal with my daughter's weaknesses, and in the midst of these battles, my own weaknesses come to light. That is how God works. He strengthens the weak and breaks down those who are strong in their own power. The truth is we are all weak and need God every minute of the day.

CONCLUSION

I wish I could talk with you right now. If I could, I would love to hear what kind of talents God has given you. And I would thoroughly enjoy watching how God desires to use you and how He plans to carry it out. He is so creative! His back is never against the wall, and you will never hear Him say, "I don't know what to do with this one. I can't figure out how to use her." I assure you that if He can use me in spite of my severely restricted life, He can and will use you.

Take a moment now to write a prayer to thank God for giving you a second chance. You may be on your third or fourth chance and if so, you've got even more to thank Him for. Praise Him for any failures you have, or are experiencing, and trust that through these failures, He is teaching and tutoring you into a new creature. Listen for God's encouragement as He tells you to hang in there and not give up. Keep in mind that just like Matthew and Mark, you and I have no idea what great things God has in store for us.

Week Five

Day 4 - Luke

"As iron sharpens iron, so one man sharpens another."
Proverbs 27:17

REVIEW

Day 1 - Fearfully and Wonderfully Made

Day 2 - Matthew

Day 3 - Mark

This week we have learned about two of the four Gospel writers (Matthew and Mark) and their God-given personalities, gifts, and place in God's kingdom plan. Though very different from one another, God had a very specific purpose for their lives involving who they were created to be. Each man found complete personal and spiritual satisfaction when he followed Jesus and His call on his life.

Today we are going to look at our third Gospel writer, "Dr. Luke." Like Mark, Luke was not one of the twelve disciples, but was a very talented, gifted, and passionate man of God chosen to write the account of Jesus' ministry here on Earth. Luke was a physician by profession and was of Greek descent. He was most likely a very well educated man in both medicine and the Greek culture. His personality was the patient type. He was a good listener and demonstrated a calm patience with people. He was intelligent, skilled at his work, and a loyal man to his friends and to his God.

BEYOND MEDICINE

The first two chapters in the Gospel of Luke span the time from Jesus' conception, to His visit to the Temple at twelve years old. While Matthew also covered the genealogy and birth of Christ in his first two chapters, Luke went beyond the listing of the facts and delved into the workings of the Holy Spirit. Though very detail oriented, Luke shows a deeply compassionate heart that was greatly moved by the Spirit of God. He was acutely aware of, and in tune with, this third part of the Trinity, and his writing reflects this with a passion.

Question and Reflect

List the references to the Holy Spirit that Luke makes in the following verses regarding:

John the Baptist (Luke 1:11-15) _____

John the Baptist (Luke 1:80) _____

Mary (Luke 1:35) _____

John's mother Elizabeth (Luke 1:41) _____

John's father Zechariah (Luke 1:67) _____

Simeon (Luke 2:25-32) _____

Luke places a special emphasis on the work, power, and presence of the Holy Spirit in the life of Christ. He mentions the anointing of the Holy Spirit on John the Baptist while still in his mother's womb. What a powerful message the Spirit must have spoken to this man of medicine. Luke is a master at emphasizing the Spirit's power, and it is a common thread found throughout both of his writings in Luke and Acts. He stresses and magnifies the power of prayer and the powerful work of the Holy Spirit when it is initiated. Of all the gospels, Luke focuses the most on the prayer life of Christ and its importance before a significant event or decision. And he never fails to mention the powerful outcome that resulted.

THE MAN OF COMPASSION

Though a great historian, Luke's knowledge of the facts never blinded him to the healing miracles of our Lord. He wrote more about the healing ministry of Jesus than Matthew and Mark put together. I wonder if as a physician, he cherished these miracles more deeply. While many desperate people turned to Luke for healing, there were no doubt times he could not restore their health. This had to be very sad and frustrating for him.

As a nurse, I know the helpless feeling of not being able to help all who are sick and in need. In many cases, we can help and heal, but when we can't, it's difficult to accept. While medicine can do many things, it pales in comparison to the healing our Great Physician can do both inside and out. Luke's witness to the power of his God, Creator, and Healer proved to deepen his faith walk. He drew closer to his God, and as a result, exhibited the wonderful attributes of God in his faithful love and compassion for others.

Read the following verses and record the person who is showing compassion.

Matthew 9:35-36 _____

Matthew 14:14 _____

Matthew 15:32 _____

Matthew 20:34 _____

Mark 1:41 _____

Mark 6:34 _____

Mark 8:1-2 _____

While Matthew and Mark mention their observations of Christ's compassion in their Gospels, Luke gives specific attention to a concern for women, children, and the poor. Not only did he make special mention of the disadvantaged, but he also went beyond writing about it and exhibited it throughout his life.

What a wonderful man this physician must have been. His writings are saturated with the gentleness and compassion of the Lord. If he were in practice today, his waiting room would be full from sunrise to sunset. Believe it or not (and I don't think I have to say this twice), not all doctors were called to be doctors. Many doctors and nurses love medicine and science, but have the bedside manners of a telephone pole. Though responsible for the care of patients, they often fail to care with true compassion. A physician such as Luke is hard to come by. He was a man of God, and he chose the perfect profession using the talents and abilities he was blessed with from birth. In fact, he was so gifted that God chose to pair him with one of the greatest men of the New Testament, Paul.

A LOYAL FRIEND TO THE END

Luke was a gentle and compassionate man blessed by God with another quality that is also highly valued and hard to come by - loyalty.

Read 2 Timothy 4:11.

Who does Paul state was the only one left with him at this point in time?

_____

_____

When Paul wrote this second letter to Timothy, he was once again in prison. Unfortunately, unlike in his earlier imprisonment, he was not held under guard in a rented house, but was instead kept in a cold dungeon as he approached the end of his powerful life and ministry. He writes in 2 Timothy 1:15 that everyone in the province of Asia had deserted him and that it was only Luke who remained with him. He was cold, lonely, and nearing his end, but God blessed him with a friend who was loyal to the very end. Just as Mark needed encouragement in his times of weakness, Paul also needed a faithful friend who would listen and care for his needs during his time of weakness.

It is believed the thorn in Paul's flesh, which was never removed, was an eye condition that resulted from his temporary blindness on the road to Damascus (Acts 9). Whatever the thorn, Paul's physical needs were great. During his ministry, he was beaten, whipped, stoned, and left for dead on multiple occasions. God so faithfully provided His servant with a good friend and caregiver in Luke. Luke was perfect for Paul's physical, spiritual, and emotional needs.

I can just envision Paul alone in a cold, dark dungeon, looking forward for the time when Luke would come to visit. Lonely, hungry, and in need of companionship, he would perk up to hear Luke's voice saying: "I am here, my friend! What do you need? How can I help you? Any messages for me to deliver? Can we pray?"

How precious a good friend is. They are truly gifts from God, and Luke was such a friend. I have no doubt that Luke helped soften Paul's bold personality, not to diminish his powerful message to the people, but to aid in reaching them for God. Luke provided a wonderful example of patience, loyalty, and unconditional love to Paul. Perhaps Luke's influence also prevented some misfires like that which happened to Mark back in the beginning. As any good friend and companion in the Lord, Luke helped cultivate and grow the goodness of Christ in Paul.

REACHING THE WORLD

Referring back to our picture of Jesus standing on a rock preaching to the masses, recall that Matthew was on the north, interpreting the message for the Jews, and Mark was on the south, explaining Jesus to the Roman (pagan) world. Luke was on the east side of Jesus and used by God to help send the Gospel message to all Gentile people.

Question and Reflect

What was Paul's calling by the Lord according to Acts 9:15-16?

_____

_____

Under what man was Paul trained in the law according to Acts 22:3?

_____

_____

Who was this man according to Acts 5:34?

_____

_____

What a perfect and powerful mix of talents, gifts, and personalities. A compassionate Gentile physician teamed with a highly educated, but disabled Jew. God truly works in mysterious ways. Notice how God never chose to remove the thorn from Paul, but instead chose to provide one who Paul needed to sustain him - Luke. Without his thorn and Luke, Paul would have gone too fast and too hard for the cause of Christ. He needed to be tempered with compassion, and seasoned with humility in order to be most effective. Even with all the knowledge Paul obtained under Gamaliel, it would have been for naught without compassion and humility.

Like Paul, I also have a permanent thorn in the flesh. I am the hare, my daughter is the tortoise, and it's no coincidence God teamed us up. He uses her to slow me down. Without her, I'd get whipped up into a tornado, only to cause more damage than good. Although hard to accept, God sometimes chooses not to heal in order to better accomplish His perfect will and plan. We must be willing to fully submit to whatever path He chooses.

CONCLUSION

Friends like Luke are a rare and precious gift. They see us at our worst, yet stick by our side through thick and thin. It was Luke who wrote in Acts 7 how Paul, his future life-long friend, "gave his approval" at the stoning death of the Spirit-filled Stephen. However, Luke still forgave and accepted Paul as a brother in Christ. Luke never failed to reflect Christ as he gave his gift of loyal friendship to Paul to the very end.

Luke knew when to listen, when to talk, when to show up, and how to love in spite of another's weaknesses, faults, and failures. He never sought to exalt himself, and his emphasis on the power of the Holy Spirit reflects the very presence of God inside him. What humility and compassion we see in this great Gospel writer.

How I pray that you not only have a true friend like Luke in your life but that you are one as well. It's sometimes hard to be a friend through times of trial and tragedy, but it's God's desire that we be faithful and true to one another as Luke was to Paul. You may be someone's only remaining friend and the one she needs to help her be more like Christ.

Write a prayer below asking God to help you be a true friend to someone. Ask Him to fill you with His compassion, mercy, and faithfulness so that the image of Christ will reflect through you as it did in the great man, Luke.

_____
_____
_____
_____
_____
_____
_____
_____
_____
_____

Week Five

Day 5 - John

" This is the disciple who testifies to these things and who wrote them down. We know that his testimony is true. Jesus did many other things as well. If every one of them were written down, I suppose that even the whole world would not have room for the books that would be written."
John 21:24-25

REVIEW

Day 1 - Fearfully and Wonderfully Made

Day 2 - Matthew

Day 3 - Mark

Day 4 - Luke

It's day five and time to head west! We've looked at the other three horizons through the eyes of Matthew, Mark, and Luke, and now it's time to see Jesus through the eyes of John. One lesson could never say enough about this youngest disciple. Many books have been written about John himself, not to mention the New Testament books he wrote: the Gospel of John, 1st, 2nd, and 3rd John and Revelation. Although it's difficult to know where to begin with this great man, I pray the Holy Spirit will anoint you with His wisdom and knowledge in order to teach and guide you in this lesson.

THIS DOMINANT PERSONALITY

This week we've seen how God powerfully used Matthew, Mark, and Luke without ever stealing from their personalities, ambitions, and goals. In fact, God enhanced their natural qualities greatly. By obediently following God, these men discovered personal and spiritual growth far beyond what they could have ever imagined or achieved on their own.

Today we are going to learn how God used John, the disciple whom Jesus loved. He was quite different from Matthew and Luke, who were more detail oriented, and most likely quieter by nature. John was more like Mark because of his dominant personality. He was very good at making decisions and taking on the leadership position. Although you would never know by his writings, John was a bold, thunderous, and sometimes abrasive person (Matthew 20:24). He was the younger brother of the disciple James, both from an ambitious, hard working family.

Unlike the other Gospels, the book of John does not reflect his natural personality. His writing is far from bold and abrasive as it is penned with utmost love. He reveals aspects of the life of Christ that are not found in the other three Gospels, and targets the broadest audience of all, writing to both believers and non-believers alike. His focus remains steadfast on Christ, His deity, and His great love for all mankind. This Gospel was written to convict the hearts of all men in order to bring them to salvation through faith in Christ.

A MAN OF PRIDE AND PREJUDICE

Although John's writings reflect great humility and love, surprisingly enough he battled greatly with the cancerous and destructive sins of pride and prejudice. Though Jesus' closest earthly friend, he fought the same sins we wrestle with today. John's principal inner conflict consisted of resisting the desire to exalt himself, and his dominant personality made this battle very evident.

Read the following verses and label each passage as either an issue of "pride" or "prejudice."

Luke 9:51-55 _____

Mark 9:38-41 _____

You may have had trouble deciding which verse to label as pride and which to label as prejudice. These two sins are much like Siamese twins in that they are always conjoined. John's prejudice glares in Luke 9 as he and his brother ask for permission to send fire down on the Samaritans. What had these people done to deserve such a death? They failed to welcome Jesus into their city. They hadn't tried to stone Him, they hadn't caused a riot, and they didn't seek to trap Him. They simply did not welcome Him. Because of this, James and John asked for the Samaritans to be destroyed. They may have made their request under the guise of loyalty and defense, but Jesus knew what was deepest in their hearts. Their desire to destroy an entire city was an act of pride toward those who did not follow Christ as they had. Their sins stirred within them such a passion that they went so far as to ask Jesus for permission to do this themselves.

Mark 9 shows John's battle with pride as we see his desire to stop a man from driving out demons in the name of Jesus because he was not "one of the twelve." John fought such inner competition that he took the matter to Jesus asking that He stop this man. It's hard to imagine John so self-centered that he would limit the work of God in order to exalt himself, giving no thought for the individual who was now free from demonic possession. How callous and selfish to think only of what would benefit him while having total disregard for his fellow man. Pride and prejudice is a cancer that afflicts all mankind but when it's in the church among God's own children, it is an utter disgrace.

Have you ever experienced or witnessed pride and competition among believers? If so, what was the result?

_____

_____

_____

_____

According to Mark 9:38-41, how does Jesus feel about such behavior among His followers?

_____

_____

Pride serves to only to divide and weaken. It always pulls us from God and breaks unity among believers. Rather than a "thank you," this man who did a good work in the name of Jesus, was met with John's proposal to stop him from doing any more such work. John's request was no different than the Pharisees and Sadducees who wanted to stop Jesus because He healed on the Sabbath. We have all seen Christians jockeying for higher positions at the expense of a fellow believer. If we haven't done it ourselves, we have certainly felt it in our hearts. This behavior greatly grieves the Holy Spirit. And just as Christ rebuked John then, He admonishes this same behavior in us today.

Does it shock you to think that the disciple whom Jesus loved battled such sins? It's difficult enough to understand how Judas could betray Jesus, but even harder to comprehend John's murderous desires on an entire city simply because they did not welcome Jesus. If that wasn't enough, he of all people desired to limit God's miracles for the sole purpose of keeping the glory among the twelve.

It's disappointing to hear these things about people we admire and look up to. It can change our view of them forever. If you feel a bit shocked that John could possess such impure qualities, rest assured, you are not alone. No one was more shocked than John himself. Though we all fall short of the glory of God, those of higher profile can so easily fall faster and farther. This beloved disciple was no exception.

As John walked with Jesus during His ministry, he watched every miracle and move. The more he watched, the more he saw of God's glory, which in turn magnified his shortcomings. Conversely, the more he saw of himself, the brighter the glory of God became, and that dear sister is the secret to his passionate writing. The love Christ had for John in spite of his pride and prejudice, ignited in John the ability to write with uncharacteristic love and compassion. What a perfect example of God's ability to take that which is bad in us and turn it around to use for His glory. While the enemy desires to use our weaknesses to tear us down, God seeks to use them for good. Amazing!

Question and Reflect

Read John 1:14. What does John write about the glory of God?

_____

_____

Read John 21:25. What did John say about all that Jesus did?

_____

_____

John never stopped watching Christ as he marveled at God's glory dwelling in flesh. He watched and absorbed everything Christ did while continually seeing the contrast of Christ's majesty against the backdrop of his own sin. As a result, John developed into a man of profound love and humility. He began to shed all his natural negative qualities and take on the attributes of Christ. The murderous desires for the lost subsided and the fear of competition fell away. His bold and thunderous personality was not removed but rather transformed by the grace and power of God. Jesus truly loved this disciple.

We all battle with pride and prejudice. They are evil Siamese twins that run rampant in our society. They are nothing new to man as they serve as wedges that keep us from having a close, intimate, and personal relationship with God. John had to reject his pride and learn humility in order to be effective in founding the Church. These qualities are also required of us as we do the work that God has in store for us. There is hope for us all and John is our prime example. Jesus saw the potential in John and allowed him to see and experience the transforming power of the Holy Spirit.

THE POWERFUL TRANSFORMATION THROUGH THE REVELATION OF JESUS CHRIST

According to Revelation 1:3, what does John write will happen to those who read the writings of this book?

_____

_____

    I can attest to the fact this is true. Reading and studying the book of Revelation always blesses me. Always. Every time. This book used to frighten me something awful, but I have been blessed to recently discover the great peace it provides through the knowledge of Christ. After all, this is how the book got its name. It is not the revelation of John, but the revelation of Jesus Christ to John. To all who read it, their prize is the revelation of Christ Himself, the Prince of peace.

    Sister, there is no greater blessing than to have more of Christ revealed to you. Only Christ can remove the pride and prejudice we all have in our hearts and replace it with humility and love. We are simply incapable of doing it ourselves. We cannot read God's Word and try to imitate the actions. We need the Spirit of the Living God residing in and transforming us. John could not change himself, and we cannot change ourselves. But John experienced an amazing transformation through Christ by watching His every move, and clinging to His side. We are called to do the same.

Read Acts 8:14-17.

From Acts 8 to Luke 9, what transformation do you see in John's behavior?

_____

_____

_____

_____

    The Holy Spirit had completely transformed John. He went from wanting to destroy the Samaritans in Luke 9, to placing his hands on them and giving them the gift of the Spirit in Acts 8. John now possessed and exhibited the grace and love of Christ to the very ones he earlier sought to destroy. His pride and prejudice subsided allowing humility and love to abound. God had spared John and the people of Samaria for a greater purpose. What an example of God's love, compassion, and mercy for us all.

CONCLUSION

    In closing, I pray that God has revealed to you how valuable you are to Him. You may not feel special in the eyes of man, but I guarantee, you are the apple of His eye! He has blessed you with your personality, abilities, talents, and desires for a very good reason. I often battle feeling insignificant in this big world, but the knowledge of Christ quickly removes any feelings of worthlessness and replaces them with the security of knowing I am exactly who He created me to be. I have a purpose and plan that is His and His alone. The same is true for you. You and I were fearfully and wonderfully created as one-of-kind. God has a special plan for each one of us and it is greater than our minds can fathom. Never let the enemy steal this nugget of truth from you.

    Take a moment to write a prayer asking God to reveal, guide, and strengthen His plan in you. Thank Him for how He created you, and ask Him to use you and your gifts for His kingdom. I promise you, He will bless your request!

_____
_____
_____
_____
_____
_____
_____
_____
_____
_____
_____

Week Six

Day 1 - Pride, the Roadblock to Intimacy

"I love those who love me, and those who seek me find me."
Proverbs 8:17

You might be surprised to know that we are just now getting into what I had hoped to begin five weeks ago. Originally I planned to teach the how's and why's of prayer way back at the beginning, but that was not God's plan. He made it very clear to me early on that learning how to pray and overcoming the challenges of obtaining a powerful prayer life were futile if certain issues of the heart were not dealt with first.

True to God's nature, He has indeed taken us on a wonderful journey. We have been up in a hot air balloon to get an aerial view of Christ and dived deep into the bottom of the ocean floor of our hearts to retrieve the shards of shattered hopes and dreams. We have seen Christ from four different perspectives through the eyes of common men, yet we are far from done. Finally, it's God's desire that we now begin to learn how to implement the power of prayer into our lives.

A PIPELINE TO GOD

Have you ever marveled at how someone seems to have a pipeline to God? We stand in awe of those who seem to hear and follow God with clarity and look upon it as a special gift that only a few are given. While we may think it's great and even wish we had this gift, we often don't believe it is available to us. This grieves my heart because it simply isn't true. To believe that only a few people can clearly communicate with God is to believe a lie from the enemy. And any time we believe the enemy, he steals blessings that are ours as children of the King. God wants us to know that we can have clear, close, and intimate communication with Him no matter who we are.

It's comforting to know that you don't have to be overly smart or super intuitive. God hears the simple prayers of a child, even a spiritual infant. You don't need to have a degree in theology, a special anointing, or learn a new language. All you need is a true desire to know God and a willingness to act on that desire. In a nutshell you need a committed heart. Will it come fast? No, probably not. Will it come easy? Don't expect this either because, like getting to know anyone, a deep relationship with God involves time, energy, and perseverance. There is no speedy formula.

EVERY DAY HAS A ROADBLOCK

Getting to know God is both simple and difficult. It is simple in that all we must do is set our heart on Him as Daniel did. But it's difficult since we struggle with daily pride as John the apostle did. Pride is the common thread that runs through each of us, and its presence hinders any possible chance of having a close relationship with God. The only way this thread can be cut is through daily submission to Him. Without this sincere act, the roadblock of pride will detour us from God at every turn. There are no exceptions to this rule.

Think of each day as a journey down a new road that is an extension from the day before and a link to tomorrow. We wake each day to begin a new voyage down a road never before traveled. Each new day offers the choice to either overcome or surrender to the sin of pride. We choose to overcome pride as we submit to God's will, which leads us closer to Him, or pursue our pride, which leads us away from Him. Our nearness to God is a direct result of the daily choices we make.

Question and Reflect

Read Psalm 10:4 below:

"In his pride the wicked does not seek him;
in all his thoughts there is no room for God."

According to Psalm 10:4, what is it that crowds out God?

_____
_____

How is the individual with pride described in this verse?

_____
_____

    A shallow relationship with God is never God's fault. His love and compassion to man is abundant far beyond that which we deserve. He is completely fair as He gives everyone the same opportunity to seek Him. Though setting our hearts on God may sound simple, it is a continuous daily battle, since our natural tendency is to set our hearts and minds on our own desires.

    In week three of our study, we learned about the wedges of sin and how God and sin are forever incompatible. When we harbor the sin of pride in our hearts, we cannot approach God on an intimate level. Pride prevents us from either drawing near to Him in the first place, or it will dissolve any intimacy we once had with Him. What is scary is that the sin of pride is so subtle and natural to us that it can make drifting from God as easy as doing nothing. All we have to do is live our life the way that comes natural to us, one day at a time, with our own best interest at heart. All Christians commit themselves to God at some point in their life, but many fail to follow up on that commitment on a daily basis. They simply don't realize that unless they consciously reinstate their commitment to Him each day, they will unknowingly drift from God.

    Life was never meant to be one long haphazard block of time that, once set in motion, is never monitored again. On the contrary, life is a compilation of countless individual 24-hour segments of time that require careful daily supervision. Any life fully committed to God is, in reality, a life that is repeatedly committed to Him day after day. No great man or woman of God makes one single commitment but rather achieves closeness with God by recommitting himself on a daily basis. There is no special anointing - just simple daily commitment to God.

SELF EVALUATION

How often do you feel you hear from God? Check one.

_____ Never

_____ Once/Twice in my life

_____ Once a year

_____ God speaks/leads me on a regular basis

When was the last time you heard a word from God? If you can't remember the time, can you recall the topic?

_____

_____

If you were able to name the last time that God spoke to you, how did you know it was God?

_____

_____

_____

_____

How often do you set aside time to be alone with God in prayer and Bible reading each week? Keep in mind the focus is on the number of times, not the amount of time. Circle one.

Once a week

2-3 times a week

3-4 times a week

5-7 times a week

More than once a day

Now compare your answers and see how they relate with one another. Does the amount of time you spend alone with God affect how often you hear God speak?

_____

_____

    I don't have to know your answers to tell you that the amount of time spent alone with God will always have a direct impact on how often you hear from God. If you can't remember the last time you heard a word from God or felt Him clearly leading you, you are spending too little time with Him. And be careful not to mistake time spent working for God in church activities as time spent alone with God. These activities cannot bring you closer to God and will not earn you greater standing with Him. Only time spent alone with Him will bring you to a more intimate relationship. There is simply no other way.

THE PREREQUISITE TO FINDING GOD

Read 1 Chronicles 28:9 below:

"And you, my son Solomon, acknowledge the God of your father, and serve him with wholehearted devotion and with a willing mind, for the LORD searches every heart and understands every motive behind the thoughts. If you seek him, he will be found by you; but if you forsake him, he will reject you forever."

According this verse, how are we to seek God?

_____

_____

_____

_____

Why are we to serve God with all of our heart?

_____

_____

_____

_____

Serving God with our whole heart is the prerequisite to finding Him. This verse tells us that we are either seeking God or we are forsaking Him – there is no middle ground. This can be a stumbling block for many Christians since they believe that forsaking God involves an all out rebellion, not just withholding a little of their life or heart from Him. When we don't seek God and give Him our time and attention on a daily basis, we are turning our backs on Him, and we will not find Him.

Are you seeking God wholeheartedly or are you forsaking Him? (Be honest, even if it hurts.)

_____

_____

_____

_____

We often lack genuine honesty when answering questions like this. But the truth remains – our level of intimacy with God measures our commitment to Him. If you cannot hear His voice, you are not in close fellowship with Him. God is occasionally quiet but if you rarely or never hear Him speak to your heart, you are not in close fellowship with Him.

I wonder by chance, does this disturb you? Have you have sought God but feel as though He will not be found? Are you doing all you know to do to find God but simply can't? It's important to understand that God never changes and makes no exceptions among His children. He doesn't associate only with those who project a certain image or do a certain work. He doesn't play favorites with some while ignoring others. He searches all our hearts, determine our motives, and responds accordingly. The pure heart draws Him in, and the deceitful heart pushes Him away.

1 Chronicles 28:9 tells us that as we approach God in prayer, He searches our heart to determine our motive. This implies that even in the midst of seeking Him, we have the capacity to do so with motives that are impure and unacceptable to Him. So often we tend to think that if we are seeking God, we are doing the greatest of all things, but according to this verse, that is not always true. Many of God's children approach Him with motives that run contrary to His will. They may be doing top-notch work for God, but deep inside they reserve part of their heart for their own agenda. These hidden ulterior motives are what keep us from finding God. He sees them and they push Him away. If we are seeking God but are failing to find Him, we can trust the cause to be one of pride and failure to submit.

Have you ever approached God with a request that ran contrary to His will?
_____
_____

What was God's response to that request?
_____
_____

MAKING A COVENANT WITH GOD

When I awoke from my "Christian coma," one of the first things I noticed was something that had been with me all along, God's faithfulness. I had wandered and rebelled for many years but He never left my side. It captivated my attention and prompted me to make a covenant with Him. I promised Him that from that moment on, I would spend time each day with Him in prayer and Bible study for the rest of my life. Even if it was just five minutes a day, I was determined to keep this promise, and to this day I have.

When I made this pledge, I was totally sincere even though I was a spiritual infant, ignorant about prayer and lacking in Bible knowledge. Nevertheless, I was determined to seek my Lord. All I knew was that He had been faithful to me through all my rebellious years, and the least I could do was be true to Him for the rest of my life. I sought Him with all my heart, and He faithfully met me each day, allowing me to get to know and understand more of Him. Because of my commitment to Him, I have learned to perceive His voice and follow His will for my life. I am not especially anointed or chosen, nor do I possess any special gift or skill. I simply committed myself fully to Him and He responded to my devotion.

CONCLUSION

Have you ever made a promise to God that you would meet Him each day in prayer, Bible study or reading? If not, I encourage you to do so. God honors those who honor Him and will bless you far beyond what you can ever imagine. If you fear making a commitment due to the time required, let me encourage you to focus on the commitment itself, not on the time involved. The problem isn't finding the time - it is finding the dedication. A dedicated heart will always find the time for that to which it has committed itself. Remember, you are entrusting yourself to God who is the creator of time. He will make sure that it is not an issue.

If you sincerely want to draw near to God and wish to make a lifelong promise to Him, I encourage you to do it now. In the space below, write a prayer telling God you are ready to commit time to Him each day for the rest of your life. Determine in your heart to seek Him and then trust Him, knowing you will not be disappointed.

_____
_____
_____
_____
_____
_____
_____
_____
_____
_____
_____

Week Six

Day 2 - The Battle of True Submission

"Submit yourselves, then, to God. Resist the devil, and he will flee from you. Come near to God and he will come near to you."
James 4:7-8

REVIEW

Day 1 - Pride, the Roadblock to Intimacy

Yesterday we talked about how pride is a roadblock to our drawing near to God. What we do with our pride each day directly affects our relationship to God. We all face the battle of pride on a daily basis. Regardless of our good intentions and the hard work we may do for God, if our motives are even slightly prideful, we will not please God, and He will not draw near to us.

So how do we deal with this sin of pride so that we can develop closeness to God? Good news: being aware of the fight is half the battle! Not knowing that we face this roadblock each day is a sure recipe for disaster. If drifting from God is as easy as doing nothing, then being unaware of our sin of pride is sure to keep us far from Him. In order to overcome this hurdle, we must first look for it each day and then decide to fully submit to God's will. Once we develop the daily habit of submission, we are then able to move on to learn how to pray. But if we don't first learn the importance of approaching God in humility, it will all be for naught. Since God is always looking at our hearts, we need to first learn how to pray with a humble and submitted heart so that God will hear and respond to our prayers. To approach Him any other way is an act of futility.

Question and Reflect

Read Daniel 10:12.
What did the archangel Michael tell Daniel were the two reasons that God heard his prayers?

_____

_____

Read James 4:3, 6-10

What does James say is the reason we do not receive what we ask of God? (vs 3)

_____

_____

In verses 7 and 8, what is the key to drawing near to God?

_____

_____

After learning about Daniel's exemplary commitment to God, it isn't difficult to picture his heart humbly submitted to God. But James writes from a completely different perspective. While Daniel lived under the old-covenant law, James, Jesus' half brother, literally grew up in the same house with the new covenant. The long-awaited Messiah had come and been placed right under his nose, but James did not recognize Him. Unable to see the forest for the trees, he simply couldn't see his brother as the Messiah. It wasn't until Jesus died that James saw Him as Deliverer and Lord. Unlike Daniel, his commitment came much later in life, but in spite of delayed belief, he was the first author to pen a New Testament book. (Though not listed first, the book of James was written first.)

The critical moment for James came when Christ appeared to him after His resurrection. (1 Corinthians 15:7) The once convoluted image of his controversial brother at long last gave way to the knowledge that Jesus was indeed the Son of God and not an illegitimate brother. With this new revelation in mind, James was able to see Christ as He truly is, a pure reflection of God, and perfect example of humility and submission to the Father. With this knowledge at hand, James wasted no time writing down these keys to obtaining true intimacy with God.

Isn't it interesting that James mentions the motives of our hearts as 1 Chronicles 28:9 did yesterday? He says we ask but do not receive because we ask with wrong motives. I can tell you from experience that writers can only write from the experiences they have lived. You simply cannot write with power and passion about that which you do not know first hand. James knew all too well the guilt of praying with wrong motives in his heart. Though raised in a godly home and the brother of the Messiah, James battled a heart that sought God with ulterior motives. He knew the struggle, and he fought it for years until his heart was revealed through the revelation of Christ. At that moment, profound healing, divine restoration, and overwhelming intimacy with God began. What a comfort we find when we finally see Jesus.

Read John 7:5.

How do you think James could live with Jesus all his life and fail to see Him as the Son of God?

_____

_____

Maybe James couldn't see Jesus because he was too close (kind of like looking for your glasses when they're atop your head.) James is a perfect example of those of us who come from religious homes, serve in many church activities, and do every good thing there is to do, yet still fall short of putting Jesus on the throne of our hearts.

James was no doubt a good man from a good home, but let's face it, he was a late bloomer. He grew up with Jesus as his big brother and still didn't believe. Maybe he suffered from spiritual farsightedness and needed distance in order to see Christ clearly. Perhaps the view of his brother was so narrow that it required seeing Him after the resurrection for things to fall in place. James no doubt possessed a heart that wanted to find the Messiah, but he suffered from very poor vision. Much like James, we too must see Jesus in our own personal and profound way in order for it to click and that, my friend, is Christ's specialty. Just as Jesus revealed Himself to his brother James,

He seeks to reveal Himself to you.

A 20/20 HEART

Once James accurately saw Jesus, his heart's vision became 20/20. He went on to become a prominent early church leader and lived the rest of his life dedicated to his brother and Lord. He died the death of a martyr, but his vision of Christ never faded. In God's grace and mercy, James was given just what he needed to see Christ fully, and once he did, he bloomed beyond measure.

Read James 1:1.

How did James describe himself as he opens his letter to the twelve tribes?

_____

_____

When Jesus reveals Himself to His children, all doubt, shame, disgrace, and disbelief are dispelled, and James was no exception. His new view of Christ convinced him beyond a shadow of a doubt that his brother Jesus was indeed the Messiah. The first words he wrote in his book are those describing himself as "a servant of God and of the Lord Jesus Christ." As a result of the revelation of Christ, he automatically knew his place; a place of complete humility and submission before God the Father and His Son Jesus.

Submission is so pleasing and attractive to God. When we submit our hearts to Him, we become malleable, curable, and then usable. Just as pride repels and pulls us away from Him, submission serves as a magnet that draws us near to the very heart of God!

Re-read James 4:7-8a.

"Submit yourselves, then, to God.
Resist the devil, and he will flee from you.
Come near to God and he will come near to you."

Fill in the blanks to list the three instructions James gives in these verses, noting their order.

_____ yourselves to _____.

_____ the devil and he will flee from you.

_____ near to God and He will _____ near to you.

James provides us with detailed steps on how to approach God, and it's no big mystery. First, we submit our hearts to Him, and then we resist the devil. Once we have done these two things, we will draw near to God, and He will draw near to us!

Read Matthew 6:24a below:

"No one can serve two masters.
Either he will hate the one and love the other,
or he will be devoted to the one and despise the other."

    The word "serve" in this verse means to "be in bondage to" or to "be a slave to." Does this ring any bells? Remember how James introduced himself in the first sentence of his book? He identified himself as a "servant" of God and of Jesus Christ. He began his letter by letting his readers, the Jewish Christians of the new church, know that he was a servant to God and Christ. This was the foundation of his message.

Is your submission to God the foundation of your life? Do you think of yourself as a servant in bondage to Christ?

_____

_____

    Remember, while it doesn't count if we act like a servant, it does if God looks at our hearts and sees a servant attitude. He isn't impressed by our busy calendars or all the activities we do for Him. God only draws close to the heart that seeks Him and His will above all else. The prayers of humble and submitted saints are lifted high to Him like sweet incense, and He savors each and every one of them.

CONCLUSION

    Do you want God to savor your prayers like sweet incense? Do you want to hear Him to say, "Bring that little one to Me. I want her close because she is truly seeking Me with all her heart. She is someone through whom I can do a great and mighty work." Many of God's children want this but their prayers are not received and accepted by the Lord due to ulterior motives that lie deep and undetected.

    Submitting to God takes a lot of practice, and none of us ever master it completely. It runs contrary to our prideful nature, which is why it must be dealt with on a daily, hourly, and sometimes minute-by-minute basis. As we end today's lesson, ask God to hear your prayers. Ask Him to show you how to submit more of yourself to Him so that He can welcome your prayers. Claim the name of a "servant" to God and Jesus.

_____

_____

_____

_____

Week Six

Day 3 - Clinging to Our Clocks

"There is a time for everything and a season for every activity under heaven."
Ecclesiastes 3:1

REVIEW

Day 1 - Pride, the Roadblock to Intimacy

Day 2 - The Battle of True Submission

Yesterday we read in Matthew 6:24 that no one can devote themselves to two masters. We will either hate one and love the other or be devoted to one and despise the other. Whatever "master" we choose to serve is also the one to whom we submit ourselves. God wants us to submit to Him with every fiber of our being because when we do, we are then (and only then) placing ourselves in the position where we can be healed, rejuvenated, and used for His great plan. It is not until we approach Him in true humble submission that we are able to approach Him at all.

We discussed earlier in our study the subtle sins of the heart. Now that we are getting down to the nitty gritty of how to obtain a powerful prayer life, this issue is more important than ever. It is common to assume that when we approach God in prayer, our motives are pure and our will lines up with His. But as we have learned this week, we all have the capacity to approach God with ulterior motives and with hearts that mean well but can run contrary to His will. Knowing and admitting you have this capacity within you is your first step to true humility before God.

A BATTLE OF WILLS

Submitting my heart to the will of God has been the hardest thing I have ever tried to do. Nursing school had its challenges, working with certain individuals throughout the years nearly drove me over the edge, and discovering that the world does not revolve around me has been a real eye opener. But the most difficult thing by far has been seeking to give every square inch of my heart to God. In the midst of my attempts to hand God all my real estate, I have discovered two things. I feel great peace when giving certain parts of my life to Him and great anxiety when trying to submit others. It's a mixed bag of continual challenges that confront us every day.

My last great battle with God's will was actually not long ago. It occurred long after I awoke from my Christian coma and surfaced in the midst of a desert of sorts, during a long time of simply being alone with God. The battle began to brew when God gave me a vision. It was a sketchy vision at best but one that was revealed several times and through several different people. It involved His purpose and plan for my life and I found the whole thing very exciting! Being a rather impatient person, once I was convinced this was not a figment of my imagination, I was energized and ready to go. I was ready to begin work the next day. Spiritually speaking, I got myself dressed and headed for the door. But there was a problem -- it wasn't time to begin.

Do you have any idea what it does to an impatient person when you tell them to do something but to first wait? It is brutal. Like fertilizer on a lawn, it only makes the enthusiasm grow. This revelation of my call followed by the instruction to wait was the perfect recipe for a battle between God and myself. And that is precisely what happened. How exasperating to finally be on the same page, only to discover our timetables were different. I wanted to start, but God said wait. This issue of timing was a real showstopper, and as it turned out, was the first of many battles He and I would have with regards to His schedule versus mine.

GOD'S PERFECT TIMING

Why would God give anyone a vision and then make him or her wait? There are many reasons, and we could never know them all. However, we are usually asked to wait for two reasons: 1) the timing of people and events around us and 2) the timing related to personal/spiritual issues within us. The second reason is probably the most important of all. As an impatient person, God knew that before I could ever fulfill His mission for me, I must first learn to submit my schedule to Him. By revealing His vision for me and then requiring me to wait, God was teaching me to submit that which was most valuable to me, my clock.

Question and Reflect

What vision or promise did God give to Abram (Abraham) in Genesis 12:1-3?

___

___

Read Genesis 15:1-6.

What vision or covenant did God give to Abram (Abraham) again?

___

___

Did Abraham believe and trust God and His promise?

___

___

Abraham was a man of great faith. He believed and trusted fully in God. His great faith drew him to the very heart of God, and as a result, he is the only man listed in the "Hall of Faith" three times (Hebrews 11:8, 11 and 17.) But even this great man of God dealt with issues of the heart that ran contrary to God's will. Though repeatedly told by God that he would become a great nation through a son from his own body, (Genesis 15:4), Abraham battled God's timetable. The difference in God's timing and his own was so vast it provoked Abraham to take matters in his own hands.

Read Genesis 16:1-4.

When Abraham agreed to have an heir through Sarai's maidservant Hagar, both he and Sarai were rebelling against God. Outwardly they appeared to be seeking the will of God, but in the end they were rejecting His timing. In a nutshell, they were tired of waiting, so they took matters into their own hands. They wanted to move things along, so they concocted their own plan to bring about God's plan. It would have been a good idea, if it had only been God's plan. But it wasn't.

Like Abraham and Sarai, we too are tempted to rebel against God by abandoning His timetable. If we are fortunate enough to get a glimpse of His plan, we inevitably fight the order He desires to carry it out. We push and prod to accomplish His will, never taking the time to grasp the wisdom and insight He so carefully weaves into His timing. Full and complete submission to His timing is crucial in all areas of our lives because without it, even the most committed heart will turn a promise into a nightmare.

An unfortunate byproduct of Abraham's rejection of God's timing was that it took him out from under God's umbrella of protection. As a result, turmoil and strife ensued. God did not stop Abraham and Sarai from carrying out their plan, and as a result, Hagar conceived a child. Typical of any man-made plan, it was not a good one, and Sarai knew it was not going to fly from the start. Once she found out about the child, she began to despise and mistreat Hagar. (Genesis 16:6) As a result, Hagar eventually ran away with her child. But God was still at work with a plan. He met Hagar in the midst of her despair and sent her back to Abraham and Sarai. She gave birth to a son and named him Ishmael, just as the angel commanded.

How does Genesis 16:12 describe Ishmael, this child born out of rebellion?

_____

_____

_____

_____

There are always consequences to sin, even when our intentions are good. Simply knowing God's will isn't enough. We must strive to be so closely tethered to His heart that even in waiting, we do not abandon His timetable. Obeying God's schedule is critical in all we do because when we fail to honor His calendar, we usher in countless obstacles and delays. All of which could be circumvented through obedience.

As foretold in Genesis 16:10, Ishmael became the father of a great nation of people, the Muslims, who are still in conflict with God's people (Israel) today. The repercussions of Abraham's rebellion thousands of years ago can still be seen and felt today, and it all stemmed from the issue of Abraham's failure to exercise a patient faith in God. If only he had known.

Have you ever stepped out of God's will in the area of timing? If so, what were the repercussions?

_____

_____

_____

_____

It is so easy to be hasty when trying to follow God. More often than not He seems to move like molasses in January. I don't know how many times I have asked God, "What in the world are we waiting for? Let's get moving before I am too old to move!" Abraham surely felt this way at his old age, and the enemy took advantage of it. Like a lion lurking in the shadows, Satan knew exactly what he was doing when he prompted Sarai to have a child through Hagar. He knew the offer would entice Abraham as well. Though a great man of God, even Abraham couldn't understand what was taking God so long to carry out His promise. His questions eventually led to doubt, which in turn led to rebellion. Oh, if we could only learn to submit our clocks to God and begin to realize how vulnerable we are when we abandon God's timetable.

Question and Reflect

Read Genesis 18:13-14 below:

> "Then the LORD said to Abraham,
> "Why did Sarah laugh and say,
> `Will I really have a child, now that I am old?'
> Is anything too hard for the LORD?
> I will return to you at the appointed time next year
> and Sarah will have a son."

Based on the Lord's question to Abraham regarding Sarai, what are we really doing when we question and resist His timing? Check one.

_____ Seeking to clarify His will

_____ Exercising our faith

_____ Doubting Him

Never underestimate the power that doubt holds in our lives. It can stop anyone from carrying out the will of God. God hates doubt and all that it does to stifle His plan. As a result, the Lord went to Abraham and confronted him directly on this sin of doubt. Though Abraham's faith was great, Sarai's focus on their elderly condition, eventually smothered both her and her husband's faith. As a couple, they began to doubt God and take matters into their own hands, which led to profound repercussions still felt today.

CONCLUSION

Have you ever tried to submit your will to God but found yourself still clinging to your clock? Sister, trust me, when we hold too tightly to our clocks, all we hear is ticking, which distracts us from hearing the voice of God. This issue of desperately holding on to our calendars is a common tool the enemy uses to take our eyes and ears off God. As we wait, listening intently to our clocks, the enemy creeps close, whispering words of doubt that tell us God has forgotten us and waiting on Him is a waste of time. Seizing the moment, he offers other alternatives under the guise of fulfilling God's plan, but in the end, they are all lies meant to lead us astray.

God never forgets us, and He never wastes time. He is the creator of time! He is always at work, even when we don't see it. He is continually at work in and around us and given the time, His plan will come to pass. Like a ticking timepiece, all the parts in God's plan are in working order, keeping perfect pace for His plan and will for your life. Put your trust in Him. Hand Him your clock, then rest in His arms as you exchange the sound of a ticking clock for the sound of His tender beating heart.

Week Six

Day 4 - Humble Yourself and Be Exalted

"To some who were confident of their own righteousness and looked down on everybody else, Jesus told this parable: "Two men went up to the temple to pray, one a Pharisee and the other a tax collector. The Pharisee stood up and prayed about himself: `God, I thank you that I am not like other men--robbers, evildoers, adulterers--or even like this tax collector. I fast twice a week and give a tenth of all I get.' But the tax collector stood at a distance. He would not even look up to heaven, but beat his breast and said, `God, have mercy on me, a sinner.' I tell you that this man, rather than the other, went home justified before God. For everyone who exalts himself will be humbled, and he who humbles himself will be exalted."
Luke 18:9-14

REVIEW

Day 1 - Pride, the Roadblock to Intimacy

Day 2 - The Battle of True Submission

Day 3 - Clinging to Our Clocks

This week we have learned how pride is a roadblock that prevents us from truly submitting our hearts to God. Yesterday we saw how Abraham's desire to do God's will was overtaken by his rebellion against God's timing and the severe historical repercussions that resulted. One thing is for sure, our battle with pride and submission is multifaceted. We can never assume we have a handle on it because when we do, we're sure to find a new version of it creeping into our lives.

Today we'll be focusing on another facet of pride which is also extremely common and subtle. The sin of exalting ourselves. Have you heard the story about the man who won a medal for his humility but had it taken away because he wore it? It sounds hilarious but humility is like that. A catch-22 in which you can't seem to win for losing. For example, have you ever reached a place of humility in your life only to find yourself proud of it? It's a frustrating thing because with God, to be proud of our humility is to lose it.

Humbleness, like the Christian walk, is a delicate road. It starts out more broad and simple, but as we seek God, it narrows to a sidewalk of sorts. As we continue to draw nearer to Him, our walkway becomes wooden planks, then balance beams, and eventually a tight rope. The closer we get to God, the smaller the rope and the more vigilant the walk.

Why is this? Why would walking closer with God be more difficult? Shouldn't it be the other way around? I don't know all the answers, but one thing I do know is the closer we get to God, the more He wants us to depend on Him. He wants us to get to the point where we are teetering on a thread so that sooner or later we'll jump into His arms and allow Him to carry us the rest of the way. This is His greatest desire, for it gives Him the most pleasure.

THE PHARISEE AND THE TAX COLLECTOR

Look back at today's daily Bible verses and read them again.

These verses speak volumes to us even two thousand years after they were written. This parable, told by Jesus, is recorded only in Luke's gospel. Luke was an excellent historian and blessed with a keen sensitivity to the Holy Spirit. His writings reveal great insight into the power of prayer and how it ignites the work of the Holy Spirit. In this parable, Luke reveals that the key to a strong prayer life depends on how we position ourselves as we approach God. In order to soak up all these vital concepts, let's begin by first breaking the parable down into smaller, more digestible parts.

Question and Reflect

To whom was this parable spoken according to verse 9?

What were these two men in the parable both heading to do?

Write word for word the prayer of the Pharisee:

Write word for word the prayer of the tax collector:

According to verse 14, which man's prayer brought him justification before God?

It's interesting that the man who was the least educated in religion, who was looked down upon by man, and spoke the fewest words, was the one who left justified before God that day. This proves yet again that anyone can approach God. It doesn't take special anointing, years of theological education, or knowledge of a secret code. All it takes is a heart that willingly chooses to humble itself before God.

What was the Pharisee's main focus in his prayer?

_____ God

_____ Himself

_____ His fellow man

_____ His own sin

What was the tax collector's main focus in his prayer?

_____ God

_____ Himself

_____ His fellow man

_____ His own sin

Describe the physical posture of each man:

Pharisee: _____

Tax collector: _____

THE PRAYER OF THE PHARISEE

It's as predictable as gravity. What lies deepest in our hearts eventually comes out in our actions. When this Pharisee prayed, he stood up and "prayed about himself." In his deep-seeded pride, he boasted about himself while pointing a pious finger at his fellow man. Even his physical posture reflected his sin of pride. Blinded by sin, he spat out a worthless prayer thanking God he was not like all other men when, in fact, he himself reflected the most wicked of hearts. His prayers were worthless that day as he chose to exalt himself rather than humbly submit to God. As a result, he left unpardoned.

There is an interesting word in verse 11, which sums up the position this Pharisee took as he approached God in prayer. Refer back to today's passage and fill in the blank:

"The Pharisee stood up and prayed _____ himself."

This word "about" also means "to". Let's exchange words and see how the verse reads now:

"The Pharisee stood up and prayed _____ himself."

Is it any wonder this Pharisee went home unpardoned? Not only did God not hear his prayer because of his prideful assassination of those around him, but also because he prayed it "to himself." God was left completely out of the picture.

THE PRAYER OF THE TAX COLLECTOR

In some ways the tax collector's prayer was much like the Pharisee's. He also prayed about himself. But God looked upon the tax collector with favor, heard his prayer, and pardoned him that very day. But what was the difference between the two? Why did one heart approach the throne of God while the other kept at bay?

The difference is found in how their hearts approached God. The tax collector, who stood at a distance, was ultimately allowed to approach God while the Pharisee, positioned at the temple, never got near to Him. The one who appeared closest to God was in fact not, while the one farthest away was the one received. With X-ray vision, God looks into our hearts to determine why we do what we do. Never distracted or swayed by the image we project, He is able to hear both eloquent and primitive prayers to discern their true meaning.

While the prayer topics of these two men were virtually the same, their hearts' focus was entirely different. They both prayed about themselves, but only one kept focus on God. This parable clearly illustrates that the kind of heart that draws near to God is one that humbly acknowledges its sin and the holiness of God. What a dichotomy. We aren't called to be clean in order to approach God. We are only called to be honest. And…what we pray about to God isn't nearly as important as the position our heart takes as we approach Him.

CONCLUSION

To which of the men in the parable can you best relate? Do you find yourself praying to yourself about yourself? Do you approach God exalting yourself as you point an accusing finger toward those around you? It's actually very easy to pray with a critical eye and fail to have genuine love and concern for someone else's welfare. Such prayers are tainted with sin and will go unheard unless we shift our focus and attention onto Him.

God has occasionally thumped my head to redirect my focus. There was a time when I was fervently praying about the critical nature one of my sisters in Christ suffered from. I prayed passionately about this situation because she bugged the tar out of me. One day God spoke his piercing truth to my heart. He said, "You are as bad as she is because you are critical of her criticalness."

Of course He was right, and quite frankly, I was a bit relieved to hear the truth. I had in fact become much like that which I disliked most in her. With the cat out of the bag, God then proceeded to show me how I was wrong in my approach to Him. He revealed to me that as I came to Him about her, it was more like a tattle tail pointing out her every fault as opposed to a loving concerned sister. I was critical and judgmental, just like the Pharisee in the parable. As a result, God could not hear and answer my prayer.

Our daily walk with God is like walking a fine line. It's easy to slip and fall, but God is always there to catch us and help us get back on track. As I wrongly approached God about my sister, He lovingly showed me the right way to pray. I recall hearing, "Okay, now try it again, but this time, don't be so critical of her. Pray as if you are standing next to her with your arm around her, not as if you are on a soapbox pointing down at her. Stand beside her looking up to me on her behalf." What a precious lesson He taught my heart that day.

As we close, ask God to help you pray with a heart that is pleasing to Him. Pay close attention to who you are praying to, making sure it is to God and not yourself. Also pay special attention to your posture as you approach Him. Seek to approach Him in humble submission, making sure your prayers are not tainted with selfish pride or judgment of another.

Week Six

Day 5 - Waiting on God

"When God made his promise to Abraham, since there was no one greater for him to swear by, he swore by himself, saying, "I will surely bless you and give you many descendants." And so after waiting patiently, Abraham received what was promised."
Hebrews 6:13-15

REVIEW

Day 1 - Pride, the Roadblock to Intimacy

Day 2 - The Battle of True Submission

Day 3 - Clinging to Our Clocks

Day 4 - Humble Yourself and Be Exalted

Earlier this week we learned how Abraham waited and waited on God's promise to bless him with descendants greater than the number of stars (Genesis 15:5.) Abraham was 75 years old when he obeyed God and left his home for the Promised Land (Genesis 12:4) only to find the land occupied by the Canaanites. But God spoke words of reassurance to Abraham by again promising that this land was for the many descendants He would provide. (Genesis 12:6-7)

How confusing it must have been for Abraham to uproot his family and travel to a foreign land in obedience to the Lord, only to find the land unavailable. Imagine the disappointment as he gazed on the Promised Land overflowing with people. How could the land be for his descendants when another nation resided there? No doubt these thoughts went through Abraham's mind just as they would have gone through ours if we had stood on that hill following a long journey of obedience. We all would have questioned and pondered God's plan as we fixed our eyes on what appeared to be an impossible promise.

GOD'S PROMISE TO YOU

Just as God promised Abraham a land with many descendants, God has made a promise (covenant) to us as well. It is a personal promise from the great "I AM", fulfilled through His Son Jesus Christ.

Question and Reflect

Read Hebrews 9:15.

What is God's promise or new covenant to you?

_____

_____

Being aware of God's promise to you hopefully gives you great comfort. For me, however, there were many years in my Christian walk in which I found little comfort in these words because they didn't seem to effect my here and now. My impatient and shortsighted soul would hear this promise and invariably say, "But I am struggling now. I want to do a great work for God but He has allowed such restriction into my life with a disabled child that I don't see how I can ever do a great work for Him."

Like Abraham, I also love God very much and my desire is to do His will. And like Abraham, I obeyed God's call when he instructed me to quit my full-time job to stay home and school our daughter. Dani was ten years old at the time, and we started her out in a first grade curriculum. I worked diligently with her each day, giving her Autism a run for its money. She made progress in some areas, although none of them were academic. I know beyond a shadow of a doubt I did what God called me to do, but in spite of all our hard work, she has never been able to complete the first grade curriculum.

For five years, I faithfully obeyed God's instruction. But just as the Canaanites occupied Abraham's land, Autism occupied the land I thought had been promised to my daughter and me. For years I sat on a hill overlooking what seemed to be a promise gone wrong until one day I realized God had never promised me a land without Autism. In fact, He had told me early on that He would not heal her in order to accomplish a greater work. Five years earlier, He had simply instructed me to quit work and home school her, but He never made me any promises about her progress. Once I realized I had wrongly assumed this promise, I began to think outside the box. Why had God called me to home school our daughter if it wasn't His desire to release her from Autism? If God never makes a mistake, and I heard Him correctly, why was I called home?

Read Hebrews 10:35-39.

To what promise do you think verse 36 refers?

_____

_____

You may have written that the promise was eternal life. Verse 39 does speak of salvation but before we assume this is the promise, let's first see if the promise matches the necessary criteria.

According to verse 36, what criteria must be fulfilled in order to receive this promise?

_____

_____

Is perseverance what is needed to receive salvation according to John 3:15?

        YES   NO

If perseverance is the key to receiving this promise in Hebrews 10:36, yet not the way to salvation according to John 3:15, then Hebrews 10:36 can't be referring to the promise of salvation.

So, what is the promise? There are as many answers to this question as there are people born. This promise in Hebrews refers to personal promises God makes to each and every one of us. His Word is His promise because what He says will always come true. When God speaks to us, whether it is through clear instruction or broad enlightenment, it is His personal pledge to us. Every word that comes from the mouth of God is a promise that is as good as done!

I love how personal this verse is as it speaks to each of us exactly where we stand. Let's read it again:

> *"You need to persevere so that when you have done the will of God,*
> *you will receive what he has promised."*
> Hebrews 10:36

If every time God speaks it is a promise, then when we learn to hear, obey, and persevere in what He has instructed, we will receive His promise. But the question still remains: what is the promise? Actually, no one knows the promises God has for you but you, and if you don't know, it's because you have not asked Him. His promises to me aren't the same as yours because His promises are custom built for you. They will never fit anyone but you. They are promises that are guaranteed to fulfill you beyond your wildest dreams.

Think of how God fulfilled the four gospel writers by using them in a way that satisfied them far beyond what they could have ever strived for on their own. God has indeed promised you eternal salvation if you have accepted His Son as Lord, but every time He speaks to you, it is a promise. A promise that is as good as done and that, dear sister, is exciting news because it assures us that He has a special plan and purpose for each of us. He doesn't want us to simply make it through life; He wants us to be whole and complete in His will. However, we must first learn to communicate freely and intimately with Him in order to hear the great promises and plans He has in store for us.

Let me be the guinea pig for a moment and use my own situation to further explain. We know that early on God told me He would not heal my daughter in order to do a greater work. We also know that He clearly called me to home school her, but the five years of schooling proved to be less than successful. If every time God speaks there is a promise, what was His promise to me? How has he accomplished a mighty work through her disabilities when she has ultimately failed to progress even though I obeyed His call to home school?

His promise to me became evident the day I realized that He not only called one but two students home for an education. True, God had called me home to school Dani, and yes, my attempt to get her into a first grade curriculum failed. But in the midst of it all, God had a plan. A plan that involved cultivating me. All this time I thought his plan only involved my teaching her, when in fact my call home really involved my being home schooled by no one other than God Himself.

According to His infinite wisdom, God allowed her disability to remain so that I would obey the call to come home. Once home, alone in seclusion, He could teach, train, and discipline me with great tender care. I had no idea that when I obeyed the call to home school our daughter, I was in fact the one being called to the classroom!

Oh sister, I can't tell you how hard it was to work so diligently for five years and still not have Dani in a first grade curriculum. I felt like a failure much of the time, and the isolation was almost more than I could bear. In spite of it all, God knew exactly what I needed in order to draw near to Him, and He loved me enough to put me in His own home school program. He knew that in my attempts to reach her in her isolation, I too would reach out to Him in my own desperate isolation. He knew the seclusion would drive me toward Him like nothing else could. And that is exactly what it did.

My years in God's home school program have been the school of hard knocks. No question about it. I didn't enroll myself. I was drafted. I had scores of ups and downs along with many tears of frustration, but through it all, God remained at my side, teaching and tutoring me all along the way. It is true God doesn't promise us a rose garden, but He does promise great things to those who love Him. Every word He says is true and that is our guarantee. He promised to do greater things through Dani's disability and He has. Surprisingly enough, His greatest work thus far has been in me.

CONCLUSION

My greatest prayer for you is that you will choose to submit to God so that you may hear His voice. Every word He speaks is a promise; He will never let you down, but you must know His voice in order to follow it. God will never lead you down a dangerous path even though many times your next step may feel like a blind one. Abraham was a great man of faith who clung to the promises of God. God has many promises for you. Ask Him to share His promises with you today.

Week Seven

Day 1 – Worship: Our Vital Perspective

"Seth also had a son, and he named him Enosh. At that time men began to call on the name of the LORD."
Genesis 4:26

How I look forward to this week, because we are going to delve into the ever-important act of worship. The way we worship is determined by how we see and perceive God. Let me say this again in a different way to make sure we grasp this opening nugget: The state or condition of our personal worship of God is a reflection of how we view Him. In choosing not to worship God, we are really choosing not to have an intimate relationship with Him. When we choose to worship in a rote or shallow fashion, we choose a distant relationship with Him. But when we seek to worship Him in spirit and truth, we are choosing to set our focus on God alone, placing Him first in our lives. These worshippers are those the Father seeks and those who develop a close and intimate relationship with Him.

When I first began to teach on prayer, worship is what I knew the least about. I scrambled for material in order to give this element of prayer proper content, yet I was still lacking. If you'll remember last week when we talked about James, the half brother of Jesus, I mentioned how writers can only write from experience. Somehow writers must have a base of experience for writing which to draw from. Otherwise they have nothing to tether their writing. This lack of experience was precisely my dilemma when I first began to teach on worship. I had little material on worship because I had so little experience with it. I thought worship was done on Sunday mornings at church and was more of a group activity than a personal offering to God. Although I knew in my head it was part of communicating with God, I honestly thought it was more for His benefit than for mine. I hadn't begun to realize the many benefits worship grants the worshipper.

As I look back, I am embarrassed at how little attention I was able to give to this act of love we are called to give to God. I simply didn't realize its importance. One thing I've learned is that though we are all unique, we are also very much alike. My thoughts and questions about worship are most likely similar to yours. If I struggled with understanding worship and its importance, no doubt others have too. My prayer is that, by the end of this week, the Holy Spirit will open your heart and mind so you will desire to worship God in spirit and in truth. This will not only please Him, but bless you greatly.

THE FIRST ACT OF WORSHIP

Earlier in our study, we learned about the throne in our hearts and our freedom to choose what we place on it. We may choose to sit on our throne ourselves or place another person on it. We may place on it earthly possessions or a prized position we hold in the community. Whatever we place on our throne is the thing we give most of our thoughts and time to and is ultimately what we worship.

Although we know we should place God on our throne, we don't always do it. This is usually not from outright defiance but often simply because we don't know Him in an intimate way. To know God is to love Him, and to love Him is to seek Him. When we see Him for who He truly is, worship will become a natural response.

Question and Reflect

Read Genesis 4:25-26 and describe when man first began to call upon or worship the Lord.

_____
_____
_____
_____

   Isn't it interesting that God deliberately mentions when men first began to call upon Him? It makes you wonder what they had done before. Did they communicate with God? Had they not worshipped before? Apparently, they communicated with God but they hadn't worshipped Him. We know this because God communicated freely with Adam and Eve and their sons, Cain and Abel. But something had changed from the time this first family walked the Earth and the time this third generation of Enosh came along. Since we know that God is never changing, we know the change did not occur on His end, but rather on man's end.

According to Genesis 4:8, what happened for the first time in history?

_____
_____

   How sad that just two generations into the history of man we see the sin of murder. What pain it must have inflicted on Adam and Eve to have once walked with God in perfect harmony and now have the sins of hatred, greed, and jealousy drive their eldest son to kill his brother. I cannot imagine their anguish. Having once lived with God in paradise, they were now banished into the cruel new world of sin. This shift must have been painful beyond what we could ever imagine. They truly felt the wedge of sin as it was hammered between themselves and God. How abandoned and frightened they must have felt. Prior to this first-time murder, their sins had been that of disobedience, lying, greed, and jealousy, but this offense brought death to sight.

What do you think this first murder would have to do with men beginning to call upon the name of the Lord in Enosh's generation?

_____
_____
_____
_____

Read Genesis 4:25 and write Eve's response to God for giving her another son, Seth.

_____
_____

I wonder how Eve felt after her one son killed the other. Did she wonder what God was going to do now? Remember, Adam and Eve had only seen God's response to their sin of eating from the forbidden tree. They had not yet witnessed His response to this horrible sin of murder. She must have wondered many things as she gazed on her lifeless child. Would God allow them to have more children or would this be the end? Would they ever see God again? Would they ever hear His voice? What could the future ever hold?

According to Genesis 4:25, from the time Eve lost her son Abel and gave birth to Seth, she pondered many things in her heart. Like the breaking of a new dawn, she saw the blessings of childbirth and the mercy of God in a whole new way. Once unsure of whether she could have another son, she passionately praised God for allowing history's first second chance. Another son meant another chance. And another chance meant hope restored. Imagine her relief when Seth came along. It wasn't the end of mankind, and God was still in their presence. Her unique situation makes me wonder if she was the one who actually set in motion the act of worship. Wouldn't the realization of God's mercy, love, and grace through the birth of Seth surely give way to worship?

Genesis 4:26 states that the generation of Eve's grandson, Enosh, is the time when men began to call upon the name of the Lord. Ever wonder why this generation? There is no doubt Eve told Seth all that had occurred in their family before he was born. Certainly, along with the bad, she shared with him the goodness of God's bringing him to replace the brother he never knew. Her worship and praise must have overflowed like lava onto this special son conceived in new mercy. How could she contain herself? She is the only woman ever to have seen the darkness of murder against the backdrop of God's holiness. Surely she worshipped God like no one had ever done before, and it made a tremendous impact on the future generations.

Sometimes it takes extreme darkness for us to see the light. This horrible murder, and the pain it ushered in, allowed Eve to see God's glory in a new way. As a result, she began to worship God so powerfully that it infected those around her, especially her son Seth. He saw in his mother an attitude of worship that he in turn passed along to his son Enosh. This profound act of praise started a movement in this third generation and so pleased God that He makes special mention of it.

In week five we learned about the great apostle John and how mesmerized he was with Christ. He began as a boisterous young fisherman with a thunderous and prideful personality, but as the Son of God was revealed to him, his loud and sometimes offensive way was miraculously transformed into a humility that headed him straight to the heart of God. The revelation of Christ to John provided the backdrop he needed to see his own ungodliness, which then helped him gain a right perspective of God and His great compassion, love, and understanding for all His creation.

Like John, Eve's ability to see the awfulness of sin against God's holiness served to alter her perspective of God. This contrast of sin and holiness led her to humbly submit herself before God giving Him praise, honor, and glory in a pure act of worship. This, is exactly the kind of worship that we must seek to offer God, for it is one of the key elements of prayer that ushers us into the very presence of God.

Question and Reflect

Does your worship have an impact on those around you as Eve's worship affected Seth and the following generations?

_____

_____

_____

Does your worship affect you in a profound way?

_____

_____

How would you rate your worship relationship to the Lord? Check all that apply.

- _____ I can't say I have one
- _____ My worship is a rote act to me
- _____ I don't understand the importance of worship
- _____ I only worship during church services
- _____ I find worship boring
- _____ My worship is infrequent
- _____ I look forward to worshipping God every day
- _____ Worship is my favorite pastime
- _____ I can't worship enough - I love it
- _____ I worship on a moderate basis
- _____ I want to learn more about worship

CONCLUSION

It is never too late to begin praising God. The act of worship is much like dancing with the lover of your soul. While His size and power is evident as you approach Him, His love still beckons you to come. Once engaged in this dance, great joy will fill your heart as you begin to sway to the gentle rhythm of His beating heart. Listen closely. Can you hear the music as it begins to play? Do you hear Him calling your name? He waits to dance with you, and longs to hold you close. Ask Him now to take your hand.

_____

_____

_____

_____

_____

_____

_____

_____

_____

Week Seven

Day 2 – Worship: Our Eternal Act

Then I heard every creature in heaven and on earth and under the earth and on the sea, and all that is in them, singing: "To him who sits on the throne and to the Lamb be praise and honor and glory and power, for ever and ever!"

Revelation 5:13

REVIEW

Day 1 – Worship - Our Vital Perspective

Yesterday we began our weeklong study on the vital act of worship. We read in Genesis 4:26 how it was in the third generation of mankind (Enosh's generation) that man began to call upon the Lord and actively worship Him. When Adam and Eve lost their youngest son Abel to the hand of their older son Cain, they witnessed God's gracious provision through His gift of another son, Seth. Through Seth, the following generation would be the first to call upon the name of the Lord. Rather than abolish His creation as a result of this horrible act of murder, God chose to bring forth a son who would bless Adam and Eve, replace Abel, and eventually lead a generation that would touch His heart deeply as they called upon His name.

WHAT WILL WE DO IN ETERNITY?

When I was a little girl, the thought of eternity scared me to death. Even knowing I would be in heaven with God didn't comfort me enough to slow the adrenaline rush. I couldn't comprehend the concept of eternity, and as a result, great stress would ensue whenever I'd think about it. It bothered me primarily because I am a very impatient person who gets bored easily. Even as an adult, I have asked God if He will have plenty for me to do in heaven. I've gone so far as to ask Him if He will give me a job. Yes, a job! I don't want to be unemployed; I want to work. I can't bear the thought of having nothing to do. I have pondered the idea of God creating another world similar to the one we are in now (but without Satan) where I could be an assistant of sorts to someone in need. I figure this would keep me fairly busy, at least for a while, in eternity.

These are my thoughts when I'm using my own brainpower. However, when I meditate on what God's Word says about the place He has prepared for us, I am comforted to know that boredom will not be part of the agenda. God is extremely creative and heaven will be a glorious place where we will never battle boredom. There will be no more pain, suffering, or sadness because God will be everywhere. There will be no need for the sun or moon, for the Glory of God will be our light (Revelation 21:23). We will enjoy harmony with one another and best of all, we will be in the presence of God the Father, and God the Son. Heaven is the place God is custom building for you even as you study this lesson. We will enjoy what He is preparing for us and more importantly; we will enjoy being with Him.

Question and Reflect

Read Revelation 4:1-11 keeping in mind that this is all going to take place in the future.

This is what John saw when the door of heaven was opened to him, and it is our sneak preview into eternity. Perhaps the enemy is making some of you feel inadequate because you aren't familiar with all the characters in these verses. If this is the case, let's review the cast of characters.

The Cast:
- The One sitting on the Throne (vs. 2) – God
- The Twenty-Four Elders (vs. 4) - Many scholars believe this is the church as a whole, believers throughout history - people like you and me!
- The Four Living Creatures (vs. 6) - an exalted order of angelic beings or cherubim (like the ones sent to guard the Garden of Eden.) These creatures are closest to the throne of God and never stop worshipping and giving Him all praise, honor, and glory.

Now that we know whom we are observing as John shares his breathtaking glimpse into heaven, let's zero in on what they are doing here.

According to verse 8, what are the twenty-four elders and the four living creatures doing?

_____

_____

Picture in your mind's eye this beautiful scene of harmony and unity as all of God's created beings worship and honor Him in one accord. This is what we will do in eternity. All believers throughout the ages will bow to the Father and the Son, giving them praise and worship for eternity.

Read Revelation 5:13 and describe who else John heard singing praises, honor, and glory.

_____

_____

John heard every living creature give praise. The Father and the Son who created all things will one day have praise, honor and glory sung to them by all living creatures. It's fascinating that somehow God revealed to John's spiritual ears the sound of every living creature in heaven, on the Earth, under the Earth, on the sea, and in the sea singing praises to God. What must that have sounded like to John? Can you imagine hearing an ant sing? Or how about a crab? Do they have vocal cords with which to sing? I don't know, but it won't matter because God will one day enable them to sing praises to Him, vocal cords or not.

What specific words did John say he heard "every living creature" sing according to Revelation 5:13?

_____

_____

_____

_____

Wow. Even the ants and crabs will acknowledge that God sits on the throne and Jesus is the Lamb. They will sing praises, and speak it in these exact words. How can this be? How can every living creature speak these very words? Lest you be tempted to discount or dilute what John says he heard, read Revelation 22:18-19.

What is the warning to those who add anything to the prophecy of this book?

_____

_____

What is the warning to those who take words away from this book of prophecy?

_____

_____

God's Word is infallible and we are to believe every word. We know that the crabs, ants, sea lions, worms, and other creatures will speak these words because John said they would in this book of prophecy. He saw and heard what is to come and put what he heard in quotation marks. Just as all of creation will one day exalt God with these very words, so shall we. Every living creature, without exception, will acknowledge the great "I AM." The question we must ask ourselves is when we worship in the future at the throne, will it be an unfamiliar act, or will it be a continuation of what we've learned to do here on Earth? It's sobering to grasp that many of God's children will worship their Creator for the very first time along with the crabs living in the sea or ants atop an anthill. We were never meant to begin worship upon arrival in heaven. We are meant to praise Him as we walk with Him here on Earth.

Earlier we learned that Christ will wipe every tear from our eyes when we get to heaven. Some of God's children will arrive to shed tears of joy after waiting so long to see the One to whom they dedicated their lives. Then there will be those who shed tears of regret for accepting Christ but never seizing the opportunity to know Him. Learning to worship God here on Earth ensures that you will not get to heaven and find yourself unfamiliar with the act of worship. Our worship here is preparation for what we will do for eternity. It should be our desire to seek Him now. Let's not wait to worship with the crab and the ant on that day in the not so distant future.

CONCLUSION

God's great power and majesty will be revealed to us the day all creation bows down to worship Him. On that day I desire to bow on knees that are limber from the practice of submission and worship here on Earth, not stiff from standing straight in selfish pride. I want my knees to bend freely not having to be broken by the hand of God.

If you are unfamiliar with the act of worship, determine to begin today. There is no better time than now to loosen your knees before God and worship. Offer Him your song of praise and lift Him high on the throne of your heart. Don't wait to join the crabs and the ants.

_____

_____

_____

Week Seven

Day 3 – Worship:

It's In Our Spirit, Not Our Location

" Yet a time is coming and has now come when the true worshipers will worship the Father in spirit and truth, for they are the kind of worshipers the Father seeks. God is spirit, and his worshipers must worship in spirit and in truth."
John 4:23-24

REVIEW

Day 1 – Worship - Our Vital Perspective

Day 2 – Worship - Our Eternal Act

This week we learned that the first act of worship commenced as Enosh's generation began to call upon the name of the Lord. The book of Revelation reveals that one day in the future, all creatures in heaven and Earth will sing a song of praise, honor, and glory to God the Father and God the Son. All creation will sing in one accord to Him who sits on the throne forever and ever.

SEEKING GOD IN THE SPIRIT

John 4:23 tells us that one of the biggest blessings of worshipping God in spirit and truth is that this is the kind of worshipper He seeks. We don't have to search for Him in a particular place or possess a certain talent. We need only worship Him in spirit and in truth. Then He will find us. It couldn't be simpler. Let's read these powerful and comforting words of Jesus again:

"Yet a time is coming and has now come
when the true worshipers will worship the Father in spirit and truth,
for they are the kind of worshipers the Father seeks."
John 4:23

What does it mean to you when Jesus instructs us to worship in the spirit?

_____

_____

Give an example of worship that is not done in the spirit.

_____

_____

_____

To worship in the Spirit means just what it says - it is an act of the spirit. To better explain, let's look at the opposite of what worshipping in the spirit is, then compare the two. Once you see the difference, you'll be better able to do as Jesus instructed us to do. In John 4, Jesus and the Samaritan woman discussed this very issue while at Jacob's well one day. Let's listen to their discussion.

Question and Reflect

Read John 4:19-24.

In verses 19-20, what was the Samaritan woman's view of worship? Check one.

_____ It is a place where you go.

_____ It was done in the spirit.

One of the very reasons Christ came to Earth was to change our view of worship. Throughout history, man had begun to turn worship of the heart into a more physical act of obedience. Worship had become a robotic act that was performed outwardly and only in certain locations, while the spirit of worship was given little to no attention.

Though despised by the Jews as a half-breed and low life, this Samaritan woman and her people held the very same view toward worship as the Jews did, but the Jews would never have admitted it. While the Samaritans had indeed mixed pagan beliefs with Jewish beliefs, both the Samaritans and the Jews viewed worship as one location, rather than an act of the spirit. The Samaritan woman explained it quite well when she said: "Our fathers worshiped on this mountain, but you Jews claim that the place where we must worship is in Jerusalem"(vs 20.)

Since they all viewed worship as a location, one reason Jesus came was to point them in the right way. Worship had absolutely nothing to do with a person's physical location and everything to do with the heart's condition. Jesus came to realign their hearts from the horizontal view of worship (location) to one that was vertical (done in the spirit.)

What is your view of worship? Do you view it as a place you go or an act of the spirit? Be honest with yourself and most importantly be honest with God.

_____

_____

_____

To check how honest you were with the question above, select the statements below that best describe your view of worship and how it affects your walk with God.

_____I view worship more as a location and therefore do not feel a close and intimate relationship with God. I am active in doing work for Him but feel more like a distant employee than His special child.

_____I view worship as an act of the spirit and enjoy my time with God in prayer and meditation. I do not feel that I must go to a certain place to meet with God for I know that I can call on Him anytime, anywhere, and I do. I feel closeness with God that sustains me throughout each day.

Do you sense God is speaking to your heart about how you worship Him?

_____

_____

_____

_____

SEEKING GOD IN TRUTH

Worship requires a spirit that humbly calls upon the name of the Lord. It does not require a particular physical location. But Jesus told the woman at the well that true worship involves two things: spirit and truth.

What does it mean to you when Jesus instructs us to worship in truth?

_____

_____

If this is difficult to answer or put into words, hang in there. Just as worshipping in the spirit means exactly what it says, so does worshipping in truth. To worship in truth simply means to approach God in complete honesty. We come to Him as our confidant to whom we can entrust all things. We go to Him with an honest heart that is ready and willing to receive His honest feedback. It may be an instruction, a measure of comfort, or a much-needed rebuke, but His response will always be that of truth.

When we communicate with God in spirit and in truth, it's like a two-way street. The rules He has set for us to follow are the same He follows Himself. Remember - every word He speaks is a promise. Just as we are instructed to seek Him in truth, we must know and expect that He will speak His truth back to us. We must be willing to accept it, even when it hurts. And the truth of God can sting like a hot poker, but it is always sure to set you free.

Many times I have approached God with what I honestly thought was the truth only to have Him reveal the real truth to me. It never ceases to amaze me that He always knows the absolute incorruptible truth because that is His nature. He will never lie or mislead us so we can trust His instructions. When we worship God in the spirit and approach Him in truth, He seeks fellowship with us. What a privilege and blessing this is.

CONCLUSION

How has God spoken to your heart today about your worship relationship to Him? Have you mistaken being in the house of worship for worship itself? Have you unintentionally fallen into the trap of focusing on how many times you have attended church in a given week or how much work you have done in His name, thinking that this is what He ultimately wants from you? If you do not feel a craving to worship God, you have never experienced true worship, for once you have danced with the lover of your soul; you will crave it again and again. Let down any walls of dishonesty and approach Him now in spirit and in truth.

Week Seven

Day 4 – Worship: It Isn't About Us

"When a period of feasting had run its course, Job would send and have them (his children) purified. Early in the morning he would sacrifice a burnt offering for each of them, thinking, "Perhaps my children have sinned and cursed God in their hearts." This was Job's regular custom."

Job 1:5

REVIEW

Day 1 – Worship - Our Vital Perspective

Day 2 – Worship - Our Eternal Act

Day 3 – Worship - It's Our Spirit, Not Our Location

This week we've learned that how we worship God reflects how we perceive Him, approach Him, and ultimately whether we draw near to Him. If we are cautious of Him, we will have a distant relationship. If we view Him as an impersonal God who simply keeps track of our actions, we will focus on what we do "in His name." But if we perceive Him as our personal heavenly Father who wants us to draw near to His heart, we will seek Him in spirit and in truth, and He will do the same with us.

A relationship with God based on this leads us to obey His every word, which brings God's rich blessings. Long before Christ died, sending the Holy Spirit to dwell in those who would believe, certain men in history had a special relationship with God that brought them especially close to Him. Job was just such a man. He walked faithfully with God and because of this, God honored him.

WORSHIPPING GOD IN ALL THINGS

One of the greatest blessings of worship is that it shifts our focus off ourselves and places it on to God. When we focus on God, we lift Him high above all things, acknowledging Him as our creator, sustainer, teacher, refuge, and defender. So often worship is something done only in response to a blessing received or a prayer answered, but these aren't the only times we should give God our praise. We are called to worship in all things.

Question and Reflect

Read Job 1.

According to verses 2-3, describe how God had blessed Job.

_____

_____

_____

According to Job 1:1 and 1:8, what five ways does God describe Job?

1. _____

2. _____

3. _____

4. _____

5. _____

What excuse did Satan give for Job's faithful walk with God according to verses 9-10?
_____
_____

How did God allow Job to be tested in chapter 1?
_____
_____

 Can you imagine getting the news you've lost everything? Four messengers approached Job with this tragic news. While each one was still speaking, the next would advance with more bad news. Soon Job realized he had nothing left but his wife and his life. Every child, servant, and piece of property was gone.

 It must have been utterly devastating. This godly man who loved his children very much, lost them all in a matter of moments. But even in the midst of tragedy, Job was not an average man. He was a man of God, and God was on the throne of his heart. Whether the times were good or bad, his love for the Lord never faltered. This was evident in how he lived his life, how he responded in the midst of great hardship, and the time it took for him to respond.

What was Job's response in verse 21?
_____
_____

How long did it take him to respond in this fashion according to verse 20?
_____
_____

 Job lived a blameless life, fearing God and shunning evil during the most prosperous times of his life. He did the same in the midst of great loss. Tragedy couldn't change him and how he felt about God. He continued to worship as he had always done because that was the foundation of his heart. What he had faithfully practiced during the good times instinctively came out in the bad. His love and dedication to God was so deeply rooted within him, that his instinctive response to calamity was to worship.

Let's re-read Job's prayer to see his heart's true reflection.

> *"Naked I came from my mother's womb,*
> *and naked I will depart.*
> *The LORD gave and the LORD has taken away;*
> *may the name of the LORD be praised."*
> Job 1:21

Could you have prayed this prayer immediately upon hearing the news Job heard that day? Explain why or why not.

_____

_____

_____

_____

Remember, worship is a choice. We all choose who, what, and when we will worship. If we only worship when things are going our way, we will never be able to respond as Job did in times of crisis. But having said that, how did Job practice worship in the bad times when he had only been blessed up to this point of testing? How did he learn to worship during times of tragedy when he had only worshipped in prosperity?

As with any skill, the primary key to success is practice. Although Job had never had to worship in tragedy, his love for God and his choice to worship during good times set the firm foundation that would later sustain him in the bad times. His faithful worship amidst prosperity was just what he needed to prepare for calamity. What matters most isn't the situations in which we choose to worship, but the dedication itself to worship. Why? Because worship is ultimately an act of the heart, not a response to a circumstance.

Read Job 1:5. What was Job's regular custom?

_____

_____

Job chose to establish worship deep in his heart long before his life was flipped upside down. He had made it his customary routine to offer sacrifices for his children just in case they had sinned and cursed God.

What kind of sins did Job say he was concerned about according to verse 5? Check one.

_____ Adultery

_____ Murder

_____ Stealing

_____ Sins of the heart

Isn't that interesting? Job was so mindful of the power that sins of the heart can have over a person, that he offered daily sacrifices on behalf of his children just in case they sinned in their heart. If he did this daily for his children, can you imagine his diligence to keep his own heart clean before God? Praise and worship was anything but rote or routine. He knew the greatness of His God and the depravity of man's heart and carefully sought to bridge the gap. Long before this tragedy ever occurred, Job honored God with intimate daily worship, and his faithfulness during the good times eliminated any search for God during the bad. What a great man and even greater example Job is to us.

GOD REMEMBERS JOB

Good news. In the midst of all this tragedy, God never forgot Job. He watched His faithful servant give honor and glory during the worst moments of his life and in return, God was faithful to bless him yet again.

> *"After Job had prayed for his friends,*
> *the LORD made him prosperous again*
> *and gave him twice as much as he had before."*
> Job 42:10

God is forever faithful to those who place Him first in their lives. Even in our darkest hour, God is watching to see whom we have placed on the throne of our heart and blesses those who honor His name. What a wonderful testimony Job's life reflects even still today. How we should strive to do the same.

CONCLUSION

Are you waiting for Sunday morning to worship God? Maybe you are waiting until you feel like it or even for a good reason. Sister, every day brings good reason to worship God. He sustains your every heartbeat and is seeking to provide you with blessings custom built just for you! Don't wait to worship God. Praise Him now. In laughter or in tears, He wants to dance with you in worship. If you are in a time of trial, praise Him for who He is so that you too can experience what Job experienced in the midst of his trial---peace with God. Choose to take your eyes off yourself and your situation and see the glory of God through worship!

Week Seven

Day 5 – Worship: It's About God!

"Early the next morning Abraham got up and saddled his donkey. He took with him two of his servants and his son Isaac. When he had cut enough wood for the burnt offering, he set out for the place God had told him about. On the third day Abraham looked up and saw the place in the distance. He said to his servants, "Stay here with the donkey while I and the boy go over there. We will worship and then we will come back to you."
Genesis 22:3-5

REVIEW

Day 1 – Worship - Our Vital Perspective

Day 2 – Worship - Our Eternal Act

Day 3 – Worship - It's Our Spirit, Not Our Location

Day 4 – Worship - It Isn't About Us

How we approach God determines how we worship Him and ultimately the level of intimacy we will have with Him. We must determine in our hearts to practice worshipping Him here on Earth since we will be doing it in heaven for eternity. True worship is done in the spirit with utmost honesty and truth. It focuses wholly on God, His plan, and His will. In a day and age where everything is about what we have, what we want, and how we look, true worship of God is the farthest thing from many of our minds. Christians are no exception.

TRUE WORSHIP AT HIS FEET

I mentioned earlier how God and I have often locked horns about when I would carry out His will. Once aware of His plan for my life, I voted we begin now while He chose later. In time I eventually learned that along with being impatient, I was also weak in the knowledge and experience of worship. Though I feverishly itched to do God's work, I was not yet ready. As much as I wanted to do His will, I could not because I did not yet know Him. These issues of impatience and ignorance are not only related, but also bound together as if by super glue, hindering our chance for intimacy with God.

I didn't realize it at the time but God had placed me on hold. I really desired to do His will but my true focus was not on Him, it was on doing His work. My desire to work hard came first while His will came second. How subtly the sin of hidden pride creeps into our hearts. To better explain, read aloud the following sentences emphasizing the bold and underlined words. Listen to the difference the emphasis brings to their meaning:

<u>**I**</u> WANT TO DO GOD'S WILL

VS

I WANT TO DO <u>**GOD'S**</u> WILL

Can you hear the sin of pride in the first sentence? The focus is ultimately on self, while the second sentence reflects a true focus on God. This subtle sin is a stumbling block for many well-meaning Christians. We see others do great things for the Lord and want to do the same. But there is just one little problem. The Lord is not our main focus. Our attention is on the fact that we want to do His will. This may sound like a play on words but this subtle shift of focus is all we need to take our eyes off God.

Trust me on this, I know. God worked long and hard to help me see what I was really doing when I cried for Him to use me. He knew that my strong desire to do His will was really a ploy to get out of staying home with a disabled child. Knowing our daughter would never grow up, get a job and become a productive citizen, I viewed my work at home as futile and worthless. My desire instead had become to skip the work at home and go on to doing great things in His name. But God is wise and didn't fall for this scheme. From the very start, He saw this seed of pride lurking hidden deep in my heart. He knew my heart's desire was to be in the world and not at home.

Fortunately God knows the condition of our hearts and guides us accordingly. Though we often fight and resist, He knows what is best. The best for me happened to be precisely what I did not want, seclusion. With great love He bottled me up from the world to be alone with Him. The top was corked and held me tight till I too began to see this sin hidden so deep within my heart.

You see, God knows exactly where to place us so we can hear Him best. Like a Genie in a bottle, I required isolation. The world was a distraction that drowned out His voice. I simply could not fully focus on Him, so He led me to a place of seclusion. Though our time together would eventually become one of solitude, it wasn't always that way. I fought feelings of being trapped and complained incessantly of being bored. Life alone at home with a disabled child was simply the hardest challenge I could have been given. But the Lord was patient during my time of breaking, and eventually I gave in and surrendered completely to His will.

After years of butting heads with God, I finally went belly up one day. He wouldn't give in to my pleas and I had run out of ideas on how to speed Him up. One day I looked up to Him and said, "Lord, I have no more energy to fight you on this. I am an able bodied person who eagerly wants to do your will but you have chosen to isolate me in this house to care for your little disabled lamb. From now on, it's fine with me if you choose to keep me home and not use me out in the world. All my days are yours to do with as you wish. If I don't leave my house today, may it somehow be to your glory. I choose to follow you, even if it involves going nowhere."

Believe it or not, this was the beginning of true worship for me. At that moment I realized that although my focus was almost on God, when the chips were down, it was ultimately on myself. I was beginning to see my subtle pride and the never-ending challenge of keeping my focus totally on Him. I had to trust Him with His plan for my life even if it meant doing what seemed like nothing. As God would have it, learning to submit to a life of isolation, gave way to new surrender. He knew my willingness to do His will had to override any plans of my own. Isolation was His method of teaching me that doing what seemed to be nothing for Him was far superior to doing a thousand good things that are not in His will.

REFOCUSED THROUGH A TIME OF WAITING

Last week we learned how Abraham and Sarah jumped the gun on God's timing to have their promised child. After waiting for what seemed too long, they concocted their own plan to do God's will, which involved having Ishmael through Hagar. Their rush to bring about God's plan resulted in an entire nation of people who today remain a thorn in the side of God's people. The problem with Abraham was that as he waited, he began to think:

I WANT TO DO GOD'S WILL

His focus began to ever so slightly shift from God's will onto his own desires, and any time we take our eyes off God, it can prove disastrous. Abraham had not learned to completely submit and as a result, God could not fully use him. Although it's vital that we seek to do God's will, we must never let our desire to do His will override our focus on Him. This may sound contradictory, but there is a difference. Distinguishing between these two concepts can be difficult and Abraham was no exception. He, like us, experienced a learning curve, which took place during the time between Ishmael and Isaac's birth (about fourteen years). It was during this time Abraham learned to relinquish the last little bit of himself and in the process, discovered worship in a whole new way.

Question and Reflect

Read Genesis 22:1-13.

After waiting so long for his promised son, God instructed Abraham to sacrifice Isaac. Why did God ask this of him according to verse 1?

_____ To punish him

_____ To punish Sarah

_____ To test him

_____ To take back His promise from him

How would you rate Abraham's level of obedience on a scale of 1-10 with 10 being the highest level of obedience?

1   2   3   4   5   6   7   8   9   10

Did Abraham intend to sacrifice Isaac? Explain.

_____

_____

_____

_____

_____

Astounding, isn't it? Years earlier when Abraham questioned God's timing about having a son, he would have certainly questioned God about killing that promised son. Now he obeyed God's command without hesitation. Through Ishmael, Abraham learned to obey God's timing, but through the additional waiting period for Isaac, he learned to obey every word from God, even those he didn't understand. Abraham's faith had always been great, but it proved even stronger now, as God called him to sacrifice. What had occurred during those years of waiting? What was different about Abraham's faith? Let's take a peek and see.

In verse 5, what did Abraham tell his servants that he and Isaac were going to do?

_____

_____

While Enosh's generation was the first to "call upon the name of the Lord", it is when Abraham was about to sacrifice his son Isaac that we find the first mention of "worship" in God's Holy Word. Here we see profound growth in Abraham's faith and obedience. His fourteen years of waiting had served to cultivate a deeper walk with God as he learned to sit at his master's feet and worship.

It's amazing what we can learn when we are quiet and still in His presence. Whether it is voluntary or forced, it serves a purpose like no other. Unfortunately, we rarely take the time to sit and worship at His feet. All the faith in the world will do us no good unless we place our entire heart's focus on Him, and not simply what He has planned. Abraham's wait was neither futile, inactive, or without purpose, for it was during this time that he learned to give the last fragment of himself to God.

CONCLUSION

It's wonderful to see how Abraham, a great man of faith, was so teachable. Even in his old age he successfully learned the lesson God intends to teach us all. Are you teachable? Do you desire to do His will? If so, does your desire to do His will override your desire to know and follow Him with utmost precision? Although doing God's will and following His most minute instruction may sound like the same thing, they are not. Tiny fragments of selfish motives can bring about great damage. Hidden agendas weaken the foundation of our walk with God and must be dealt with before we can move on in His will.

Whether you are on hold like Abraham or placed into isolation like me, God seeks to teach you in a way that will draw you closer to Him. He knows exactly where you are and precisely how to use your situation to bring you near to His heart. Wherever you are now, stop what you are doing and focus your attention on Him. Forget your own plans and goals, even if they involve Him, and simply sit at His feet in worship. Don't let your desire to accomplish His will override your desire to know Him. Ask Him to help you focus completely on Him and show you the lessons He has for you where you are. Give Him that last little bit of yourself.

_____

_____

_____

_____

_____

_____

_____

Week Eight

Day 1 - Our Daily Bread (Part 1)

"Keep falsehood and lies far from me; give me neither poverty nor riches, but give me only my daily bread."
Proverbs 30:8

One day when Jesus returned from time alone in prayer, the disciples asked Him to teach them how to pray. They knew He had something special and they wanted it too. He spoke to them the words we now know of as the Lord's Prayer. Though this prayer serves as our example of how to pray, reciting it over and over in a routine fashion was never the intent. Our Lord would never tell us what to say word for word, as this would violate the very freedom He so highly respects: our free will.

Instead, it is His desire we pray from the heart using our own words. The Lord's Prayer is simply a guide, which gives us four key elements to implement into our prayer life. The elements ultimately bring us closer to the heart of God, breathing new life into our walk with Him!

FOUR KEY ELEMENTS OF POWERFUL PRAYER

Let's look at Matthew 6:9-13 to see these key elements of prayer:

"Our Father in heaven, hallowed be your name, your kingdom come, your will be done on Earth as it is in heaven.	WORSHIP
Give us today our daily bread.	PROVISION
Forgive us our debts, as we also have forgiven our debtors.	CONFESSION
And lead us not into temptation, but deliver us from the evil one."	GUIDANCE/ PROTECTION

In our study thus far, we have already covered two of these four elements. We went over the importance of confession during the first five weeks of study as we learned to uncover deeply hidden sin in our hearts, and we also covered the element of worship last week as we learned to dance with the lover of our soul in praise. This week we will cover the element of provision and next week (week nine) we will cover guidance and protection.

WHAT IS OUR DAILY BREAD?

Often we read the words "daily bread" and think this term only applies to people of the Bible who had to kill and prepare food for their every meal. But God's Word is eternal, and what He spoke to His people then still speaks and applies to us today. The more I read and learn about His ever-living Word, the more amazed I am at how it speaks to my own heart and applies to my quiet isolated life here in the middle of the USA. Wherever you are and whatever you are doing, His living Word applies to you too. It's a marvelous thing!

Do you ever feel strange asking God for daily bread when you don't have to worry about where your next meal is coming from? Most of us only think about food when it's time to eat or we're hungry. Few of us ever worry where our next meal will come from enough to go to God in prayer about it. But regardless of how well-nourished we are, Jesus included this element in His prayer, and we are to model our prayers after His.

Why did He instruct us to pray for daily bread when it doesn't appear to apply to us as residents of the best-fed country in the world? The bread Jesus was speaking of was not referring only to the sliced loaves we buy in the supermarket. As with every word of God, it has a much deeper meaning. Let's read the following proverb to expand our view.

Question and Reflect

"Keep falsehood and lies far from me;
give me neither poverty nor riches,
but give me only my daily bread."
Proverbs 30:8

What four things does the writer of this Proverb ask God to keep from him?

1. _____

2. _____

3. _____

4. _____

What is the one thing he asked God to give him?

As you read this Proverb and see what the writer asked, what might lead you to believe he is not referring only to the bread we eat?

_____

_____

_____

_____

As we break down the words of this Proverb, it becomes evident that daily food was not the primary focus. What the author asks for and what he asks to be kept from does not correlate with food. Why would he ask to trade lying, falsehood, poverty, and riches for daily baked bread? If we do not limit this verse to only meaning food, it opens up a whole new dimension in our prayer lives.

Consider the four things the writer of this Proverb asked to be taken from him: falsehood, lies, poverty, and riches. What part of his body do you think he was most concerned with? Circle one.

      The Mind   The Stomach   The Heart

These four things all refer to issues of the heart and not the stomach or the mind. But, how can we know this for sure? Perhaps you selected the mind as your answer. How do we know for sure he is referring to the heart? After all, they are so closely linked.

The mind and heart are indeed very closely related but the mind is always a passenger to the heart. Don't miss this gold nugget. All that we think and do is motivated by what lies deepest in our hearts. Though our minds and hearts work in tandem, when all is said and done, our minds simply carry out the will of our heart. The writer of this Proverb was most concerned with his heart as we read his following verse,

> *"Otherwise, I may have too much and disown you*
> *and say, `Who is the LORD?'*
> *Or I may become poor and steal,*
> *and so dishonor the name of my God."*
> *Proverbs 30:9*

Oh, the wisdom of Proverbs. In a nutshell, the writer was asking God to provide his life with a balance that would help him keep his eyes steadfast on Him. He was saying, "Lord, don't give me too much of anything lest I forsake You. Just give me what I need and even then, only give me that which will not distract me from You." No mention of the stomach or mind, only his heart. He speaks of commitment and honor, both of which originate in the heart.

Question and Reflect

Have you ever asked God to limit your daily provisions in order to keep you focused on Him? Why or why not?

_____

_____

_____

_____

Do you find that your heart has strayed from God as a result of anything you have, or do, in excess? Explain.

_____

_____

_____

_____

Some of you may wish your pens were filled with invisible ink as you answered the questions above. Let me assure you----we all are guilty of living in excess. Personally, I love clothes; outfits in particular. I can't get enough of them. I have no problem buying specific shoes and purses to go with a particular outfit. It's a blessing my budget doesn't fit desire because it keeps me from slipping into the dangerous territory of excess. It's easy for me to occupy my mind with thoughts of coordinating an outfit from my closet or shopping for a new outfit. By giving too much time and attention to these thoughts, I can subtly slip God off my throne and replace Him with an outfit. Sounds silly but it's true and we do it all the time.

The reality is that all the clothes I love are but temporary threads that will one day perish. God knows I enjoy them and He's let me take pleasure in them, but within limits. It's easy to overdo it when it comes to shopping, eating, analyzing, criticizing, doubting, spending, controlling and working. We are all vulnerable. You name it and someone will find a way to over do it. We are all prone to the sin of excess and this is exactly why the writer of this Proverb asked God to keep him in balance. He knew his heart had a strong potential of straying from God.

CONCLUSION

Are you in the habit of asking God to limit anything that might distract you from Him? So often we approach God with requests for things we think we need when in reality, we need to ask Him to limit those things that hinder our walk with Him. Sister, nothing we can ever do or have is worth sacrificing a close intimate relationship with God. John said it best in 1 John 2:17: " The world and its desires pass away, but the man who does the will of God lives forever." While you may be saved and guaranteed eternal life, focusing on anything other than God is to abandon Him. Take a moment now to ask God only for your daily bread. You may need to ask Him to take some bread off your table. Heed the wisdom of today's Proverb and ask Him to give you only what you need. Sometimes less really is more.

Week Eight

Day 2 - Our Daily Bread (Part 2)

"Keep falsehood and lies far from me; give me neither poverty nor riches, but give me only my daily bread. Otherwise, I may have too much and disown you and say, `Who is the LORD?' Or I may become poor and steal, and so dishonor the name of my God."
Proverbs 30:8-9

REVIEW

Day 1 - Our Daily Bread (Part 1)

We learned yesterday that asking God for our daily bread isn't necessarily asking for the bread we eat. Rather it's asking God to protect us through limitations in order to keep our heart right with Him. A well-fed stomach never guarantees a close walk with God, but a healthy Spirit led heart will. The writer of this Proverb knew this and asked God to impose limits on his life. He asked God to keep from him falsehood, lies, poverty, and believe it or not, he even asked God to keep him from becoming too rich. His focus was God, his heart, and lastly on himself.

As you learn to knit this element of prayer into your life, you'll find it helpful to think of daily bread more as your "daily provision." When God feeds us, He feeds us in every way in order to make us new creatures in Him. Amazingly He does it all while never tampering with our unique personalities. We simply become better versions of what we once were.

Question and Reflect

God seeks to feed us in three main areas: Physically, Mentally/Emotionally, and Spiritually. These three components comprise our entire being. When we allow Him to feed them all, we become all He originally designed us to be. When we, on the other hand, choose to feed one area more than another, we become imbalanced and eventually drift away from Him. Only when we allow God to keep these areas of our life in check can we be most useful to Him.

List examples of needs we have in the following areas.

Physical:

_____

_____

Mental/Emotional:

_____

_____

Spiritual:

_____

_____

Of these three areas, which do you think is most important?

_____

_____

With which area do you most often seek God for help in?

_____

_____

Now, prioritize these three areas of your life by listing them from the one you focus on most often in line #1, down to the one you focus on least in line #3.

1. _____

2. _____

3. _____

Were you able to be honest with yourself? Did you have trouble prioritizing these components of your make up? It may comfort you to know that we don't have to list these three distinct areas of our lives by name in order to prioritize them. Somehow we instinctively sense their presence and arrange them to our liking. We may not always put them in the correct order, but we all shuffle them around one way or another. It takes but a simple look at how we live our lives to see how we prioritize these areas of our lives.

Below are three extreme examples of fictional Christian women. As you read their stories, you'll see it isn't hard to see what they place first in their lives and where they fall short.

Prosperity Patty –

Patty focuses most on her physical well being. As a Christian, she feels she deserves the best things in life because, after all, doesn't God's Word state that He will provide us with all the desires of our heart? Patty's goal in life is to receive all the physical blessings God can provide her, and she is claiming each and every one of them!

Intellectual Ilene –

Ilene's primary focus is on her own brainpower. Her goal has always been to seek the highest education and this goal has not gone unmet. With honors, she graduated from the most prestigious university in the country and was flattered to accept employment at a well-known corporate giant. Saved as a teenager, Ilene attends her local church but isn't able to participate a great deal due to her grueling work schedule. As a result of hard work and dedication to her employer, she is quite successful. Her near photographic memory guarantees a sure trip up the corporate ladder. She knows God has blessed her with a powerful mind and she takes full advantage of it by dedicating it to her profession.

Spiritual Stephanie -

Stephanie has her eyes entirely on God. She accepted Christ three years ago and loves her Lord with a passion. Stephanie spends much of her day in prayer and is committed to only serving Him. She works at a local discount store part time but doesn't associate with her fellow employees due to the fact they aren't saved. She witnesses to all of her customers by putting a tract in their bags even though her employer has forbidden it. Because of this infraction, Stephanie is on probation, but she refuses to comply, saying she'd rather be fired than turn her back on God.

Can you relate to any of these women? I don't know about you but I can relate to Patty and Stephanie, but I haven't a clue what it's like to be Ilene. If our brains were cars, mine would be an old Volkswagen bug. It'll get me there but it won't be fast, smooth, or comfortable. Nevertheless, I've learned to be thankful for my little brain because intelligence is not a stumbling block for me. I have many things that trip me up but aptitude is not one of them. Writing every word of this study has required total reliance on God. It doesn't say much for me but magnifies the Lord.

Question and Reflect

Though Patty, Ilene, and Stephanie are extreme examples, they give us an idea of how useless we can be to God when we focus only on one area of our life. God is a God of balance and precision. He desires to nurture us in all these areas in order to use us in a way that will provide complete satisfaction.

Read Exodus 35:30-35.

According to verse 31, what three skills did God give Bezalel?

1. _____

2. _____

3. _____

How did God give him these skills (verse 31)?

_____

_____

According to Exodus 35:10-19, how were Bezalel and the other skilled craftsmen called to use their skills?

_____

_____

_____

_____

_____

_____

      The NIV Bible says God gave Bezalel skill, ability, and knowledge in all kinds of crafts. Both he and Oholiab were given all the skills they needed plus the ability to teach the people how to build the Tabernacle. The same is true for us. Once we allow the Holy Spirit to dwell inside us, we have all we'll ever need to accomplish that which we are called to do and no area of our life will be neglected. The New Living Translation Bible states it beautifully when it says,

> *"The Lord has filled Bezalel with the Spirit of God,*
> *giving him great wisdom, intelligence and skill in all kinds of crafts."*

      While all three areas of our being need balance, our Spirit is the one we should tend to first. Why? Because, like the hub of a wheel, a spirit balanced by God keeps the heart and mind strong and steady-bringing all together in harmony. With all areas in line, we not only receive God's peace that passes all understanding but also gain more than we could ever ask or imagine. What wonderful blessings there are to be had when we live balanced in God.

      Bezalel's life is a perfect example of one so blessed. Whoever this man was prior to the building of the Tabernacle, God singled him out as project manager for this delicate job. He knew all about Bezalel and his family and handpicked him from the multitude to build His first earthly dwelling place.

Draw a line connecting each gift of the spirit to the correlating area of Bezalel.

Gift of the Spirit	Correlating Area of Bezalel
Wisdom	Mental/Emotional
Intelligence	Physical
Skill	Spiritual

Bezalel's life is perfect example of the daily bread Jesus was referring to when He instructed His disciples. This bread we are to ask for permeates every area of our lives, going far beyond feeding our physical bodies. It feeds our hearts and minds, giving us wisdom to hear His instructions and ability to carry them out.

Imagine if Bezalel had tried to build the Tabernacle as Patty, Ilene, and Stephanie would have. If he were like Patty, he would have prayed, then simply waited for the Tabernacle to drop out of the sky, since all we have to do is ask and receive. If he were like Ilene, he would have labored for years designing a Tabernacle of his own creation, not God's. And, if he were like Stephanie, he would have most certainly received the wonderfully detailed plans of God's intent but never been able to teach and work with those also called to help build the Tabernacle.

CONCLUSION

Only God's daily bread can provide us with that perfect balance we need to be truly productive in life. Daily bread is so much more than carbohydrates! It is the sustenance we need to be complete, content, and fruitful in the Lord. God's daily bread nourishes our body, mind, and soul. Some of us need to feed certain areas of our life more, while other areas to go on a diet. Whatever you need, you can trust God to accurately calculate your needed intake to make you healthy, happy, and strong. All you need is a heart that receives the Holy Spirit, like Bezalel.

What area of your life is God drawing attention to? Does that area need more nourishing or does it need a reduction? Write what you sense God is revealing to you and ask Him to give you balance.

Week Eight

Day 3 - A Spotlight on Prosperity

"Do not love the world or anything in the world. If anyone loves the world, the love of the Father is not in him. For everything in the world--the cravings of sinful man, the lust of his eyes and the boasting of what he has and does--comes not from the Father but from the world. The world and its desires pass away, but the man who does the will of God lives forever."
1 John 2: 15-17

REVIEW

Day 1 - Our Daily Bread (Part 1)

Day 2 - Our Daily Bread (Part 2)

This week we have talked about how much more we receive when we allow God to give us what we need instead of all we ask for. It's human nature to ask for things that are often not good for us. For this very reason God, in His infinite wisdom, does not grant us all we ask.

Unfortunately we live in a time when the "name it and claim it" philosophy is popular. It's so well liked because it feeds our hearts' selfish desires. Naming a blessing from God and claiming it as done is dangerous since we often harbor undetected sins deep within our hearts. Wanting something badly enough to claim it in the name of God can easily lead us down a very selfish path, which leads us away from Him. It is my prayer that you will hear the Holy Spirit speak to your heart on this issue and receive His perfect and pure instruction.

PATTY PROSPERITY

Remember imaginary Patty from yesterday? She's a great representative of those who approach God as if He were a short order cook. A personal and intimate relationship with God is often never a consideration and certainly not likely when this mindset is dominant. Satan loves it when we dare to expect things of God. This enticing focus on self is one of the most common tools the enemy uses, and it is a highly effective one at that.

Early on in my Christian life, I only approached God when I wanted something. Whether I received what I wanted or not, I would eventually go my own way. God was like a drive-through window or casual acquaintance. We are all guilty of doing this one time or another and it is a classic sign of spiritual immaturity. No one who really knows God in a personal and intimate way will treat Him like a short order cook. When we have truly placed God on the throne of our hearts, telling Him what to do isn't an option because submission will be our first priority. Only hearts deceived by the enemy dare demand what they want from God, refusing "no" for an answer.

Is it wrong to name a promise of God and claim it? No, not at all. God's Word is full of promises, but we must be very wary of claiming self-centered promises about which we have never truly consulted God. Many claim promises assuming God approves-anything from a designer purse to the cure of a life-threatening illness. Can God heal or provide anything we ask? Yes. As creator of the world He can do anything. However, it is because He is the great "I AM" we must never claim anything that we have not first taken to Him and laid at His feet. You see, the question is not "Can He?", but rather, "Is it His will?" Claiming something that we have not first taken to Him in prayer, is nothing short of being a tool of the enemy's, designed to take your eyes off God.

It is so easy to claim healing from an illness without first taking it to God. We are likely to do this because from our human perspective, we can't understand why God would not desire to heal. Even His Word says He is the Lord who heals us (Exodus 15:26). The problem with claiming this promise without first laying it at God's feet, is that it prevents us from tapping into His infinite wisdom, knowledge, and plan. Failing to carefully consult Him in all we do, and in every situation, is bound to lead us away from God's will into enemy territory.

Our goal is to securely fix God on the throne of our hearts so that all our wants and desires come second to His, even issues of life and death. Can God heal you or a loved one of a deadly illness? Can He provide you with a better lifestyle? Can God do anything we ask of Him? While the answers to these questions are all "yes", the question we should ask ourselves isn't can He, but is it His will?

Why wouldn't it be God's desire to heal someone of an illness? This is a legitimate question and one I asked God for years on behalf of our daughter. In time, He blessed me with the understanding that not only does He heal, but He heals every time, just not always in the way we want Him to. When we don't get what we ask, it's important to remember that all of God's decisions are based on wisdom that far surpasses our own. He sees everything of the present as well as the future. He has a perfect plan and an ultimate goal, which may or may not involve the healing of an illness.

When physical healing does not take place, how exactly is God healing? When I asked God to heal our daughter, He not only chose not to, but He told me He had no plans to. I have to admit that caught me a little off guard. I never expected this answer from Him. It had never crossed my mind. In spite of my narrow vision, He revealed to me that His wisdom far surpasses my own and that He could actually do a greater work through her disability - and He has! He has healed me of a multitude of infirmities as a result of not physically healing Dani. It's a truly puzzling way to conduct business, but that's how God often works. In the end His plan is always better.

Look at the great apostle Paul for example. He had a thorn in the flesh, which he asked God to remove three times yet each time God said "no." Why would God not heal this man through whom He had chosen to do such a great and mighty work? Couldn't God do more through Paul had He healed him? Apparently not or God would have done so. Instead He made way for Paul's greater need, one of humility and dependence on God. To gain this would alleviate any temptation to rely on his own strength, ultimately making Paul more effective. A greater work was indeed accomplished in spite of Paul's weakness. He was never healed of what he originally asked to be healed of, but God provided a greater, more complete healing---one of full and complete submission.

Have you ever asked God for something and been told "no"? Do you now understand why He didn't allow it or still resent having been told "no"? Explain.

_____

_____

_____

_____

If you still have regrets, ask God to reveal the greater purpose in His answer. List some possible reasons why God's "no" was to your benefit.

_____

_____

_____

_____

It's important to remember that we never really have a clue as to what's best for us in the long run. Our plans are nearly always tainted with selfish desires and ulterior motives. But God's plans are forever pure and never tainted with motives that would harm us. They always work for our good and His glory. He knows precisely what will bless us most. What we ask for may be good, but His plan involves giving us more than we can ever imagine. Given this, how could anyone claim to know the will of God? Furthermore, why would we claim anything that has not first been laid at His feet?

BUT... GOD PROMISES TO PROSPER US

The enemy often tempts us to focus on the wealth of God in order to take our eyes off God Himself. The "prosperity path" is a dangerous and slippery slope, which can easily tempt us to focus our attention on God's hand and not His face. At the risk of sounding like a scrooge, I ask that you not just listen to me, but seek the wisdom of the Holy Spirit on this highly debatable topic. It's true God seeks to prosper His children, but to focus on the gift and not the Giver, is a tragic error.

The enemy is hard at work enticing us to take our eyes off of God. He tempts us to crave earthly wealth, which serves only to narrow our definition of prosperity. Please never forget the reality of this truth. His tactics are designed to be subtle and they often throw well-meaning Christians off track. I encourage you to ask God to show you how the enemy may be doing this in your life, so you will not be led astray.

Question and Reflect

In your own words, define what it means to be "prosperous."

_____

_____

_____

_____

Webster's Dictionary defines "prosperous" as:
- Marked success or economic well-being
- Enjoying vigorous and healthy growth
- Flourishing

Compare your definition and Webster's definition. Do you think prosperity is something for the present or future? Circle one.

        Present   Future

In Jeremiah 12:1b, what question does Jeremiah ask God?
_____
_____

Read Deuteronomy 28:1-2 and 15. According to these verses, whom does God bless and whom does He curse?
_____
_____

In your opinion, do Deuteronomy and Jeremiah contradict one another? Explain.
_____
_____
_____
_____

     What Jeremiah saw going on around him is something we have all seen and questioned at one time or another. Why do the wicked prosper? Is it God who is blessing them? If He isn't actively blessing them, why is He allowing them to prosper? Why do corrupt CEO's of crumbling large companies walk away with millions of dollars when the modest employee walks away with virtually nothing after years of hard work? Why is the pornography industry booming like never before when it is a blatant affront to God? Why do the wicked seem to prosper so much more than God's people?

SATAN'S PROSPERITY VERSUS GOD'S PROSPERITY

Read Matthew 4:1-11.

According to verses 3, 6, 8, and 9, in what three areas did Satan tempt Jesus?

    1. _____

    2. _____

    3. _____

Satan has no authority to offer the eternal blessings and promises of God. What he offers is meager and paltry at best. He offers only that which was given to him by God. Earthly possessions and short-lived prestige are all he has to lure us away from God's true prosperity. Matthew 4 says Satan tempted Jesus in the areas of flesh, power, and pride. He approached Jesus during His most vulnerable time, the end of a 40-day fast, when He was most hungry and tired. He knew to dare not approach Jesus at full strength.

As you read how Satan enticed Jesus, would you say he tempted him with things of the present or future?

_____

_____

Read Jesus' reply to each of Satan's temptations in verses 4, 7, and 10 and circle the sentence that best describes all of His responses.

- He outwitted the enemy
- He kept total focus on God and His Word
- He stumped the enemy
- He debated with the enemy

Christ came as our example, and at the very onset of His ministry, He showed us how to respond when tempted by the enemy. We are to simply stay focused on God and His word since they are our anchor that will never lead us astray. They are the same today as they were yesterday and will be the same tomorrow. Satan tempted Jesus with things of the world 2,000 years ago and he tempts us today in the same fashion. He'll do anything to take our eyes off God. His formula is simply, temporal satisfaction in exchange for eternal consequences.

Read Hebrews 11: 1-2 and 32-40.

Hebrews 11 is often called the "Hall of Faith." From Abel to the prophets, God commends the faith of His people. One by one He lists the names of those who believed in Him and acted in obedience. They demonstrated what faith is; being sure of what we hope for and certain of what we do not see. Why does faith please God so much? Because, faith involves having a heart set on Him, not the things of the world.

According to verses 39-40, why didn't those of great faith get to see what had been promised to them?

_____

_____

_____

_____

This, dear sister, is the difference between the prosperity of the wicked and prosperity of God's children. Children of the enemy can only receive the things of the world because that is all Satan has to give. God's children receive blessings far greater than this world can ever contain. Our rewards are eternal, and many will only be seen and enjoyed when we go to live with Christ. We must never seek only the earthly prosperity. Instead, we must keep the faith and hold fast to the promises of our Lord and Savior Jesus Christ!

CONCLUSION

Do you find yourself wanting your prosperity now? Are the eyes of your heart fixed on the hand of God or are they set on God Himself? Take a moment to thank God for all the times He has said "no" to you, preserving for you a greater blessing in heaven. Praise Him for His great wisdom and love, and ask Him to help you seek His face like never before.

Week Eight

Day 4 - Daily Bread for the Mind

"We demolish arguments and every pretension that sets itself up against the knowledge of God, and we take captive every thought to make it obedient to Christ."
2 Corinthians 10:5

REVIEW

Day 1 - Our Daily Bread (Part 1)

Day 2 - Our Daily Bread (Part 2)

Day 3 - A Spotlight On Prosperity

This week we've learned that asking God for our daily bread goes far beyond simply feeding our physical bodies. This bread is uniquely designed to feed our mind, body, and soul, keeping all parts balanced and in harmony. Prosperity Patty was our example of one out of balance as she focused chiefly on earthly things. In futility she sought earthly prosperity and missed all God had in store for her. The prosperity path is a dangerous trail the enemy seeks to lead us down. It's designed to shift our focus off God's face and on to His hand, centering only on what He can provide us.

INTELLECTUAL ILENE

We also got a glimpse of Intellectual Ilene. She is the one with the photographic mind. The one I cannot begin to relate to. Saved as a teenager, Ilene whizzed through high school and college as if it were a recreational activity. She used her brainpower to climb the corporate ladder and was quite successful. Her problem, however, was to rely solely on the brainpower God gave her and not on God Himself.

As powerful as Ilene's mind was, it did not have the power to override what was deep within her heart. She and her career sat high on her throne, living out the truth that though the heart and mind work closely together, the heart always takes the lead. In fact, our hearts and minds work so closely together it's hard to tell which is doing what. The heart directs, while the mind thinks, reasons, plans, and organizes ways to carry out the will of the heart. They are incredibly tight partners.

OUR HEART'S PARTNER

For much of this Bible study, we have worked on heart issues but today for the first time, we are going to talk about its close partner----the mind. When Jesus instructed His disciples to ask for their daily bread, He meant not only physical nourishment, but also nourishment for their minds.

Question and Reflect

What do you think it means to ask for daily bread for your mind?

_____

_____

_____

_____

Given that our hearts and minds are so closely knitted together, it's important to address them both. We cannot work on one without also working on the other. Let's first look at how the enemy feeds our minds.

Yesterday we learned that Satan has no authority to offer the blessings and promises of God. All he has to offer is the measly earthly things he possesses. Although God is the creator of all things, Satan has been given authority to rule over the world. Unlike God, he is not all-powerful, he does not know everything, and he cannot be everywhere at once. He is an angel created by God and he has limitations.

An important seed to plant deep in our heart is the knowledge that although Satan can place thoughts in our minds, he cannot read our minds. Why is this so important? Because it reassures us that he cannot penetrate or control our minds. Though he can place thoughts in our heads, he ultimately has no control, short of any we hand over to him. In a nutshell, our minds are our own to feed and nourish as we desire. We can choose things of God or lies of the enemy. Whatever we choose, that is what will be carried out in our lives.

Read Isaiah 32:6 describing the person whose mind is led by the enemy. Fill in the blanks.

"For the fool _____ folly, his _____ is busy with evil: He _____ ungodliness and spreads _____ concerning the LORD; the hungry he leaves empty and from the thirsty he withholds _____."

Do you see how detrimental it is when we let the enemy influence our minds? It not only affects us but hurts those around us as well. The mind led by the enemy spreads its tentacles in all directions, causing great heartache and pain. Only a fool allows the enemy to run rampant in her mind.

Since the enemy cannot overtake our minds, any ground he has is that which we've given him. He can pester, nag, badger, and harass but he can never overtake the mind of a child of God. He is nothing more than an angel who has gone bad. He isn't God, he didn't create you, and he cannot control you. His only hope is to try to influence your thoughts with the hope to one day affect your behavior. The good news is we have the upper hand.

Since Satan only has the power to distract us, there are three things we must do to remain close with God:

1. Keep our heart's focus on God at all times
2. Fill our mind with God's Word by memorizing Scripture
3. Meditate on His Word day and night

Read Isaiah 26:3 and Romans 8:6-8. How does God bless our minds when we keep them steadfast on Him and allow the Spirit to take control?

_____

_____

_____

Isn't peace what we are all looking for in life? Jesus knows peace is our key to happiness, which is why He instructs us to ask for His daily bread. In doing so we are saying, "Lord, give us this day the peace that only comes through You!" When we ask for this, God is good to always give us not only what we need, but so much more. He is so multifaceted that He is simply unable to bless us just one way. His generosity is far more abundant than one blessing could supply. Therefore, when we receive His peace that passes all understanding, many other powerful gifts will naturally follow!

Read Job 38:36. What additional gift do we get when we set our mind on God?

_____

_____

The gift of understanding is our key to true peace. Just as the heart and mind work in tandem, so do understanding and peace. You simply cannot separate the two. When was the last time you were frustrated or angry with someone because you could not understand them? This helpless feeling that comes from being unable to control certain situations, or people, is very unsettling. This helplessness is a thief that inevitably robs us of our peace.

Describe a time when you felt or unable to understand a person or situation and how it made you angry?

_____

_____

_____

_____

There isn't enough ink and paper to tell you how many times I have become angry and frustrated over that which I could not comprehend. My little Volkswagen brain has a low threshold for knowledge. Our daughter has been a puzzle since the day she was born and challenged my economy-sized brain on a daily basis. Almost every time we take her to the doctor we hear, "Never seen that before." It used to grate on my nerves, but after eighteen years, I've learned to chuckle in my heart and say, "Lord, you have truly made her a unique creation."

Through the years God has taught me that I will never find peace on my own. There are too many things I do not know. I can't understand my daughter, many people, politics, and much of the time, I do not understand myself. The limitations of my brain will never permit me to find peace in the world or within myself. It is only something that can be found when I allow the Holy Spirit to reside in me.

CONCLUSION

Are you blessed with a brain like Ilene's that runs as smooth as a Cadillac, or are you stuck with a VW brain like mine? No matter what God has blessed us with, we all need His daily bread. The Ilenes of the world cannot find true peace by relying on their own brainpower, and neither can those of us with more limited abilities. We all need understanding to find the peace we so desperately crave. But it cannot be found through intellect. It can only be found by allowing God to nourish our minds with the peace of His Holy Spirit.

Is your mind focused on God each day? Do you ask Him to bless your mind with His wisdom, knowledge, and understanding? When you ask for these things, God will answer you and bless you abundantly.

Week Eight

Day 5 - Daily Bread for Our Spirit

"The fruit of the Spirit is love, joy, peace, patience, kindness, goodness, faithfulness, gentleness and self-control. Against such things there is no law."
Galatians 5:22-23

REVIEW

Day 1 - Our Daily Bread (Part 1)

Day 2 - Our Daily Bread (Part 2)

Day 3 - A Spotlight On Prosperity

Day 4 - Daily Bread for the Mind

This week we've learned about many different kinds of daily bread. We've learned that the bread we need to feed our bodies is really the least of our worries. Matthew 6:26 tells us God cares for even the birds of the air, and if He feeds them, how much more will He do for us? God faithfully feeds all of His creation. He provides for His children's mental and emotional needs and above all, seeks to nourish our spirit.

What exactly is our spirit? It is our soul, the part of us that will live in eternity. As humans, we were created differently from all other animals in that we were given souls that will live forever. Our spirit animates us, giving us life. Webster's dictionary uses the word "breath" as the first word to describe "spirit." It is that invisible supernatural existence that possesses the human body.

We've also talked about how closely linked the mind is to the heart and how the mind is always a passenger to the heart's motives. These two elements of our being travel through life intertwined like a vine. But they are not the only passengers on the journey. There is yet another.

While our hearts direct our bodies, and our minds plot the course, our souls ride along as well. As if in the back seat, it quietly goes where the heart and mind lead. There is one main difference among the three. The one in the backseat will live on into eternity. The heart and mind steer the way, but the soul reaps the consequences in the end. What the heart and mind determine to do during our life affects our soul for eternity. It's a sobering thought.

A BALANCED SPIRIT

Earlier this week, we read about Spiritual Stephanie, our fictional example of one so spiritual, she alienates those around her. She was out of balance even though she appears to be walking with God. But how could she be out of balance? Did she get too much of God? Does this mean we should ration our time with Him or at least monitor it closely?

If you have ever known a Spiritual Stephanie, you might be inclined to answer yes. This type of person can be too extreme to enjoy. But before we prescribe this medication of limiting our time with God, let's first be sure we have accurately diagnosed the problem.

We know that God is a God of peace, perfection, and balance. We also know that when our lives are in balance, it is the sign of a strong, healthy walk with God. Anytime we are off balance in any area of our life, we have strayed from His side to some degree. Balance can never be achieved by limiting our time with God. In fact, the only way to find balance is through spending quality time with Him. So Spiritual Stephanie's problem is not God, or the amount of time she spends with Him. This leaves only one alternative: the problem lies with Stephanie.

Question and Reflect

Read Galatians 5:16-26.

If we live by the Spirit, what will we do according to verse 16? Check one.

_____ We will not associate with sinners

_____ We will not gratify the desires of our sinful nature

_____ We will spend all of our time alone in prayer

_____ We will alienate ourselves from those around us

List the 15 acts of the sinful nature according to verses 19-21.

1. _____   9. _____

2. _____   10. _____

3. _____   11. _____

4. _____   12. _____

5. _____   13. _____

6. _____   14. _____

7. _____   15. _____

8. _____

Read James 3:13-16 below:

"Who is wise and understanding among you? Let him show it by his good life, by deeds done in the humility that comes from wisdom. But if you harbor bitter envy and selfish ambition in your hearts, do not boast about it or deny the truth. Such "wisdom" does not come down from heaven but is earthly, unspiritual, of the devil. For where you have envy and selfish ambition, there you find disorder and every evil practice."

In verse 14, what two things can we harbor in our hearts that are unspiritual and from the devil?

1. _____

2. _____

What two same ungodly characteristics are listed both in Galatians 5 and James 3?

1. _____

2. _____

    Isn't that interesting? Galatians names fifteen detestable acts that characterize a sinful nature while James lists only two - the same two tucked smack dab in the middle of the list in Galatians. At first glance it may appear that the two James mentions are less harmful compared to the ones in Galatians. Wouldn't you agree that sexual immorality, impurity, debauchery (extreme indulgence in sensuality), idolatry, witchcraft, hatred, discord, jealousy, fits of rage, dissension, factions, drunkenness, and orgies sound far worse than selfish ambition and envy? And what would this have to do with Spiritual Stephanie and her time with God? Let's revisit James 3 to find the cause of her imbalance. James lists two kinds of wisdom. Wisdom from God and wisdom from the devil.

Let's compare the two:

Describe wisdom from God (James 3:17-18):

_____

_____

_____

_____

Describe wisdom from the devil (James 3:13-16):

_____

_____

_____

_____

    Did you realize you could receive wisdom from the devil? We often think of wisdom as only a good thing, but the Bible says we can actually receive wisdom from the devil. Wisdom is defined as having knowledge or understanding with no mention of whether it is good or bad. What determines whether we receive godly or ungodly wisdom is whom we choose to follow (James 3:13). The fruit that comes from our deeds indicates whose wisdom we follow. But again, how does this apply to Stephanie. and more importantly, how does it apply to us?

Let's re-read Stephanie's story.

Spiritual Stephanie has her eyes entirely on God! She accepted Christ three years ago and loves her Lord with a passion. Stephanie spends much of her day in prayer and is committed to only Him. She works at a local discount store part time but doesn't associate with her fellow employees due to the fact they aren't saved. She witnesses to all of her customers by putting a tract in their bags even though her employer has forbidden it. Because of this infraction, Stephanie is on probation, but she refuses to comply, saying she'd rather be fired than turn her back on God.

What good fruit can you see as a result of her deeds?

_____

_____

Which kind of wisdom is she following?

_____

_____

Is the presence of love, joy, peace, patience, kindness, goodness, faithfulness, gentleness, and self-control evident in her life? If not, what does her life reflect?

_____

_____

While Stephanie does not commit sexually immoral acts, get drunk, or practice witchcraft, she does show selfish ambition and that, in and of itself, is a cancerous sin that will penetrate every area of her life. Selfish ambition is one of the fifteen disgusting and ungodly acts of the sinful nature and is not to be taken lightly. Whenever we harbor selfish ambition, we are following the wisdom of the devil, which will lead to discord and evil practices (James 3:16).

What possible selfish ambition might Stephanie be harboring in her heart?

_____

_____

_____

_____

I can tell you from experience, it's a battle leaving the feet of God. I often find it much more enjoyable to spend time with Him than with people. He always speaks the truth, He loves me with an unconditional love, He never lets me down, and He is always stable and secure. His phone line is never busy and He has an extravagant amount of patience with me as I learn at my slow pace. I love sitting at my Lord's feet because that is where I am most safe.

But God doesn't call us to sit at His feet and never leave. While called to commune with Him, we are also called to go out into the world. That is the great commission! If we all behaved as Stephanie, we would be islands that never unite, failing to reflect Christ and negate the call. How can we prevent falling into a trap like Stephanie who honestly sought God?

Read John 6:48-51. What is the only bread that can feed and save our soul?

___

___

Jesus, the Son of God, is our daily bread. He is the only bread that can nourish and satisfy our soul, giving us the peace we all crave. Sister, Jesus is all we need, now and forever. He feeds the body, mind, and soul all at once, providing us with the strength, wisdom, and understanding we need to be fruitful in life. He heals us even when it isn't the healing we asked for. He sees the past, present, and future all at once and knows exactly what it takes to make us whole. The concept is simple but often overlooked. Seek, submit, and obey.

CONCLUSION

Have you asked God to feed your spirit with the daily bread of His Son? Are you seeking the only bread that can feed your soul, or are you feeding yourself with the empty food of selfish ambition? Christ is the only nourishment for our soul. He sees through any Christian camouflage you may be wearing. He knows if you are seeking Him for your own gain or in true humility. He knows whose wisdom you follow and He sees the fruit of your deeds. Ask Jesus to feed your soul today so that His light will begin to shine through you!

___

___

___

___

___

___

___

___

___

___

___

Week Nine

Day 1 - Standing Firm

"Finally, be strong in the Lord and in his mighty power. Put on the full armor of God so that you can take your stand against the devil's schemes. For our struggle is not against flesh and blood, but against the rulers, against the authorities, against the powers of this dark world and against the spiritual forces of evil in the heavenly realms."
Ephesians 6:10-12

Congratulations! We are finally here! We have made it to our last and final key to effective prayer: asking God for His guidance and protection. We've learned the importance of worshipping the One we have chosen to follow and how to ask God to show us the hidden sins, confess them and ask for His Holy bread. After doing these things, it is critical we ask for His guidance and protection.

We live in hostile enemy territory as Satan's targets. This is not because of who we are but rather to whom we belong to. Satan couldn't care less about you and me individually: we are but litter in his puny plot to thwart God's mighty plan. His only concern lies in hindering those who work for God.

Last week we learned to ask God for His daily bread for our minds. We also learned that Satan is very limited in power. Only a fool allows him to run rampant in her mind, and any ground he has gained is ground we have literally given to him. He can never overtake our mind because he is nothing more than an angel gone bad. He can pester, nag, and frustrate you, but he is not God. He didn't create you and he cannot overtake you. He can only try to influence your thoughts with the hope of influencing your behavior. The ultimate control is in our hands.

This coming week we will be learning about spiritual warfare and our need for God's guidance and protection. All Christians experience spiritual warfare, but only a few recognize it for what it truly is and even fewer fight the battle. This may be difficult to comprehend but more common than you might think. Many live as if ignorance were bliss when in fact ignorance is a tragic mistake.

HOW DO WE FIGHT THE ENEMY?

Picture a battlefield filled with Christians under attack from every direction. Imagine the various reactions each individual might have to the attack. Some people run, some cover their heads, some fall to the ground, some plead for mercy. Some give in to the enemy, some fight with all their might, and some deny the battle exists at all.

Whether you are a Christian or not, we are all under attack. Some how and in some way the enemy has implemented his plan of warfare on you. Your reaction, whatever that may be, may be yours and yours alone, but God is only pleased with those who resist the enemy. Sister, may it be our desire to fight. I pray you will never run, cower, cover your head, fall to the ground, give in, or deny the reality of this battle. But determine to fight with the strength of the Lord. Once we learn to do this, victory is ours!

In what realm are we fighting our battle (Ephesians 6:12)?

_____

_____

     We are at an extreme disadvantage as we fight an enemy that is unseen. The battle is not physical but one that is not only hidden but fought in our minds. It is a conflict that is supernatural, ultimately fought in the heavenly realms. Our fight does not require physical skill. It requires mental aptitude and a focused heart. Our ability to maintain focus on God determines the outcome. When we remain stable, strong, and balanced in the midst of battle, we are winning the war.

     How do we fight this unseen enemy and keep our balance in the middle of war? God's Word provides excellent instruction on handling the enemy and his warfare. When we implement these clear instructions in our lives on a daily basis, we will be amazed at their effectiveness.

Question and Reflect

Before we learn to fight this unseen enemy, let's first take a personal inventory.

Check what best describes the spiritual warfare you typically experience in your life.

    _____   I cannot detect any

    _____   I can only think of a few instances of warfare in my life

    _____   I am aware of it almost on a daily basis

If you have detected warfare in your life, do you defend yourself against the attacks and if so, how?

_____

_____

Do you find your methods of defense effective?

_____

_____

     If you are unable to detect warfare in your life, this is your week sister! While no one likes warfare and we should never seek out the enemy, the worst thing to do is deny we are in this battle. Putting our heads in the sand while the war goes on around us will not keep us from getting dirty. It is imperative that all of God's children be aware of warfare. This is why He has given us instructions on how to defend ourselves.

Read Ephesians 6:10-20.

From where does our strength come (verse 10)?

What are we to put on for this battle (verse 11)?

Once armed, what are we instructed to do (verse 11)?

How many times is this instruction given?

Notice we are to put on the "full" armor of God and once we do, our instruction is to stand. God tells us specifically what to put on and why, then tells us four times to simply stand there.

Does putting on armor, then just standing, sound like an effective defense against the enemy?

If standing and doing nothing sounds foolish to you, you are not alone. This instruction is one we easily glaze over either because we don't give it much thought or find it doesn't make sense. We accept what it says but we don't fully take it to heart. In many respects, putting on the full armor and simply standing sounds a bit confusing. After all, why would we gear up for war and not move? How can we fight the enemy positioned in one spot?

These are good questions that should not be ignored but instead taken to God so He can help us understand. Remember, it is our goal to follow every word that comes from the mouth of God. We must never pick and choose what parts of His Word we obey, but decide to obey it all. If God says put on the armor, then we must put on the armor. If He says put on the armor and stand, then we must do exactly that. Our aim is follow His commands to the letter. To put on the armor then duck, turn away, run away, debate with, cower, or plead with the enemy, is not an option.

Read Exodus 14:13-14.

Fill in the blanks listing the three instructions Moses gave the people before they crossed the Red Sea (verse 13).

"Do not be _____."

"_____ firm."

"_____ the deliverance the Lord will bring you today."

Name the great benefit Moses states will occur if they follow God's instruction to stand firm.
_____
_____

    In the midst of being pinned between the enemy and the Red Sea, Moses instructs the people to stand. Here again is this command. Though simple, it must have been difficult to carry out. Imagine standing there as death approached. The thunder of the army roars in your ears as the cool sea breeze blows against your back, reminding you of the water blocking your escape. I cannot imagine the fear anymore than I can imagine my leader's voice instructing everyone not to move. How could anyone survive if they didn't at least fight back?

    Planting yourself in one spot during battle sounds ludicrous. but God told his people to stay put and not be afraid for a very good reason…so they could watch! Once calm and quiet in the midst of this battle, they were able to not only witness, but also understand and remember His great power and love for them. He wanted to bless them with great faith so he provided them with a front row seat to this historic performance.

    Oh, what a great and mighty God we serve! His love is so vast that He will instruct us to stand as disaster approaches just so He can bless us with the opportunity to witness His enormous power and love. When times get tough and we take our eyes off God, we miss the opportunity to watch Him do great things. This is why we must obey His every Word, even when we don't understand. To stand firm in faith is to witness the movement of God's mighty hand and be blessed.

Has fear ever robbed you of the joy of watching God act on your behalf? Explain.
_____
_____
_____
_____

Have you ever fled the scene and missed a great work of God?
_____
_____

CONCLUSION

Has the enemy pulled the wool over your eyes? Are you aware of the warfare he is waging against you? God desires for you to be aware that you are a target of the enemy, which is why He has given us clear instructions on how to protect ourselves. Denial of the warfare is a tool of the enemy and a very effective one at that. He knows if he can keep you in denial, he will have you wrapped around his evil finger.

Ask God to help you see the warfare and stand firm with your eyes fixed on Him. When you see the great and mighty work He desires to do on your behalf, your faith will grow and God will be pleased!

Week Nine

Day 2 - The Armor of God

"The LORD looked and was displeased that there was no justice. He saw that there was no one, he was appalled that there was no one to intervene; so his own arm worked salvation for him, and his own righteousness sustained him. He put on righteousness as his breastplate, and the helmet of salvation on his head; he put on the garments of vengeance and wrapped himself in zeal as in a cloak."

Isaiah 59:15b-17

REVIEW

Day 1 - Standing Firm

This week we are learning about spiritual warfare. Though invisible, it is very real and all around us. Unfortunately, many Christians are either unaware of it or choose to ignore it, which leads to a weak and vulnerable spiritual condition.

A close and dangerous partner to denial is the one who disregards or discounts spiritual warfare. This person, who I call the "poo-pooer," says, "Oh, I don't need to worry. I am fine. I don't see any warfare going on. If I leave the devil alone, he'll leave me alone." If you or anyone you know believes this, be very, very careful! While we are not to seek a fight with the enemy or fear him, his presence is still real, and he does pursue God's children. He has an intricate and precise plan set to destroy every child of God. Any thoughts that lead us to believe otherwise are lies straight from the enemy, and when these lies are believed, they give him a foothold in our lives.

GOD PRACTICES WHAT HE PREACHES

Read Ephesians 6:10-20 and name the six pieces of armor we are instructed to put on to prepare for spiritual warfare.

1. _____ 2. _____

3. _____ 4. _____

5. _____ 6. _____

God provides us with six pieces of armor which, when used, will protect us from the enemy's attacks. Did you know that the very armor our Lord provides for us He also uses Himself? As you read today's verse, did anything stand out to you? Did you perhaps notice which pieces of armor Isaiah wrote that God wore?

Re-read today's Bible verse at the beginning of our lesson and name the two pieces of armor God put on.

1. _____

2. _____

How remarkable. This verse wonderfully magnifies the uniformity of God, leading me to trust Him even more. His Word is always true and never changing. He will never say one thing then do another, and what He instructs us to do, He Himself also does. Imagine the privilege of donning the very same armor God places on Himself! Our armor is the same armor that He places on His Holy head and breast. What an honor to be His child. Who says God isn't a personal god? Who dares label Him as a distant, far off, and uncaring Father? Nothing could be further from the truth.

Clothing is a very personal thing since it is worn directly on the body. I never share my clothing with anyone and I by no means share headwear (you know because of head lice). But here we see the great "I AM" giving us the very helmet and breastplate He Himself uses. Now I know God doesn't have to worry about us giving Him head lice, but in our sin He gladly clothes us with His own personal and Holy garments. Oh sister, I hope this draws your heart closer to Him by helping you see how much He truly loves you. He gives us what He Himself wears to gain victory over the enemy. How it touches my heart to see His great love and affection for us. We are truly prized children of the King.

THE ARMOR

Why do you suppose God gave us six pieces of armor to wear when He Himself wears only two? A safe answer would be "because He's God" which is true, but let's dig a little deeper to fully understand and appreciate why we wear three times more armor. It's important to learn what it is we are to wear, why we are to wear it, and how it is meant to protect and preserve us. Then we will be able to put it on and stand firm in the midst of battle.

BELT OF TRUTH:

This is the Word of God, our first line of defense against an enemy who is the author of all lies. This belt is to be secure around our waist in order to provide an unshakable, unchanging stability at the very core of our being.

BREASTPLATE OF RIGHTEOUSNESS:

This is the Righteousness of God. When we accept Christ as our Savior, we are instantly and permanently made righteous before Him (Philippians 3:9). It is a gift from God that can never be taken away, but one the enemy seeks to erase from our minds. Satan loves to remind us of our faults and failures to cause us to pause or question as we walk with God. Even though we are in right standing with God, we must daily remind ourselves that in His eyes, we are accepted as holy. We are not worthless but in fact worthy. We are no longer sinners but saints. Meditating on these truths will protect our hearts with the knowledge that we are precious in His sight. Then we won't hesitate, but walk with confidence wherever He leads us.

GOSPEL OF PEACE:

This is the knowledge of God's Word. Planting God's Word in our hearts and minds brings His peace. A peace that passes all understanding. It is calm in the midst of the storm and tranquility in the presence of the enemy. It is the unexplainable, invaluable victorious presence of God!

SHIELD OF FAITH:

This is what pleases God. It is our only movable weapon of defense. It is used to extinguish Satan's fiery darts that come at us from every direction. Satan is very creative in his attacks and knows which way to aim his arsenal in order to make contact with our vulnerable spots. When our faith is steadily focused on God, we literally quench Satan's flaming arrows. What great power lies in the faith of those whose hearts are set on God.

HELMET OF SALVATION:

This helmet serves to protect our minds, which are the battlefield of spiritual warfare. A mighty and powerful headdress, this helmet serves to protect our minds from the lies of the enemy by keeping our focus on salvation in Christ. In war, a helmet is not an optional piece of armor. The best armor in the world is useless to a soldier if his mind is not stable and sound. As warriors in this unseen war, we need God's wisdom planted firmly in our minds to keep us focused on His truth.

SWORD OF THE SPIRIT:

This is the Word of God, the only offensive weapon we have. While other pieces of armor defend us against the enemy's attacks, the Sword of the Spirit is the one piece used against Satan in an offensive way. It causes him to flee every single time because he cannot withstand the power and purity of God's Word. He can twist it but he can never bear up under it. He can recite it, but he cannot fight it. Great power is at our disposal when we hide the Word of God in our hearts and minds.

Question and Reflect

Compare our armor with the armor God wore for battle in Isaiah. Why do you think God put on only two of the six pieces?

_____

_____

_____

_____

_____

We are instructed to put on six pieces of armor. These six pieces can be divided into two categories: 1) armor we receive once and for all at salvation and 2) armor we must put on daily.

ARMOR OF GOD	
Temporary Armor	Permanent Armor
• Belt of Truth	• Breastplate of Righteousness
• Shield of Faith	• Helmet of Salvation
• Gospel of Peace	
• Sword of the Spirit	

God is the great "I AM" which says it all and is His defense against the enemy. Think about it: He doesn't have to put on truth because He is truth. He doesn't have to put on the gospel of peace because He is the Word and the Word is peace. He doesn't have to protect Himself with the shield of faith because He is protection for those who have faith in Him. He is all we need to fight the attacks of the enemy. While all armor comes from God, it is His righteousness and salvation that overcomes Satan and brings victory. Therefore, when waging war against the enemy, all He needed was the breastplate of righteousness and helmet of salvation to move His mighty arm. He is all the other armor!

The helmet of salvation and breastplate of righteousness are our permanent pieces of armor. We receive them when we accept Christ and they can never be taken from us. The other four pieces of armor, the belt of truth, shield of faith, gospel of peace, and sword of the Spirit, are pieces we must put on each day. We are not called to passively wait for someone to dress us either but instructed to intentionally apply it each day. It is a daily discipline we must implement in our lives. As pawns in this heavenly war, without God, we are nothing. Our only hope lies in the One who is literally our armor.

Since we know that the armor we are to put on involves God's Word and our minds, what can we do to arm our minds against the enemy's attacks?

_____

_____

_____

_____

Our instructions are simple: read, know, and meditate on the word of God. Place it in your heart and meditate on it day and night. Know the truth, believe it, and use it as your sword against the devil. Don your armor every day, making it a part of every fiber of your being so that when the enemy launches his attack, you are ready for the fight.

CONCLUSION

Are you putting on the armor of God or is it in your Christian closet dusty and unused? If you have not been donning your armor, how is the battlefield of your mind? Is it filled with God's peace, or is the enemy hard at work distracting it? Is your mind stable and strong in God's truth, or confused by lies of the enemy? Are the arrows from the enemy pelting you day in and day out, or are you sheltered behind an ample shield of faith? Are you sure of your salvation and confident of your righteousness before God, or do you believe the enemy's lies that you are worthless and useless?

Sister, you may think you are fine not wearing God's armor but the battlefield of your mind tells the true story. Confidence, faith, and a firm stand in the midst of life's battles tell whether you are wearing God's armor or if exposed areas exist. The first step to putting on this armor is admitting you need it. Don't deny the existence of warfare or your need for protection against the enemy. Write a prayer thanking God for His sufficient armor and determine to put it to good use each day.

Week Nine

Day 3 - Bondage of the Enemy

"Now the Lord is the Spirit, and where the Spirit of the Lord is, there is freedom."
2 Corinthians 3:17

REVIEW

Day 1 - Standing Firm

Day 2 - The Armor of God

Spiritual warfare is something I have known about and actively battled for many years. However, I remember a time when I was in the middle of great warfare and didn't have a clue what was going on around me. Those days were very frustrating. I would look at my circumstance as something I should be able to control and found it very unsettling when I couldn't. It was in the midst of the greatest of wars that I began to realize my battle was not of the world, but was spiritual warfare the enemy had begun way back in my early years. Once open to the reality of this warfare, I ran toward God like a frightened little girl. Shaking in my boots close to His side, He began to teach me the truth about warfare. It was then I found the peace and security that had eluded me for so long.

THE BATTLE OF INSECURITY

Insecurity has been my primary battle all my life. Maybe you struggle with it too. I function well in life and as far as I know, have been considered normal, but I never fully felt up to par with those around me. I would always look at the good in others and compare it to the bad in me. Any good qualities I could name about myself I would invariably nullify with the bad.

Completely unaware of it, all those years of feeling insecure were in fact a highly effective tool Satan used to keep me sedated. His goal was to prevent me from realizing that I was special and God had a special plan and purpose for me. Isn't it puzzling how we Christians can believe in a great and mighty God but still feel worthless or inadequate deep within? When it happens, and it does all the time, it is warfare. Although it makes no sense for those saved by the grace of God to feel insignificant, the enemy often uses this war tactic because it works quite well.

Satan's devices are similar to those used by elephant trainers. To keep an elephant confined, a trainer will tie a heavy chain from one of its ankles to a post in the ground. Over time as the elephant feels the resistance of the strong chain, he will cease to resist to the point where the trainer can place a small rope around his ankle and manage to keep him contained.

The enemy works much the same way. We grow up in harsh enemy territory and quickly learn to cower to his intimidating assaults. Once we choose Christ, we are no longer bound to the enemy. We are treasures of God and free from the enemy but so often continue to believe we carry a yoke that in reality is no longer there. With freedom from bondage and strength available in Christ, we continue living as if bound by the enemy. Intimidation is a mighty effective tool.

Question and Reflect

Can you think of one or more tools the enemy uses to keep you bound? Circle one.

Yes   No

Name tools the enemy uses on you and how they keep you bound.

TOOL   HOW IT BINDS YOU

- _____   _____
                                              _____
                                              _____

- _____   _____
                                              _____
                                              _____

- _____   _____
                                              _____
                                              _____

- _____   _____
                                              _____
                                              _____

Lack of confidence is the number one tool the enemy loves to use on women. He uses it for one reason. It works! Without a thought, we can feel insecure in a multitude of areas. Just name it and we'll find a way. It doesn't even have to be a good reason; just give us one and we'll hand over the confidence.

There are two ways we can respond to insecurity when it comes our way. How we choose to respond determines how much of a stronghold we allow the enemy to have in our life. When our response becomes drastic and the enemy gains good ground, the insecurity is played out via underachieving or overachieving-neither of which reflect a heart balanced in the Lord. By some strange quirk of nature, I have found myself on both sides of the spectrum. At times, I can feel so utterly worthless that it tempts me to wallow in despair, while other times I feel as though I can teach a college course to wannabe workaholics. It's as if I have the world by the tail and can do anything I set my mind to do. Either circumstance, when extreme, prevents true harmony with God.

How do you think <u>under</u>achieving can work against true submission to God's will?

___
___
___
___

How do you think <u>over</u>achieving can work against true submission to God's will?

___
___
___
___

Draw a line matching each word to its quotation:

Underachieve   "I choose to trust and follow God wherever He leads me."

Overachieve   "I trust God can do anything, but He would never use me to do a great work."

Heart balance with God   "I'm not sure of God's call on my life but I'm working hard doing what I want and finding success at it."

When we underachieve, or fail to believe that God has a special plan for us in His kingdom, we work against Him. It's similar to saying, "Yes God, I believe You created the universe and You can do anything but I don't believe You can use me for Your good will." On the other hand, overachieving can easily lead us from the heart of God by taking us in a direction that we have chosen for ourselves, apart from God. As women in a performance and works oriented society, we need to be very careful not to be caught up on either end of this spectrum. We must seek to keep our eyes only on God, then find, accept, and carry out His perfect will for our lives.

Do you feel you are in God's perfect will or do you feel the enemy and his lies have sidetracked you? Explain.

_____

_____

_____

_____

Are you at peace with your life at this point in time? Explain.

_____

_____

_____

_____

Read the words the prophet Jeremiah wrote to the Israelites while exiled in Babylon:

"For I know the plans I have for you," declares the LORD, "plans to prosper you and not to harm you, plans to give you hope and a future. Then you will call upon me and come and pray to me, and I will listen to you. You will seek me and find me when you seek me with all your heart. I will be found by you," declares the LORD, "and will bring you back from captivity. I will gather you from all the nations and places where I have banished you," declares the LORD, "and will bring you back to the place from which I carried you into exile."
Jeremiah 29:11-14

CONCLUSION

We are like the exiled children of Israel as we live and dwell in enemy territory here on Earth. God's plan is to prosper us, and our chief weapon against the enemy is the hope of our future with Christ. The enemy doesn't want us to realize that God has a plan for us and he certainly doesn't want us to discover it. Instead, He wants to lead us to destruction far from prosperity, and he will whisper any lie in our ear to distract us from God's will.

Dear sister, we all hear lies from the enemy, but none of us will ever be able to distinguish his lies from God's truth until we read and know the Bible. We need to fill our minds, the battlefield, with God's powerful weapons that thwart the enemy's attacks. We need His wisdom and knowledge to guide and protect our hearts and minds. Every single word of God exposes the dark lies of the enemy and enables us to experience healing, restoration, confidence, peace, and power in our lives. This is what God intends for us to have!

How I pray for God to reveal to you all the lies the enemy is telling you. His lies are subtle and far too great for us to detect without God's wisdom residing in us. God is faithful, and He desires for you to clearly see and follow Him wherever He leads. Ask God to survey the battlefield of your mind and show you any territory that is unprotected. Ask Him to prepare you for war so you can stand your ground against every strike of the enemy.

Week Nine

Day 4 - Attacks of the Enemy

"Pray continually; give thanks in all circumstances, for this is God's will for you in Christ Jesus."
1 Thessalonians 5:17-18

REVIEW

Day 1 - Standing Firm

Day 2 - The Armor of God

Day 3 - Bondage of the Enemy

As I opened my living room blinds one morning, the enemy suddenly attacked at full force. It wasn't like a freight train, but rather, more a subtle seduction. That's how it caught me off guard. I opened the blinds to a beautiful sunny day, completely unaware the enemy was waiting like a lion in the bush. I looked through the slats to see what I had seen a hundred times before: the neighbor taking her youngest daughter to junior high school. Her daughter is a few months younger than our daughter Dani and their entire family is a delight. She and her husband have two wonderful girls, both close in age to our son and daughter.

As I watched their car pull out of the driveway and disappear down the road, time seemed to grind to a halt as I listened to these words whispering in my ear, "Just think, after she takes her daughter to school she'll have the entire day to do as she pleases while you are stuck at home with a disabled child. What kind of a god do you serve who keeps you so trapped in this house? How can He love you? Your life will never change and you will never be free."

I will never forget those venomous words as they spit in my ear. I heard them clearly, never taking the time to identify their source. Like weights on my soul, I gave them permission to capture my freedom as I walked away from the window, eyes cast down in despair. I didn't know it at the time, but it was the enemy whispering those lies in my ear that morning. It wasn't the first time, nor would it be the last time, that he would point out the restrictions in my life. He had done it countless times before, only this time, I listened and meditated on the deceit.

By 11 am, I was in a state of depression. The enemy had masterfully guided me into a corner by badgering and intimidating me to the point where I was spiritually curled up in a ball. In no time at all, I had become a participant in his plot to destroy the day. Like a parrot, I too began itemizing all that was wrong in my life, blaming everything on our daughter's disability. I began to think, "How *could* God love me and let this happen? Why *am* I cooped up when I want to serve Him with all my heart? Why do I have to give up my life for a child that will never become a productive member of society? What good is my life anyway? It's all a total waste and God doesn't care. Why does my neighbor have two normal children and I don't? If I only had a normal daughter, I would be happy."

Just a few lies was all it took to send me into a tailspin. The battlefield of my mind had all the armor needed to fight the enemy, but I hadn't put it on that morning. Spiritually I was naked, standing in the middle of a war. Looking back, I now see how the enemy led me to his dark corner that morning. I'm grateful it happened so I can give you a first hand account of how the enemy seeks to lead us far from the truth of God. Satan has no power to force any of us into a corner, but he can certainly influence us to the point where we go voluntarily. And when we do, it is a huge mistake. I pray you will learn from my error and be spared from any seductions by the enemy.

SATAN'S METHODICAL PLAN

The following is a step-by-step process the enemy used to engage his warfare on me that morning. Circle any steps that sound familiar to you:

    Step 1 – The enemy spoke his lie to me

    Step 2 – I listened to the lie

    Step 3 – I took my eyes off God and His truth

    Step 4 – I pondered, then began to meditate on the lie

    Step 5 – I began to participate by adding to his lies

    Step 6 - I sunk deeper and deeper into despair

Have you ever experienced this kind of subtle warfare?
_____
_____

Are these steps down to the pit of despair a common trip in your life?
_____
_____

Does the enemy use the same topic or tool to seduce you into despair?
_____
_____
_____

    I eventually crawled out of the corner away from the enemy's toxic lies, but it took some outside help, a phone call from my husband to be precise. As usual, he called asking how my morning was going to which, without hesitation, I informed him how totally ensnared I felt. I told him what I saw when I opened the blinds and that I would forever be trapped with no hope for the future. Quickly he realized the enemy was hard at work on me, and just as the enemy had led me down toward the pit of despair, my husband, in his great love and wisdom, began to show me the way back up. He pointed out our godly family and how the Lord has blessed our lives, including our little disabled lamb. He reminded me of our happy marriage and how content and happy Dani is because of this. Through the phone line he reached down into the pit I was in and lifted my chin up, encouraging me to refocus on God.

Just as I had chosen to turn away from God that morning, it was my choice to get my eyes back on Him again. My husband couldn't do it for me. I had to do it myself by deciding to stop this downward descent. The enemy hadn't abducted me that morning; he simply lured me away. The battlefield of my mind was vulnerable to attack, and it was no one's fault but my own.

Question and Reflect

Have you ever made the mistake of listening, then meditating, on the poisonous lies of the enemy?

_____

_____

What happened when you meditated on his lies?

_____

_____

_____

_____

_____

Satan's lies are sometimes so subtle that I still have trouble identifying them. Nevertheless, I have learned that the most important thing to do at the onset of an attack is to go to God in prayer, then take it to a close and trusted friend. Battling the enemy on our own is never an option. Trust me - the enemy will tell you not to concern anyone with your problem and that your problem is piddly, but don't listen to him. Instead, fight this spiritual battle in the spiritual realm---fight him with prayers of the saints!

Read Ephesians 6:18.

Under what occasion does Paul tell us to pray?

_____

_____

What kind of prayers and requests are we to pray?

_____

_____

Who are we to pray for?

_____

_____

There is no occasion in which we are not instructed to pray. There is no condition or concern that is too piddly for God, and there is no child of God that does not deserve the gift of prayer. God cares about everything you care about and wants you to come to Him with everything. He wants us to share prayer needs with one another so we can unite in the power of intercessory prayer. Satan tempts us to believe our problem is too insignificant because he knows that when we do, he can then begin to isolate us in a corner and brainwash us with his lies.

Read 1 Peter 4:7 and 1 Peter 5:8.

What two things does 1 Peter 4:7 say we should be so we can pray?

1. _____

2. _____

What two things do 1 Peter 5:8 say we should do to stand firm against the enemy?

1. _____

2. _____

Sister, we are called to take control of our minds. We need to have clear, alert, controlled minds in order to pray effectively and stand firm in our faith. You don't have to be mentally ill to have a mind that is out of control - you simply need to lack focus on God. The enemy engages his warfare in our psyche and he can attack at any given moment. We don't even have to leave home to be under fire and it doesn't have to feel like a freight train. So often times we don't have a clue we've been targeted. Sometimes all it takes for him to launch an assault is opening our blinds on a beautiful sunny day and seeing a neighbor drive her daughter to school. When that time comes, we need the armor of God.

CONCLUSION

Determine now to take your every thought captive and make it obedient to Christ (2 Corinthians 10:5). Clinging to God's truth is key to standing firm against the enemy's attacks and it isn't impossible. You can do it! Ask God to you keep your mind alert, controlled, and focused on Him, then determine to stand firm in your faith. Ask Him to help you detect the subtle lies that trigger spiritual tailspins and alert your mind to the enemy's tactics. He will do it!

_____

_____

_____

_____

Week Nine

Day 5 - Detecting Subtle Lies

"Finally, brothers, whatever is true, whatever is noble, whatever is right, whatever is pure, whatever is lovely, whatever is admirable--if anything is excellent or praiseworthy--think about such things. Whatever you have learned or received or heard from me, or seen in me--put it into practice. And the God of peace will be with you."

Philippians 4:8-9

REVIEW

Day 1 - Standing Firm

Day 2 - The Armor of God

Day 3 - Bondage of the Enemy

Day 4 - Attacks of the Enemy

We learned from 1 Peter 5:8 that Satan prowls around like a roaring lion seeking someone to devour. Like a wild cat stalking its prey, he is subtle, quiet, and nearly undetectable. It may sound frightening that someone so mysterious is out to get you but remember, as God's children, we are not alone. God has given us armor that He Himself uses against the same enemy. This issue of Satan's subtleness is one that deserves attention since it can be very difficult to detect and is his signature move.

After sharing about my tailspin when I simply opened my living room blinds, you may wonder how we can ever be able to detect such clever tactics of the enemy. If doing such an innocent daily routine can turn into great warfare, what chance do we have against this unseen foe? Such fearfulness can prompt us to do precisely what the enemy wants us to do, recoil. If he can't keep us ignorant, he wants us scared, but both are completely unnecessary. You can detect even the subtlest tactics of the enemy, and we will learn how to today.

Will the enemy never again sucker you? No, I'm sorry, I can't guarantee that. But you can get a good handle on the warfare he typically engages on you in order to better detect when he is trying to lead you astray. Becoming aware of this is half the battle. Learning the precise tactics he uses on you gives you an upper hand, allowing more and more victories in your life. It's a simple process of observing and learning about what is going on around you.

RED FLAGS

How can we detect an invisible enemy whose warfare is so subtle? How can we stand firm in the Lord and avoid spiritual tailspins? Just as Paul instructed the Ephesians to put on the full armor of God in Ephesians 6, he also instructed the persecuted church in Philippi to stand firm in the midst of their warfare.

Question and Reflect

Read Philippians 4:4-9.

What can we do to guard our hearts and minds from becoming anxious (v. 6)?

_____

_____

_____

_____

On what eight things does Paul instruct us to keep our minds focused (v. 8)?

1. _____   5. _____

2. _____   6. _____

3. _____   7. _____

4. _____   8. _____

What common denominator do all of these instructions have?

_____

_____

    Notice how Paul instructs us to arm the battlefield of our mind with things that are good, right, accurate, dignified, uncontaminated, outstanding, and divine. These are all things of God! Satan's method of attack is to lead us away from the peace of God by whispering lies, which is exactly what he did to me at my front window that bright sunny morning. I heard the lies, then began to listen to them more intently as they said, "Just think, she is taking her daughter to school and will have the entire day to do as she pleases while you are stuck at home with a disabled child. What kind of a god do you serve who keeps you so trapped in this house? How can He love you? Your life will never change and you will never be free." The more I listened, the more I believed.

    Take in the quality of these words. Every one of them was pessimistic, destructive, and ugly. They were negative toward God, my daughter, my neighbor, and me. Like a compass, they were designed to lead me in the direction of doubt. Once there, I would begin to question God's love for me, invariably lose hope, and enter into despair. This is precisely what happened. I began to think less of myself, and then quickly lost sight of all God had done for our family. The enemy had my attention everywhere but on the truth of God. All that I learned through our daughter's disabilities and how I had drawn near to God because of them flew out the window. The optimistic truth was gone, now replaced with depressing lies. And to think, I allowed it all to happen.

Compare what I did that morning at my window (meditating on the negative) with what Paul instructs us to meditate on in Philippians 4:8. What is the key to detecting the subtle warfare of the enemy?

_____

_____

_____

_____

Have you ever used this key to detect warfare in your own life?

_____

_____

_____

_____

The key to detecting the subtle tactics of the enemy boils down to learning to distinguish positive thoughts from negative ones. It's really that simple. Anything good comes from God and anything bad, including our thoughts, comes from the enemy. That's why we are told to take every thought captive. While Satan cannot read our minds, he will feed us bad thoughts and ideas to prompt us to act upon them. It is our job to capture them and evaluate whether they are good or bad before we allow them to take root in our heart. Remember, what we allow into our hearts is that which will eventually come out in our actions and deeds.

Think of capturing each thought as running it through a "mental detector." Once the thought is scanned, it is then labeled as either positive or negative. If it is negative, tell Satan to get behind you and ask God to replace it with His truth. Jesus did this exact thing when Satan tempted Him in the desert. He detected the lies, rejected them, and then fought back with the truth of God. Just imagine how different my morning would have been if I had done this. One thing is for sure; I wouldn't have wasted three hours in that dark corner listening to my accuser spit his hideous lies at me. You see, detecting these negative lies is so important to our walk with God because whenever our minds are focused on God, negative feelings cannot reside in us. The two are mutually exclusive. That, dear sister, is not only good news, but also the key to detecting and deflecting the subtle lies of the enemy. Once we learn to do it, victory is ours.

TAKING EVERY THOUGHT CAPTIVE

How exactly can we capture every thought that goes through our head? It sounds so time consuming, doesn't it? I mean every thought? How in the world can God possibly expect us to do this and still have time to live our daily lives? Thoughts come and go at lightning speed and to capture each one sounds like an insurmountable task. It may sound overwhelming, but to think or believe it can't be done is to be duped by the enemy from the very start. This is possible or God would not have instructed us to do it. Like anything in life, it is a skill that takes time to learn. You start with a little then work your way up.

It's like learning to ride a bike. As little children, we don't start out on 10 speed bikes. We start with tricycles then move on to bicycles with training wheels. In time, as we gain enough skill, we remove the training wheels and before you know it, we are off on two wheels. No matter who we are or what we ride, we all start with the tricycle and progress up. The skill of capturing every thought is exactly the same. You first start off small and then work your way up. But how do we start? How do we begin to capture every single thought? Hang in there because God never leads us to a dead end. He is always there to show us the way!

HOW TO BEGIN

Capturing every thought begins by simply deciding to take a general inventory of your thoughts.

Question and Reflect

Circle your answer to the following questions.

My general personality can be characterized as:

    Positive   Negative

I surround myself with people who are:

    Positive   Negative

My relationship with my family members is:

    Positive   Negative

My conversations are usually:

    Positive   Negative

In any given month, the majority of my days are:

    Positive   Negative

My week so far has been:

    Positive   Negative

My morning so far has been:

    Positive   Negative

My thoughts and feeling at this moment are:

    Positive   Negative

These questions are a good springboard toward learning how to take captive every thought. As you look at your answers, what is the dominant tone of your life? Were more of your answers positive or negative? Do your answers reflect a happy person? If not, why? The first few questions uncover the general attitude of your life, while the latter represent your life in a more detailed manner. Your answers as a whole divulge whether or not the peace of God resides in your life. Knowing your true condition is your first step toward victory, and learning to distinguish good thoughts from the bad, enable you to filter out the bad. This is how we protect our minds from the enemy.

Knowing what to look for in spiritual warfare is much like tending a garden. If you've ever had slugs, you know what I mean. They are those slow slimy creatures that catch you off guard when you see them because they're rarely seen. They come out after dark, do their dastardly deeds, then retreat to who knows where. I had slugs eat at my hosta lilies for years and never knew they were the culprits. It wasn't until I put two and two together that I realized I had in fact seen evidence of their existence for many years.

It was my mother who helped me solve the mystery. One day as she approached my front door she said, "Oh, you have slugs." Since none were crawling out in the open, I asked how she knew. That's when she pointed out the long trails shimmering on my sidewalk. Trails I had observed for many years. I had never known how those marks got on the pavement. They were simply there and that was that. They were signs of a threat, and I hadn't a clue.

Satan is much like a slug as he attempts to damage our lives while remaining undetected. Though rarely seen, he too leaves signature clues behind. Maybe you've seen evidence of the enemy's presence in your life but haven't labeled it as such. Perhaps your life shimmers of pride, insecurity, greed, jealousy, or gossip. Maybe you struggle with your temper or covet things of your neighbor. These are slimy trails of the enemy. They mean the enemy is on your property and trust me, he wants more than your hosta lilies. He wants to destroy your life and do as much collateral damage as possible.

CONCLUSION

Sister, do you desire to take every thought captive? It won't always take great effort and concentration, and it guarantees your protection. Capturing every negative thought doesn't prevent the bad things of life from happening. We will still have people problems and bad days, but in the midst of those trying times, if we dwell on all that is true, noble, right, pure, lovely, and excellent, Satan and his chaos will flee, leaving us with the peace of God.

It excites me to think of the freedom you can experience with the knowledge you now have. The battlefield, that was once so vulnerable, can now be fully protected with the armor of God. You know there is an enemy, but you also know how to gain victory in God. By choice you can now run each thought through a "mental detector" and filter out the bad, leaving only that which is good.

What great hope we have when we rely on God's word to guide, direct, and protect us. I pray you are determined to arm yourself with His word and allow it to fully protect you. When you do, there is no telling where the Lord will lead you! Ask God to help you in your warfare. Thank Him for giving you the very armor He Himself wears, and determine to wear it each and every day for the rest of your life.

_____

_____

_____

_____

_____

_____

_____

_____

_____

_____

_____

Week Ten

Day 1 - The Narrow Road

"Enter through the narrow gate. For wide is the gate and broad is the road that leads to destruction, and many enter through it. But small is the gate and narrow the road that leads to life, and only a few find it."
Matthew 7:13-14

When I first began writing this Bible study, it was like being asked to walk on water. I had never done it before. It was very scary and a lesson in complete dependence on God. I never knew from one day to the next what I was going to write, and it wasn't until the middle of the study I began to see God's plan for it. It was like being a passenger in a station wagon sitting in the very back seat facing backward. I never knew where we were heading and could only see where we had been. At first I was nervous, but after a few months I began to sit back and relax.

The ride seemed to be running rather smoothly, so I learned to occupy myself by enjoying the scenery of where we had been. God never allowed me to sit in the front seat. Perhaps He thought I'd go for the wheel, which I probably would have. But through it all I have learned more than I ever imagined, and I am so glad I took that first step off the shore and onto the water.

As God led the way in the writing of this study, He didn't tell me what was coming next and for quite some time, He didn't tell me how long it would be. I didn't know if it would be six weeks long, or if I'd come to a brick wall and never finish. At week six, I got a sense that I was smack dab in the middle of the ocean because spiritually, when I looked around at each horizon, I could see no land. It was just God and me. Somehow I knew then I had reached the middle of the study and it would only be a matter of weeks before the other shore would come into view.

As we begin our last and final week together, I see the shore approaching. I have mixed emotions about our journey coming to an end because I have grown attached to you as a sister in Christ. I already miss you because soon you will go off on your own journey with the Lord and I will be off as well. Having never crossed this big body of water before, I have no idea what God has in store for me. I only know that it is good. I am also excited for you because God has great plans that will make your heart happy and content beyond measure.

As I prayed and asked God how He wanted to end this Bible study, I felt He wanted the last week to wrap up all the other nine weeks by helping us learn how to actively seek Him. We have covered many fundamental issues in our study together and have dug deep into our hearts, but now it's time to implement all we have learned into a faithful walk with God each day. This entire study was designed to draw us closer to God, and now we must learn to walk with Him each and every day.

Too few Christians learn how to draw near to God in a close, intimate, and personal way. Even fewer learn to remain steadfast at His side all their days. But sister, you and I are not going to fall away. We are going to cling to our Lord until His return! We are going to have tears of joy, not sadness or regret, when we gaze on the Lamb of God. We are going to not only discover, but also carry out the plan He has custom-built just for us. We are going to experience the peace of God, which is rightfully ours even in the midst of warfare, and be a beacon of light in this world of darkness!

Question and Reflect

Read Deuteronomy 10:12-13.

What five things does God ask His people to do?

1. _____
2. _____
3. _____
4. _____
5. _____

Why does He ask this of them? Circle one.

- To control them
- To scare them
- To override their free will
- For their own good
- All of the above

Read Deuteronomy 11:18-25.

How does God advise His people to put into practice these things asked of them?

_____
_____
_____
_____

    Our Lord is so great. He is always faithful to provide instructions with the commands He gives. He isn't a distant, far off God who barks out orders then watches us fumble as we try to find a way to carry them out. He tells us exactly what to do and how to do it so that we can receive His blessings. He tells us to fear and love Him, to walk in His ways, and serve Him by observing all His commands. He wants us to be blessed and He wants to be the one to bless us!

According to Deuteronomy 11:18 and John 1:1-2, what are God's commands?

_____

_____

God's commands are His Word, and the Word is Jesus, and Jesus is God! How profound. Each time you and I reach for our Bibles, we are literally reaching for Him. When we plant His Word in our hearts, lives, and homes, we are infusing every part of our life with the great "I AM." What a privilege to have the God of all creation ask us to tap into His power so He can bless us. What more could we possibly ask for?

Given that God offers such abundance, why do you think so many disobeyed what God asked of them in Deuteronomy 10:12-13?

_____

_____

_____

_____

It can all be summed up in one word: rebellion. Anytime we turn our backs on God by disobeying His Word, we are rebelling. It may be as deliberate as when someone has full knowledge of God and still chooses to turn away from Him. Or it may be a rebellion based in ignorance. Both are tragic and addressed by God.

" Fix these words of mine in your hearts and minds; tie them as symbols on your hands and bind them on your foreheads. Teach them to your children, talking about them when you sit at home and when you walk along the road, when you lie down and when you get up. Write them on the doorframes of your houses and on your gates, so that your days and the days of your children may be many in the land that the LORD swore to give your forefathers, as many as the days that the heavens are above the Earth."
Deuteronomy 11:18-21

In Deuteronomy, God addresses each form of rebellion and tells us how to extinguish it. First, He addresses willful rebellion by telling us that we must make a conscious choice to fix His Word in our hearts and minds so it comes forth in all aspects of our lives. Second, He addresses ignorant rebellion by telling us to teach His Word to our children.

Did you know we will be held accountable for those we do not teach? Failing to instruct our children in God's Word encourages them to rebel out of ignorance. Wow. What a sobering thought. We will actually be held responsible not only for our own rebellion, but for those whom we encourage to rebel. Once again, we see our call to be united as one body, teaching, and supporting one another. Keeping God's Word to ourselves isn't good enough. We must pass it on to others.

Are you encouraging your children to rebel by not sharing the good news of Jesus Christ?

You don't have to be a parent to be guilty of not teaching children. God's children are all around us. We work with them, we mix and mingle with them, we live next door to them, and we walk past them on the street. Opportunities come up all the time for us to share Christ, but we must first step out of our comfort zone. You don't have to know the Bible from cover to cover to share what God has done for you. Your walk is a testimony to those around you. Our daughter has never spoken a word, and yet somehow, God uses her to testify to His great love and mercy. I don't know how He does it, but He does. It is the work of the Holy Spirit in and through her, and it's amazing to see. If God can use a child who has literally never spoken a word, how much more can He use you?

CONCLUSION

How determined are you to learn God's Word? Are you determined to let it permeate your life and share it with others? The enemy is smooth as he whispers his lies, saying we can't learn God's Word or we need a formal education in order to understand what it says. But that isn't true. As today's Bible verse says, the road to life is narrow but even so, nothing is impossible with God! His Word is alive and His Spirit will teach you if you are seeking Him with all your heart.

This week I will share some pointers to learn how to understand God's Word and grow abundantly. Ask God to place a desire in your heart to walk with Him each day for the rest of your life. Ask Him to show you how to dig deep into His Word and take away any anxiety the enemy may be tempting you to feel.

Week Ten

Day 2 - Daily Discipline

"Your statutes are wonderful; therefore I obey them. The unfolding of your words gives light; it gives understanding to the simple. I open my mouth and pant, longing for your commands."
Psalm 119:129-131

REVIEW

Day 1 - The Narrow Road

When our daughter was about three years old, it was evident she was in total bondage to Autism. She never cried for my husband and me, she never wanted to be held, and she was virtually walled off from the world around her. As each day passed, it broke our hearts to see and feel the growing chasm between us. One day, in an act of desperation, we made a conscious decision to attempt to rescue her. Our plan was to enter her world with the goal of bringing her out into ours.

From birth, Dani never liked being held and out of respect for her wishes, we didn't hold her as much as we wanted. We knew she needed physical contact and tried countless times to give it to her, but she would never allow it. I learned in nursing school that touching and holding an infant was vital to human growth and development, and it always nagged at me that we could not hug and embrace her. What bothered me most was she didn't want it.

One day God gave my husband and me the idea to do a therapy on her. One we'd never heard of. We decided if every human being needs the physical contact of holding and cuddling in order to grow and develop, we would hold Dani even if she didn't want it. Talk about tough love! We had to literally force our affection on her. It seemed so mechanical and invasive that I really wasn't sure it was going to end up being a good thing.

I'll never forget the discussion my husband and I had as we were developing this plan. One day as we drove down the road, I said to him, "What gives us the right to force her into our world? Think about how much pain and suffering we have in our world. Do we really want to bring her into it? Maybe she would be happiest where she is." In response, my husband replied with calm wisdom saying, "But there are a lot of good things in our world, too. You and I are two good things in this world that she is missing and we have a lot to offer her." When he said this, I knew he was right. We had to make her do something she wouldn't at first want to do but in the long run, would benefit her greatly.

Each day I began to do what we called "hold therapy." I would wrap her arms and legs around my body and hold her firmly as she began to scream. Our plan was to let her fight until she quit crying long enough to feel my loving embrace, even if it was just for a few moments. If she would just for one moment receive some comfort while in my arms, I thought she might come and join us in our world. As she screamed in misery, I would hold her close, gently telling her everything was all right. We predicted that she would most likely collapse from exhaustion before she would voluntarily give in and that is exactly what happened. The first time I tried this, she screamed for 40 minutes solid until she finally collapsed in my arms. This went on for a week before the time each day began to shorten. Soon we were able to hold her without a fight.

Today she sits with us on the couch and enjoys a good cuddle like any other child. Though she still is not as affectionate as a child without Autism, she continues to get better. Although many people clearly see her disability, they don't see the Autism when they meet her today. She shakes hands and will on selected occasions even give a hug. She acknowledges us as her parents and is now in our world enjoying all the things life has to offer. It took our conscious decision to force her to do something she at first did not want to do, but I can't tell you how much it has paid off in the long run. It gave us our little girl.

Question and Reflect

Do you sense that God wants a closer relationship with you?

_____

_____

Are you fighting His efforts to draw you closer to Him?

_____

_____

If you are resisting His call to draw nearer, why do you think you are hesitant?

_____

_____

_____

_____

So often we choose to stay in our own world, not because it's better, but because it's most familiar. We would rather chase after things of the world than pursue the blessings of God. We read, watch, and listen to all sorts of things throughout our day, giving little time to studying His Word. As a result, we miss many great things the Lord has in store for us. If we want to receive a greater blessing we must make a conscious decision to do what we may not want to do at first.

I am so glad God showed us how to rescue our daughter from her world. Along with helping her, it also showed me how I isolate myself from the One who loves me the most. It was difficult to do, but has been worth it. Sister, you and I must determine to do the same when it comes to our heavenly Father. We are no different than Dani when we fight His loving embrace and we suffer greatly when we insist on staying apart from Him in our own world.

Read Psalms 119:103. How does the Psalmist describe what God's Word is to Him?

_____

_____

How would you describe what God's Word means to you?

_____

_____

_____

_____

The Psalmist speaks of the many blessing that come from studying God's Word. He describes the Word as honey. Doesn't that sound wonderful? There is nothing like golden honey on a hot biscuit fresh out of the oven. It almost makes me salivate just thinking about it. This is how the Psalmist felt about God's Word. He loved its taste, found that it nourished and regenerated his soul, and had grown to love it to the point where he savored it like honey in his mouth.

Do you ever crave God's Word like sweet honey (…or maybe chocolate)?

_____

_____

Satan doesn't want you to have a taste of God's Word. He knows that if you have one drop, you'll want more. He also knows that as it nourishes you, it weakens him. He will tell you that you don't need it, or have the capability to understand it, but don't believe these lies. God wrote His Word for you and through the power of the Holy Spirit, He will make it possible for you to understand it. You deserve to read, know, and understand God's Holy Word because it was written for you!

READING YOUR BIBLE DAILY

We know God's Word is like honey and if we get a little of it, we will want more. We also know the enemy doesn't want us to have any of it and battles us every step of the way. How are we to begin? How did the Psalmist begin? What was his first step toward learning God's Word?

He began where we all must begin. By simply reading it. We read a little each day until we begin to taste the sweetness. Job meditated on God's Word so much that he treasured it above his daily bread (Job 23:12). Can you say the same thing? It took me years to get to the point where I treasured God's Word. For quite some time, I read it only out of my commitment to the Lord. As much as I love Him, I didn't fully understand what I was reading, but because of my commitment, I continued. In return, God honored my efforts by teaching and guiding me all along the way. He taught me even when I didn't know I was learning. Now that's a good teacher!

I remember when His Word first began to taste sweet. I was working full time and began to notice increased difficulty in putting my Bible down in the morning in order to get ready for work. I had to be at work at 9:00 am and would have to dress and feed Dani and myself. I had made my commitment to God to spend time each day in prayer and Bible study for the rest of my life and was beginning to grow closer to Him. This closeness became evident when it was so hard to end my time with Him in the morning. I began getting up earlier each morning to have more time with Him, but still ended each study saying, "God, I am so sorry I have to leave for work now. You know I love you and wish I could spend all morning with you, but I have to go. I love you. Good bye."

My spiritual lips had acquired a taste and it left me thirsting for more. God, in all His love and mercy, honored my thirst for Him by eventually bringing me home permanently. Now I get His sweet honey each day until I am full to the brim. He is so gracious and respectful to those who love Him and put Him first. All it took was for me to dedicate time to Him each day and He took care of the rest.

Have you dedicated time to spend each day with God, even if it's just five minutes?
_____

_____

You can begin to get a taste of His sweet honey by simply reading one chapter of God's Word each day. You can read the Bible in a variety of ways. Take a look at the following options and select one or two you would like to try in the next year.

GENESIS TO REVELATION. Go at your own pace reading the Bible a little each day, cover to cover, until you are finished.

READING THE BIBLE IN A YEAR. Use a chart that assigns certain chapters to look at each day that allows you to read through the entire Bible in one year.

A PROVERB A DAY. The book of Proverbs has 31 chapters, which correlates with the maximum number of days in any given month. By reading a chapter in Proverbs each day, you are learning the wisdom of God and how to put it into your heart, mind, and daily life.

ONE PSALM A DAY. Psalms, a book of poetry based in strong theology, is the source of many of the hymns we sing today. The Psalms sing praise to God and are excellent to assist you in meditating on God and His holiness. There are 150 chapters in the book of Psalms. If you read three chapters a day, you will read the entire book in about 8 weeks.

THE FOUR GOSPELS. It is always a blessing to read about the life of Christ. Choose to read two chapters a day beginning in Matthew and read until you finish John. Seek to find the similarities and differences each gospel writer brings out.

These ideas are but the tip of the iceberg! There are all kinds of ways to read the Bible, and you can do whatever you feel led to do. You can read any single book out of the Bible, all of Paul's epistle letters, all of John's letters, read about the old testament prophets, find out who the judges were in the book of Judges, read about all of Israel's kings, choose a book you know the least about, or come up with any other creative ideas. God will teach and guide you through all of His Word, you only need to be determined to begin and decide to never end.

If you have read through the Bible already, don't let the enemy tell you there is no need to do it again. God's Word is inexhaustible, and to think you cannot glean any more from it is pride, which puts a wedge between God and you. Believing we don't need to read His Word each day is guaranteed to lead us far away from Him. We will never know all there is to know from God's Word and in a strange way, this gives me great comfort. I don't want to reach the end. Maybe it's because I get bored so easily, but I love that He is so multifaceted. Learning about God and walking with Him is a continuous, never-ending journey. It is never boring and will always keep you on your toes.

CONCLUSION

Sometimes in life there are things we need to do that we don't want to do. Seeking God through the reading of His Word is one of them. If we truly believe and trust in God, we will do what He asks us to do and plant His Word in our hearts everyday. The benefits of reading His Word are innumerable. Read Psalm 119 and note some of the benefits that stand out to you the most. List a few below and ask God to bless your life with them.

_____

_____

_____

_____

_____

_____

_____

_____

_____

_____

_____

_____

Week Ten

Day 3 - Our Teacher and Our Reminder

"But the Counselor, the Holy Spirit, whom the Father will send in my name, will teach you all things and will remind you of everything I have said to you."
John 14:26

REVIEW

Day 1 - The Narrow Road

Day 2 - Daily Discipline

In our final week together we are learning how to walk with God. For nine weeks God has shown us how to draw near to Him, but we can't stop there. He knows we are prone to drift away and He doesn't want this to happen. Instead, He wants us to walk closely by His side every day for the rest of our lives. He wants to protect and guide us in all that we do so that He can lavish us with all His bountiful blessings. But it takes discipline and determination on our part to seek Him daily because God will never force Himself on us. He wants us to want Him and will never override our free will.

TURNING BACK TO GOD

For many of us, the task of finding God is a difficult one. Some of us may have known Him well at one time and then drifted away, while others have never walked with God in an intimate and close way. Regardless of the track record, we need to focus on the fact that God is approachable and His Word is available for us to receive, absorb, and understand. When we read His Word, we will be transformed and made new.

There are two basic rules to following God:

1. Follow Him and His commands and be blessed

2. Turn from Him and His commands and be cursed

Could it be any simpler? Could He be more clear? There are mysteries of God that we will never understand, but this is not one of them. Following God and receiving His many blessings are made as clear as crystal because He wants us to obtain them. If following God is so clear, why does it tend to be so difficult for us? One of the primary reasons is our own free will. Some people simply don't want to follow God. Others want His blessing but don't want to commit to Him. Then there are those who want to follow Him and receive His blessing, but they don't know where to begin. They want to read His Word, but they truly don't understand it and how it applies to them. Although this is quite normal, the enemy will tell you that God's Word is not understandable and it doesn't apply to you. The good news is God's Word is understandable and it does apply to us today!

Question and Reflect

Read Deuteronomy 30:1-20.

      By the time Moses spoke these words to the nation of Israel, they had turned their backs on God many times and he was nearing the end of his life. In spite, after seeing all the miracles God had done on their behalf, they failed to trust Him and obey His commands. They easily drifted out from under God's protection and rebelled by doubting and complaining, which made God very angry. In Deuteronomy 30, God reached out to his people, telling Moses to reiterate His two main rules to them. He told them that no matter what they had done in the past, His covenant with them was still active and so were His two rules. They had the choices. Follow His commands and be blessed, or turn their backs on Him and be cursed.

      In verse 3, the Lord promised He would restore their fortunes and have compassion on them if they returned to Him and obeyed His commands. He promised that no matter how bad their situation was, or how far they had been scattered throughout the land, He would restore them (verse 4). He also promised that the original blessing given through His promise to Abraham, Isaac, and Jacob, would be theirs once again if they only turned back to Him and followed His commands.

What did God say He would do to their hearts if they returned to Him (verse 6)?

_____

_____

What would be the result of God doing this to their hearts (verse 6)?

_____

_____

What does God say about His commands in verse 11? Check one.

    _____They are hidden and must be found

    _____They are not too difficult or beyond your reach

    _____They are impossible to understand

    _____They are only for a few chosen people to understand and follow

Where does God say His word is not located (verses 12-13)?

_____

_____

Where does God say His Word can be found (verse 14)?

_____

_____

God's consistency is such great comfort. Though we may waver and wander, God and His Word will forever remain the same. It is always available and ready to heal us in order to bring us closer to Him.

Read today's Bible verse John 14:26.

What two things does Jesus tell His disciples the Holy Spirit will do for them after He is gone?

_____

_____

The words Jesus used to comfort His disciples are the same words that console us as well. This verse has sustained me each day that I have worked on this study over the past nine months. As I followed God's lead from day to day, not knowing what was in store, I meditated on the fact that His Spirit is our personal tutor. For those who think they aren't smart enough to understand God's Word, this is a great relief. Good sound Bible teaching, reading the Word of God for ourselves, and allowing the Holy Spirit to be our personal tutor, is all we need to know the living God.

Did you know you had your own personal tutor? Did you know your teacher not only knows the Holy Word but also *is* the Holy Word? If you have accepted Christ as your personal Savior, the Holy Spirit resides in you. When you sit down to read your Bible, ask God to reveal His Word to you in a new and fresh way and He will, because it is His desire.

The Holy Spirit is like a Post-It note. When we can't remember something we know we learned in the past, all we have to do is ask God to remind us. He knows our limited brain capacity and that we cannot comprehend or remember all His nuggets of truth. But thankfully, He doesn't expect us to. He only asks that we learn His Word, trust it, obey it, and rest in it. He loves coming to our aid, and I have grown rather fond of letting Him. It's proven to be much less stressful.

Have you ever realized the Holy Spirit is your teacher and reminder? If not, how different would your life be if you did?

_____

_____

_____

_____

I am convinced that not being an intellectual, like our fictional Ilene in week eight, has its advantages. To remember things, I write nearly everything down because I can only think of one thing at a time. If I need bread at the store and don't write it down, that mental list will fly out of my brain as soon as my mind goes on to something else. I used to think I was afflicted with a severe case of dim-wittedness. But the closer I have grown to God, the more I see that my limited capacity to learn and remember things serves a greater need: keeping my walk closer to Him.

I talk to God all the time and am continually asking Him to remind me of something or teach me something new. And do you know what? He absolutely LOVES it! He loves it when we ask questions and come to Him with our problems. There is nothing more obnoxious than a child who doesn't know something, but won't admit it. They need help, but they won't accept it. God wants to help us and would much rather we ask repeatedly, than never ask at all.

Why does God love to be our teacher when we ask Him questions?

_____
_____

God loves it when we come to Him for guidance because He enjoys our company. It's that simple. He created us to worship and fellowship with Him and when we don't, He misses us. Even in our weakness and frailties, He enjoys our company because we are His. Sadly, many of His children turn from Him and go their own way, rejecting Him and all He wants to give. God is all-powerful and can handle rejection, but it still breaks my heart.

CONCLUSION

Has the enemy blinded you from seeing God as your teacher and reminder? It should bring a big sigh of relief to know you don't need a formal education in the ministry to do His work. All you need is the divine education of time alone with God in daily prayer and Bible reading. The good news is it's not only free, but also earns great heavenly credits!

Ask God to help you understand His Word and reveal something new about Him today. Ask Him to help you be dedicated to Him and His Word each and every day.

_____
_____
_____
_____
_____
_____
_____
_____
_____

Week Ten

Day 4 - The Lonely Road

"Small is the gate and narrow the road that leads to life, and only a few find it."
Matthew 7:14

REVIEW

Day 1 - The Narrow Road

Day 2 - Daily Discipline

Day 3 - Our Teacher and Our Reminder

In our final week together, we are learning how to walk with God. For nine weeks, the Lord has shown us how to draw near to Him. Now it is time to fully commit ourselves to walk with Him all the rest of our days. This takes great determination for several reasons. It can be controversial, trying, confusing, and lonely. Not long ago God warned me of how lonely this road would be, and it has proven to be one of the most valuable lessons He has ever taught me.

I was asked to head up a prayer team to lead our church in prayer for our building project. My partner and I met and worked out a plan of action. We set up four designated times a month for the entire church to come and pray over the pews and for those who would soon be sitting in them. We would pray for their salvation, their involvement in the building campaign, and for God to lead and guide them. We advertised this event to the entire church in the weekly mailers and anticipated a reasonable turnout given our church's thousands of members. The first week, eight people showed up. Although I expected more, I was happy with eight. The second week, four came. The third week was the biggest surprise of all, and one God used to teach me this valuable lesson.

It was a bright sunny Saturday morning and 11:00 am was the scheduled time to pray over the pews. Arriving at 10:30 am I arrived to turn on the lights and music, then sat to read my Bible as I waited for the people to arrive. From 10:30 am until 11:00 am, there wasn't a soul in the huge sanctuary other than me. At 11:00 am sharp, I glanced around the sanctuary, which was quiet as a tomb, and was amazed to verify not a single soul had arrived. In a bit of denial I resumed my reading as I sat and waited. 11:10 am rolled around, and still not another soul. At 11:20 am, I took one last disbelieving look at my watch and turned to give the sanctuary another scan. There was no one there but me. I couldn't believe my eyes.

Realizing no one was coming, I looked back at my Bible and began to cry. It was awful. With a tear welling up in one eye I said, "Lord, I am so sorry! None of your people showed up. I did all I could to get them here but no one came and I am sorry. I don't know what else I could have done." It may sound strange, but at that moment, I felt such sympathy for the Lord. I know He is God Almighty, Creator of all heaven and Earth, but I felt so sorry for Him. What were the odds that out of 4,000 church members, no one would show up to pray? It absolutely boggled my mind as I sat there stunned.

A tear was about to fall onto the page of my Bible when the Lord spoke to my heart. As clear as a bell He said, "Nancy, if you truly want to follow me the way you say you want to follow me, it's a lonely road and you'd better get used to it." He spoke no other words, yet I knew what He was telling me. He was instructing me to pray over all the pews myself, alone, with Him. God was testing my faith that day to see what it would do when left completely alone. Would I give up and go home because no one else came, or would I believe, trust, and obey?

With great sadness, I began to pray over the pews that sunny morning. No one else ever came and I confess that as I went from pew to pew, it was quite humbling. I kept thinking how several thousand people were invited to come, yet not one showed. What are the odds? At any rate, there I was alone, left to do this monumental task.

As I walked from pew to pew, I talked to God a lot. I talked His ear off as a matter of fact. I asked what good my little prayers could do and why He hadn't sent others to help. His word says that where two or more gather, He will be there. But it was only me! Would He hear my lone prayers from huge a sanctuary? I asked Him a lot of "why" questions that morning, and He kindly listened as I did the job.

By the time I finished praying, I had begun to realize that the failure of anyone to arrive was not really an act of the people as much as it was an act of God. It's incomprehensible that not one person out of 4,000 showed up. God had evidently kept everyone away that day to teach me a lesson He couldn't have taught otherwise. The time had come for me to learn firsthand how lonely the road of Christianity can be. God wanted me to understand that, though I will feel alone at times, I am never truly by myself. He is always at my side leading and guiding the way, and I must never rely on others to keep me company. I am to do His job, even if it means doing it alone.

Question and Reflect

It is easy to feel lonely and discouraged as we walk with God. Satan loves to isolate us and tell us lies of defeat. He works hard to convince us that walking this road with God isn't worth it. His goal is to make us feel so alone that we will be tempted to go back to a place where we have company around us once again. He doesn't care where we go as long as it isn't the path God has chosen for us. But we need to remember that following God can be a very discouraging and lonely road at times. That's just the way it is. I am not saying that being all alone is a prerequisite to the Christian life, but if you are growing in Christ, your close friendships will most likely decrease in number, leaving you to feel lonely at times.

Re-read today's Bible verse below and circle the words that refer to this loneliness we can experience as we walk with God.

"Small is the gate and narrow the road that leads to life,
and only a few find it."
Matthew 7:14

We've heard how small the gate is and how narrow the road is, but have you noticed that few people find it? While this verse is referring to salvation, it also reflects the volume of traffic we will come across on the Christian road. It does not say the road is so narrow that we will have to walk single file with our hands on the shoulder of the guy in front of us. This road is a narrow, not well-traveled road, and inevitably lonely at times.

Have you ever been disappointed by a feeling of loneliness in your Christian walk? Explain.

_____
_____
_____
_____

The greatest education we could ever receive is walking alone with God, against the odds. In doing this, we choose to be alone with God in a time of private teaching and tutoring. This lonely road is paved with fertile ground that serves to teach us things we could not learn in the company of others.

Read the following verses and name whom God isolated in order to educate and bless them in a profound way.

1 Kings 19: 1-18: _____

Daniel 10:4-9: _____

Mark 1:12-13: _____

Luke 1: 60 and 80: _____

Galatians 1:11-19: _____

Revelation 1:9-11: _____

God met each and every one of these men while they were on their lonely road. Elijah fled in fear for His life and God met him in the desert under the broom tree. He nourished Elijah enough to then lead him to Mount Horeb where God met him yet again to give further instructions. Daniel was standing on the bank of the Tigris River when God appeared to him. Although he started out standing with other men, they all fled when the Lord arrived, leaving Daniel alone gazing on the great vision. Paul was led into the Arabian Desert to be alone with God for three years after his dramatic conversion on the road to Damascus. John the Baptist and Jesus were both led to the desert by the Holy Spirit to be taught and strengthened in a special way. The apostle John saw the vision of Christ while in prison, alone on the isle of Patmos.

Isn't it wonderful what God revealed to these men? Think of the life changing blessings they received when they were alone, ready, and willing to receive God's instruction. In every one of these situations, these men had no one around them and therefore received great comfort, strength, and instruction from the Lord. If any human had been with them, it simply would not have been the same. God wanted them alone so that they could receive the profound education He had to offer them as their personal teacher.

CONCLUSION

Corporate worship is a wonderful thing and something we will do in heaven together for eternity. However, God is a very individual god and He wants to meet with each of us in private. When we are alone, we are able to hear Him speak the things He has to say just to us on a personal level. This is how He guides and directs us in our own unique and personal way.

Do you feel lonely and isolated in your walk with God? If so, you are in the company of some of the greatest men of the Bible. Jesus knew what it was like to be alone and abandoned and He knew we would feel the same way. In John 12:18, He promises us He will never leave us as orphans and will send the Holy Spirit to give us His guidance, wisdom, comfort, and peace.

Sister, you may feel alone but you are not. God is with you, guiding you every step of the way. He is your personal instructor. The only way we can persevere on this lonely road is to keep our eyes on Jesus. If we have our eyes on anything else, we will stumble. We were never meant to travel this road alone. We were meant to walk it with God at our side!

What great love, compassion, and mercy our Lord has for His children. If you feel all alone, set your eyes on God. Ask Him to reveal Himself to you like He did to Elijah, Daniel, John the Baptist, Paul, John the apostle, and His own Son, Jesus. Ask God for the determination to stay on the road He has set for you.

_____

_____

_____

_____

_____

_____

_____

_____

_____

Week Ten

Day 5 - Your New Journey with God

"Be strong and very courageous. Be careful to obey all the law my servant Moses gave you; do not turn from it to the right or to the left, that you may be successful wherever you go."
Joshua 1:7

REVIEW

Day 1 - The Narrow Road

Day 2 - Daily Discipline

Day 3 - Our Teacher and Our Reminder

Day 4 - The Lonely Road

Thump! Did you feel that? I think we just touched shore. Our journey together has come to an end. But before we disembark and say good-bye, let's take advantage of our last few moments together. It has been a pleasure to spend ten weeks with you. I commend you for hanging in there and pray you have drawn nearer to God through this study. I pray you will never be the same - I know I never will.

When I was a little girl in the first grade, I had trouble seeing the black board and what the teacher was writing on it. I wondered why no one else had a problem reading what she wrote. Although I had no clue I was not seeing as well as the other kids, my last name hastened a quick diagnosis. I was a Williams, which meant I was at the end of the alphabet and in the back of the classroom. When the teacher realized I couldn't see the board, she told my parents and soon, I had my first pair of glasses.

Do you know the first thing I noticed when I got my glasses? I could see the individual leaves at the top of the tall tree in our front yard. Standing at our front door and looking out at that tree, I thought, "I never knew I was supposed to be able to see those leaves way up there!" I'll never know why I didn't notice the clouds high in the sky, or the little threads in our carpet, but for some reason, I was amazed that I could see the individual leaves at the top of that tall tree.

My ignorance of my own poor eyesight is much like the ignorance many Christians have when it comes to their own view of God. There is so much more of Him to see than we are ever aware of, but sadly, we settle for seeing only a small part, thinking that's all there is to Him. But dear sister, God wants us to know Him and know Him well. He doesn't want us to see Him like I saw the leaves on the top of that tree, unclear, and out of focus. He wants our vision of Him to be keen and sharp because when it is, it is an awesome revelation! How I pray that this Bible study has improved your vision of God. I hope you never cease to stand in awe of the great "I AM." Our journey together may be over, but your journey with God will never end. He has a new exciting, rewarding, and fulfilling journey for you, and I promise you will enjoy it immensely.

Let's take a quick spiritual inventory to see how God has spoken to you through this study. It's always important to periodically check our spiritual growth to be sure we are indeed growing. You will be filling out a self-evaluation today, which you don't have to share with anyone unless you desire. It is only an aid to help you reflect on what God has done for you. As you read each question, think of your intimacy with God when you first began this study ten weeks ago compared to the intimacy you feel with Him now. After you have completed your evaluation, we will meet together at the end to say our final good-byes.

Self Evaluation

Compared to when I began this study ten weeks ago:

My desire to communicate with God today has (circle one):
- Lessened
- Remained the same
- Increased
- Drastically increased

My comfort level in approaching God is (circle one):
- The same as before
- Still somewhat hesitant
- More free to approach Him
- Completely free to approach Him

My desire to seek a deeper relationship with God has (circle one):
- Not increased
- Increased mildly
- Increased moderately
- Increased greatly

You may want to flip back through your study and review what you have learned as you answer the following questions.

What I have learned most about God is:

_____

_____

_____

_____

_____

What I have learned most about the enemy is:

_____

_____

_____

_____

_____

_____

What I have learned most about my own heart is:

_____

_____

_____

_____

_____

_____

My commitment to follow God wherever He leads me is (circle one):

- The same
- Somewhat stronger
- Greatly increased
- I am fully committed

The most important thing I discovered when I journeyed down to the ocean floor of my heart is:

_____

_____

_____

_____

_____

_____

The dive to the ocean floor of my heart changed my walk with God in the following ways:

_____
_____
_____
_____
_____
_____

The following best describes how I feel as a unique individual created by God for a unique plan and purpose (check one):

_____ I don't feel unique or believe that God has a special plan for me

_____ I see that God has created me unique, but don't know the plans He has for me

_____ I now realize I am special in His eyes and know He will use me for His glory if I let Him.

The most important thing I have learned about pride is:

_____
_____
_____
_____
_____
_____

The most important thing I have learned about my own pride is:

_____
_____
_____
_____
_____
_____

What I have learned most about Worship is:

_____
_____
_____
_____
_____
_____

This study has changed my prayer life in the following ways:

_____
_____
_____
_____
_____
_____

Before this study I <u>never</u> knew the following things about Spiritual Warfare:

_____
_____
_____
_____
_____
_____

Learning about Spiritual Warfare has changed my prayer life in the following ways:

_____
_____
_____
_____
_____
_____

My determination to walk with God wherever He leads me has (circle one):

- Dwindled
- Stayed the same
- Increased
- Increased drastically

CONCLUSION

Dear sister, they are calling us to exit the boat, and in a few moments, we will be stepping out onto a new shore. Haven't we had a great adventure together with our Lord? We have been on a hot air balloon ride and dived deep to the ocean floor of our hearts. We've met some of the godliest men of the Bible, and in our last few moments together, reflected on how this journey has drawn us closer to God. It has been a wonderful experience and I am so glad we've been able to share it together. I have some beautiful mental pictures of our trip and I trust you do too. I will miss you greatly but promise to keep you in my prayers, since we are sisters in Christ.

Let's end our time together by reading the last words Moses spoke to the Israelites as he handed his leadership over to Joshua and went on to be with the Lord:

"Be strong and courageous.
Do not be afraid or terrified because of them,
for the LORD your God goes with you;
he will never leave you nor forsake you."
Deuteronomy 31:6

As we leave one another and step onto the shore of this new land, remember - God has already gone before you! He has prepared your path and your way. He will never leave you or forsake you because He is faithful, loving, and seeks to bless you beyond measure. Believe that. Stand firm in your faith and you will never be in need. I love you and hope that one day soon our paths will cross again.

Good-bye!

If you would like to contact Nancy Douglas
regarding how this Bible study has impacted your life,
you may contact her at oliveleaf@kc.rr.com.

www.ingramcontent.com/pod-product-compliance
Lightning Source LLC
Chambersburg PA
CBHW080333170426
43194CB00014B/2546